Contributions to Management Science

The series *Contributions to Management Science* contains research publications in all fields of business and management science. These publications are primarily monographs and multiple author works containing new research results, and also feature selected conference-based publications are also considered. The focus of the series lies in presenting the development of latest theoretical and empirical research across different viewpoints.

This book series is indexed in Scopus.

More information about this series at https://link.springer.com/bookseries/1505

João Leitão • Vanessa Ratten
Editors

Strategic Innovation

Research Perspectives on Entrepreneurship and Resilience

Springer

Editors
João Leitão
Department of Management and Economics, NECE - Research Center in Business Sciences
University of Beira Interior
Covilhã, Portugal

Vanessa Ratten
Department of Management, Sport and Tourism, La Trobe Business School
La Trobe University
Melbourne, VIC, Australia

ISSN 1431-1941 ISSN 2197-716X (electronic)
Contributions to Management Science
ISBN 978-3-030-87111-6 ISBN 978-3-030-87112-3 (eBook)
https://doi.org/10.1007/978-3-030-87112-3

This Springer imprint is published by the registered company Springer Nature Switzerland AG.
The registered company address is: Gewerbestrasse 11, 6330 Cham, Switzerland

Foreword

The Role of Strategic Innovation in Change

The cliché is that the global COVID-19 pandemic has created a decade's worth of digital transformation. The rate of change has been significant given the alterations to work and social life. It is a pleasure to provide the foreword for this edited book titled *Strategic Innovation-Research Perspectives on Entrepreneurship and Resilience*. Given my expertise and knowledge, I will comment on the innovations that have taken place from a strategic perspective in the football industry. This industry provides a good way to understand how certain industries are utilizing entrepreneurship and resilience in order to survive in the global marketplace.

Suddenly, football clubs in lockdown had their supply lines cut off and found themselves in a position where they could not play. Fans could no longer come to the stadium to watch their teams and revenue of ticket and hotdog sales was being lost at an alarming rate. Lockdown exposed a lack of agility and innovation in the current business model of football, but clubs did their best to try and bring the beautiful game back to the fans and make a few dollars on the side. The Quarantine Cup was just one example of how sports clubs turned to esports as one way to do that. With no physical games to play, players entered playing FIFA soccer streamed to fans through Twitch. For many fans, it was the first time they would have experienced esports or Twitch.

All industries have been disrupted due to COVID-19 and digitalization, and football is no exception. The rise of AI and robotics is a great area to watch for football. In the field, AI offers potential to improve video assistant refereeing (VAR) and ultimately could do away with referees entirely. In fact, AI and robotics could ultimately replace players or managers entirely in the future. Players at the highest level are expensive and vulnerable, so ultimately, AI, robotic players, or virtual and extended reality could be the next frontier of innovation for the beautiful game. The boundaries between esports and football continue to blur and as a global demand for 24-7 entertainment continues, the answer to the next pandemic may be a more virtual approach to football. Football clubs have a powerful and influential reach and innovation can also be harnessed to help solve societal issues and motivate fans to healthier behaviors through physical and digital (phygital) innovations. When football clubs speak, fans listen.

So, if the role of innovation ultimately is to allow football teams to win, engage, and help fans, how will the game evolve in the twenty-first century and what will winning mean in the long run? Football will continue on the path of innovation and continue to give the fans what they want—emotion, interactive, amazing entertainment on a global scale. Innovations for new technologies for competitive advantage, training, fan engagement, and the game itself are evolving at a pace never seen before. There are great opportunities therefore for football to work with other innovative organizations, governments, and researchers to create new pathways for open innovation. This will allow football clubs to innovate, evolve, and help to improve society while still retaining what we (the fans) love about the game.

Our beautiful game of football is forever changing, innovating, and evolving: going all the way back to 1878 when Fergus Suter moved from Darwen FC and then Blackburn Rovers to become (controversially) the first recognized paid professional footballer. Pushing the boundaries and using innovation to gain a competitive edge has always been an important aspect of the game. We have seen improved lightweight clothing, aerodynamic balls, and rule changes such as offside, designed to keep the game more competitive. Rule innovations such as the golden goal introduced to make extra time more open and competitive had to be quickly scrapped because they had the opposite effect. Teams, players, leagues, associations, and manufacturers have innovated on the pitch since there was a pitch to play on. The ultimate purpose of innovation in the field is winning and leveling the playing field to make sure football continues to be the world's most popular sport.

In recent decades, we have seen the rise of data and technology in football (sportstech). In a traditional industry like football, this has not always been an easy transition. According to PwC's 2019 annual survey of decision-makers in sport, the majority recognize the value of innovation, but less than half have a clear strategy in this area. So, for all the brilliance and passion within football, often the decision-makers are bereft of time, money, resource, and expertise to innovate. They are also often tied up in rights and what they are allowed to do, which can also stifle open innovation. Football clubs and players are often pulled in various directions through partners, sponsors, players, agents, and associated contracts. Often, the key purpose is directing finance, time, and energy to winning on the pitch and then other innovative aspects are secondary.

Fan engagement is obviously important to football clubs—we have all heard the old adage "without fans, football is nothing"—however when it comes to innovation, the priority is often winning with the hopes that the fans will be more likely to follow a winning team. Despite this, football clubs at all levels of the pyramid have used websites, social media, and smartphones to innovate to try and reach new audiences over the last decade. Most clubs are on a journey of digital maturity to become people focused and data driven, properly capturing and using data through (evolving) FRM (fan relationship management) systems. The ultimate goal is a

360-degree view of the fan data in order to reach as wide an audience as possible with the right offer at the right time. More tickets and shirts sold means more revenue and better players, which (hopefully) means more wins on the pitch—a wide but full circle.

As one Leeds fan aptly put it on social media "We're all Avatars now." Clubs re-ran old matches on social media and turned (initially) to Ifollow for a digital season ticket. For the first time ever, older season ticket holders watched whole games on their old laptop or smartphone. Clips through social media and foundations stepped up their care for the community schemes. Everyone held their breath that football would start again—that fans could be in the stadiums and wondered what would happen to Euro 2020 and Copa America?

The very fact that most fans already had a smartphone and football clubs were all present on social media with the ability to live stream to those devices meant that the game could continue even without fans in the stadium. Digital innovation therefore saved the day (to an extent). What lasting changes these innovations will bring will become clearer over the coming decades. We do know though that esports and sportstech continue to grow at incredible rates and the new generation of season ticket holders consume football in a different way from their parents and grandparents. Football clubs need to keep innovating and adapting to keep up with the pace of technology and change, "hyperdigitalized" and always on fans.

University of Salford, Greater Manchester, UK

Alex Fenton

Acknowledgments

Editing a research book is always a time-intensive task that requires long hours and dedication. Thus, we thank Prashanth Mahagaonkar for his help and insight in this process. It is much appreciated. We thank the authors for their contributions and hard work in producing each chapter. We also thank the reviewers of each chapter who helped in refining and making each chapter better. Joao would like to thank his family. Vanessa would also like to thank her family—Kaye, David, Stuart, Hamish, Tomomi, and Sakura. Thank you for supporting me and helping me.

Contents

Contributors

Chinthaka Aluthgama-Baduge Derby Business School, University of Derby, Derby, UK

Khairul Hidayatullah Basir Faculty of Agriculture, Universiti Islam Sultan Sharif Ali, Gadong, Brunei Darussalam

Erhan Çankal Department of Finance and Banking, Ankara Yildirim Beyazit University, Ankara, Turkey

Ahmet Kibar Çetin Department of Economics, Ankara Haci Bayram Veli University, Ankara, Turkey

Elena Conde Facultad de Deporte, Catholic University of Murcia, Murcia, Spain

Adriana Ana Maria Davidescu Bucharest Academy of Economic Studies, Bucharest, Romania

Håkon Ege FURIM Institut, Oslo, Norway

Marleen Hofland-Mol Erasmus University, Rotterdam, Netherlands

Lisa Kalina Institute for European Sport Development and Leisure Studies, German Sport University, Cologne, Germany

Minjung Kim Texas A&M University, College Station, TX, USA

Nining Latianingsih Politek Negeri Jakarta, Jakarta, Indonesia

Chul Won Lee Yonsei University, Seoul, South Korea

João Leitão Department of Management and Economics, NECE - Research Center in Business Sciences, University of Beira Interior, Covilhã, Portugal

Iis Mariam Politek Negeri Jakarta, Jakarta, Indonesia

Louis Moustakas Institute for European Sport Development and Leisure Studies, German Sport University, Cologne, Germany

Brent D. Oja West Virginia University, Morgantown, WV, USA

Talis J. Putnins University of Technology Sydney, Ultimo, Australia

Duminda Rajasinghe Nottingham Business School, Nottingham Trent University, Nottingham, UK

Vanessa Ratten Department of Management, Sport and Tourism, La Trobe Business School, La Trobe University, Melbourne, VIC, Australia

Christina L. Rudatin Politek Negeri Jakarta, Jakarta, Indonesia

Antonio Sánchez-Pato Facultad de Deporte, Catholic University of Murcia, Murcia, Spain

Arnis Sauka Stockholm School of Economics, Stockholm, Latvia

Hülya Ünlü Department of Economics, Cankiri Karatekin University, Çankırı, Turkey

Petrus Usmanij La Trobe University, Melbourne, Australia

Nuri Görkem Yönkul Cankiri Karatekin University, Çankırı, Turkey

Claire C. Zvosec Louisiana State University, Baton Rouge, LA, USA

List of Figures

Chapter 11

List of Tables

Strategic Innovation-Strategies for Entrepreneurship and Resilience

Vanessa Ratten and João Leitão

Abstract Innovation should by design have a strategic purpose in order to make a difference to society. The strategic purpose can have an associated positive or negative connotation depending on its impact and usefulness. The aim of this chapter is to understand how strategic innovation can be utilised for entrepreneurial purposes thereby adding to the existing literature on strategic innovation but embedding an entrepreneurship perspective in a more direct way. This helps to understand how strategic innovation has been used in times of crisis and how firms can build their resilience through strategic planning.

1 Introduction

For innovation to be successful, it needs to be well thought out and planned (Charitou & Markides, 2003). This means there is some form of strategy going into every innovation decision (Govindarajan & Trimble, 2005). Whether this actually happens each time an innovation is developed is a matter of perception as some strategies can be unplanned (Ferreira et al., 2017). This chapter will focus on introducing the concept of strategic innovation to the reader, which is embedded into each chapter of the book, thereby making an important contribution to the strategic management, innovation management and entrepreneurship fields. In addition, each chapter focuses on resilience in terms of how entities cope with change. This is useful in the current economic and social climate characterised by the Covid-19 pandemic (Ratten, 2020a, 2020b).

V. Ratten (✉)
Department of Management, Sport and Tourism, La Trobe Business School, La Trobe University, Melbourne, VIC, Australia
e-mail: v.ratten@latrobe.edu.au

J. Leitão
Department of Management and Economics, NECE - Research Center in Business Sciences, University of Beira Interior, Covilhã, Portugal
e-mail: jleitao@ubi.pt

J. Leitão, V. Ratten (eds.), *Strategic Innovation*, Contributions to Management Science, https://doi.org/10.1007/978-3-030-87112-3_1

Strategic innovation is different to traditional forms of innovation as it embeds a planning approach to each decision made regarding the change (Grillitsch et al., 2019). This makes it helpful in reshaping current innovation processes in order to embed new thought processes. Hamel (1998, p. 8) defines strategic innovation as the "capacity to reconceive the existing industry model in ways that create new value for customers, wrong-foot competitors, and produce new wealth for stakeholders." Within this definition there is a recognition of the non-linear nature of innovation that makes it hard to predict. It also highlights the need to outmanoeuvre competitors in the quest to be the dominant market leader (Markides, 1997). This can be difficult due to the competitive reality of the market where there is an emphasis on profit marking activities. Thus, stakeholders need to be considered when making any strategy decisions (Diaz-Carrion & Franco-Leal, 2021). Stakeholders can exist in both direct and indirect ways through their connection with a company. Other definitions of strategic innovation also take this same approach by focusing on the changes within the business model through value creation purposes. For example, Schlegelmilch et al. (2003, p. 118) define strategic innovation as "the fundamental reconceptualization of the business model and the reshaping of existing markets (by breaking the rules and changing the nature of competition) to achieve dramatic value improvements for customers and high growth for companies."

The Covid-19 pandemic has required entities to break the rules in adapting to new market conditions, and as a result, improving innovation efficiency is a major goal of most entities (Pitt & Clarke, 1999). Innovation enables entities to increase their competitiveness and withstand competitive pressures. In the knowledge economy, innovation is power so it must be cultivated (Ratten & Usmanij, 2021). This means reengineering management approaches to incorporate more innovation.

Innovation fundamentally is about new ideas and strategies that make a positive difference to society. Strategic innovation involves both strategy and innovation. The combination of both schools of thought is useful in the global marketplace that requires entities to foresee change. Other terms such as product development and value innovation have been used to describe strategic innovation. Value innovation is a term that has gained popularity due to its recognition of the outputs of the innovation process (Apostolopoulos et al., 2021). This means when analysing innovation the output in terms of usefulness should be considered. This will help in understanding whether the innovation has been successful and made a difference to society. Kim and Mauborgne (1999, p. 43) describe value innovation as something that "makes the competition irrelevant by offering fundamentally new and superior buyer value in existing markets and by enabling a quantum leap in buyer value to create new markets." This means value is evaluated by the market at the time it is produced. It can change depending on surrounding market forces that might emphasise a certain new type of product, service or process. Value should therefore introduce something in favour of a specific individual or entity. This can occur through reshaping existing conditions.

2 Entrepreneurship and Resilience

Resilience as a concept refers to the ability to bounce back from hardship. In times of crisis, being resilient enables an individual to accept new conditions and to adapt to the environment. This capacity to recover from difficult life events is a personality trait that can be learnt over time. As there may be unforeseen obstacles that individuals need to overcome having a resilient mindset is important. It takes time and effort to be resilient. Even if people are resilient, there still is some kind of emotional upheaval associated with change. This means individuals need to manage their stress levels in order to cope with new circumstances. Resilience is sometimes associated with mental toughness due to the need to acclimatize to new conditions. This means being emotionally intelligent can make a difference to how a person perceives change.

The main components of resilience are having a positive and adaptive attitude to change that enables new conditions to manifest in the business environment. This means individuals need to be aware of changing conditions in terms of how this will affect their current condition. Individuals who adopt a mindfulness approach are better able to adapt to the change. Everyone experiences twists and turns in their lifetime but what is important is to have a positive perspective. These changes can differ in magnitude from small alterations that are easy to deal with to more significant and traumatic events. Not everyone will adjust to change in the same way as it depends on their psychological profile but also living conditions. This means each individual brings a unique thought process as to how they analyse the change. Generally, most people accept change as part of their existence but others will be sceptical about whether the change is required.

Resilience gives individuals the strength to proceed in times of hardship. This is important in order to process change and utilise healthy coping mechanisms. Resilient people tend to be more optimistic about change and realise that it normally means hardship for a short period of time. Those people lacking resilience are normally more pessimistic and negative about change. Therefore, they need to tap into support systems in order to obtain help. This can enable them to work through the problems caused by the change.

3 Overview of Chapters

There are 11 chapters included in this book. This chapter has provided an overview of strategic innovation in terms of entrepreneurship and resilient approaches. The second chapter titled 'Workplace Innovation with Baby Boomers: The Role of Job Crafting for Performance and Well-being' by Minjung Kim, Brent D. Oja, Claire C. Zvosec and Chul Won Lee focuses on how entrepreneurship and innovation can be utilised in the workplace. This provides an interesting setting for understanding the ways workplaces can strategically implement innovation. The third chapter titled

'Aligning Strategic MSME Entrepreneurship to Local Government Policy: A Case Study of a Tourism Village in Bogor Indonesia' by Nining Latianingsih, Iis Mariam, Christina L Rudatin, Petrus Usmanij and Vanessa Ratten focuses on strategic innovation in an emerging country context. Thereby offering a novel view as to how entrepreneurship policy can be used in times of hardship through strategic innovation principles. The fourth chapter titled 'Exploring Entrepreneurial Diversity: A Fascination or Frustration?' by Chinthaka Aluthgama-Baduge and Duminda Rajasinghe focuses on strategic innovation through an entrepreneurial diversity perspective. Thus, taking a new approach as to how entrepreneurial can incorporate diverse schools of thought. The fifth chapter titled 'Financial Constraints to Innovation Activities Revealed Barriers Versus Deterring Barriers: Evidence from Turkey' by Hülya Unlu, Erhan Cankal and Ahmet Kibar Cetin highlights the constraints to innovation that result from financial hardship. Thereby providing a useful discussion on how resilience can be built through strategic change. The sixth chapter titled 'Entrepreneurship, Education and Athletes: Entrepreneurship Within European Dual Career Programmes' by Louis Moustakas, Lisa Kalina, Antonio Sánchez-Pato, Elena Conde and Håkon Ege analyses the use of entrepreneurship, innovation and resilience in sport. This involves a focus on how athletes due to their competitiveness can also utilise strategic forms of innovation. The seventh chapter titled 'How to Craft the Entrepreneurial Spirit: Entrepreneurship Education in the Dutch Creative' by Marleen Hofland-Mol analyses the entrepreneurial spirit that is evident in the creative sector. Thereby focusing on strategic innovation in terms of creativity and entrepreneurship. The eighth chapter titled 'Empowering Community Out of Poverty: A Case of Kampong Bolkiah Community Development Centre, Brunei Darussalam' by Khairul Hidayatullah Basir focuses on community forms of strategic innovation. The ninth chapter titled 'How Does the Effect of Absorptive Capacity on Innovation Capacity Change According to Countries' technology manufacturing value added levels?' by Nuri Görkem Yonkul and Hülya Unlu analyses how technology can be used in strategic innovation. The tenth chapter titled 'Reinforcing the Labour Market Resilience. Exploring the Relationship Between Minimum Wage, Official Economy and Informal Economy Using Granger Causality and Scenario Simulations' by Adriana AnaMaria Davidescu discusses the role of the labour market in strategic innovation. The eleventh chapter titled 'Uncovering the Main Characteristics of Shadow Economies in Romania and Moldova for Strengthening the Labour Market Resilience' by Adriana AnaMaria Davidescu, Talis J. Putnins and Arnis Sauka focuses on how innovation can be used in shadow economies, thereby offering a useful perspective about the role entrepreneurship and resilience plays in the labour market.

4 Conclusion

In conclusion, this chapter has presented a broad overview of what strategic innovation is and why it is important for entrepreneurship. In these times of extreme change, it is useful to remember the way innovation can be used in a strategic way in order to alleviating change. This is useful particularly in times of crises that require strategic forms of innovation in order to solve pressing society problems.

References

Apostolopoulos, N., Ratten, V., Petropoulos, D., Liargovas, P., & Anastasopoulou, E. (2021). Agri-food sector and entrepreneurship during the COVID-19 crisis: A systematic literature review and research agenda. *Strategic Change, 30*(2), 159–167.

Charitou, C. D., & Markides, C. C. (2003). Responses to disruptive strategic innovation. *MIT Sloan Management Review, 44*(2), 55–63A.

Diaz-Carrion, R., & Franco-Leal, N. (2021). Social and strategic innovation: Extending the varieties of capitalism to Asian countries. *International Entrepreneurship and Management Journal*, 1–22.

Ferreira, J. J., Fernandes, C. I., & Ratten, V. (2017). Entrepreneurship, innovation and competitiveness: What is the connection? *International Journal of Business and Globalisation, 18*(1), 73–95.

Govindarajan, V., & Trimble, C. (2005). Organizational DNA for strategic innovation. *California Management Review, 47*(3), 47–76.

Grillitsch, M., Hansen, T., Coenen, L., Miörner, J., & Moodysson, J. (2019). Innovation policy for system-wide transformation: The case of strategic innovation programmes (SIPs) in Sweden. *Research Policy, 48*(4), 1048–1061.

Hamel, G. (1998). Strategy innovation and the quest for value. *Sloan Management Review, 39*, 7–14.

Kim, K. W., & Mauborgne, R. (1999). Strategy, value innovation, and the knowledge economy. *Sloan Management Review, 40*(3), 41–54.

Markides, C. (1997). Strategic innovation. *Sloan Management Review, 38*(3), 1.

Pitt, M., & Clarke, K. (1999). Competing on competence: A knowledge perspective on the management of strategic innovation. *Technology Analysis & Strategic Management, 11*(3), 301–316.

Ratten, V. (2020a). Coronavirus (covid-19) and entrepreneurship: Changing life and work landscape. *Journal of Small Business & Entrepreneurship, 32*(5), 503–516.

Ratten, V. (2020b). Coronavirus and international business: An entrepreneurial ecosystem perspective. *Thunderbird International Business Review, 62*(5), 629–6a34.

Ratten, V., & Usmanij, P. (2021). Entrepreneurship education: Time for a change in research direction? *The International Journal of Management Education, 19*(1), 100367.

Schlegelmilch, B., Diamantopoulos, A., & Kreuz, P. (2003). Strategic innovation: The construct, its drivers and its strategic outcomes. *Journal of Strategic Marketing, 11*(2), 117–132.

Workplace Innovation with Baby Boomers: The Role of Job Crafting for Performance and Well-Being

Minjung Kim, Brent D. Oja, Claire C. Zvosec, and Chul Won Lee

Abstract This chapter focuses on innovation via job crafting (i.e., employee-based innovations to job design), specifically for the "baby boomer" generation. The authors offer a conceptual model of the outcomes of baby boomers' job crafting strategies. Specifically, when older (and more experienced) employees have more control over the design of their job responsibilities via job crafting, they are able to use their unique knowledge of their organizations and roles to provide innovations regarding their job tasks, relationships, and perceptions. Consequently, participating in job crafting is thought to support their performance and well-being. The authors also propose that baby boomers are likely to be "active sport tourists" and volunteers at community-based sport and leisure events by using skills learned from active participation in job crafting (e.g., efficiently adjusting their work schedule and increased leadership capacity). Overall, the model proposes that job crafting can provide an organizational competitive advantage by supporting organizational and individual performance and the well-being of baby boomer employees.

M. Kim
Texas A&M University, College Station, TX, USA
e-mail: m.kim@tamu.edu

B. D. Oja (✉)
West Virginia University, Morgantown, WV, USA
e-mail: boja@mail.wvu.edu

C. C. Zvosec
Louisiana State University, Baton Rouge, LA, USA
e-mail: clairez@lsu.edu

C. W. Lee
Yonsei University, Seoul, South Korea
e-mail: wakeford@yonsei.ac.kr

J. Leitão, V. Ratten (eds.), *Strategic Innovation*, Contributions to Management Science, https://doi.org/10.1007/978-3-030-87112-3_2

1 Introduction

The baby boomer generation is generally thought of as those born in the United States between 1946 and 1964. January 1, 2021, marked an important milestone in that everyone in the baby boomer generation had turned at least 65 years old. One may think that older baby boomers, who were born between 1946 and the mid-1950s, have already retired, but 54% of employees in the United States are likely to retire after age 65 or plan to delay retirement (Transamerica Center for Retirement Studies, 2020). In addition, baby boomers are healthier, wealthier, and better educated than previous cohorts of retirees (Patterson & Pegg, 2009). When the retirement period arises, employees experience anxiety about retirement itself, health care, and other aspects of social life in adulthood (DeVaney, 1995), and the cohort of baby boomers is no exception.

The employee life cycle has four stages, encompassed in the term HIAR, which stands for "hire, inspire, admire, and retire" (Reh, 2019). Compared with other stages, retirement planning as a life transition is crucial for employees' postretirement well-being, and the role of employer support with respect to retirement cannot be overstated. Generational differences among employee groups reflect dissimilarities in work values, attitudes, and expectations (O'Bannon, 2001), so employees show different levels of workplace outcomes, such as job satisfaction and work–family conflict (Beutell & Wittig-Berman, 2008). Employees who are within other stages of the employee life cycle (e.g., hire, inspire, admire) and other generations may consider how an organization handles and provides services for the retirement of senior employees. Although the notion of a lifelong workplace no longer holds, the ways by which to consider an employee's retirement is important not only to employees who are close to retirement but also to current ones who will eventually arrive at this stage of their careers.

As the fourth industrial revolution has reshaped the way we work and interact with others, the types of skills that are in demand have also changed. According to the World Economic Forum (2020), the most sought-after competencies in workplaces today are analytical thinking and innovation, active learning, complex problem solving, critical thinking and analysis, and creativity. In these dynamic and innovative work environments, what are the roles of baby boomers and how do they influence younger generations of employees? How can organizations maintain or even augment meaningful work among baby boomers? From managerial and organizational perspectives, what can organizations do for younger baby boomers during the remainder of their careers, other than offer financial and health benefits?

To answer the above-mentioned questions and apply innovative practices in workplaces to gain a competitive advantage, we used job crafting principles, a form of job design, as managerial strategies for ensuring that baby boomer employees are better prepared for retirement physically and psychologically. Job crafting refers to "the physical and cognitive changes individuals make in the task or relational boundaries of their work" (Wrzesniewski & Dutton, 2001, p. 179). In the proposed conceptual framework, job crafting is expected to function as a means of enhancing organizational performance and augmenting employee well-being. The discussion has significant implications for managers, human resource professionals, and leisure programmers on developing plans to promote baby boomer employees' post-retirement well-being.

2 Literature Review

2.1 Baby Boomer Employees

As a cohort of employees, approximately 70% of baby boomers plan to work past age 65, are already working past age 65, or plan to work indefinitely (Transamerica Center for Retirement Studies, 2020). While all generations face uncertainty during economic turbulence, such times are particularly concerning for baby boomers approaching retirement (Buonocore et al., 2015). In relation to the baby boomer generation, Macunovich (2000) detailed, "Its legacy was a population bulge destined to leave its imprint on each phase of the life cycle as it passed through" (p. 2). This sentiment has been echoed by the U.S. Department of Health and Human Services (2021), calling the better understanding of the work, leisure, and general lifestyle preferences of this generation an important challenge.

Age and generation have a significant impact on how employees manage emotional regulation, stress, and well-being; as the general workforce ages (a large subset of which is baby boomers), organizations need to continue to adapt in relation to understanding the characteristics of and maintaining the productivity of older employees (Scheiber & Zacher, 2013). Considering this notion – and the sheer number of baby boomers from a population standpoint – it is critical to learn more regarding sustaining and improving employee well-being, particularly during the pre-retirement years (Mäkikangas et al., 2016). Generational diversity in the workplace is important, and although baby boomers make up an important segment of the workforce, managing work-life balance and workday scheduling could differ from generation to generation. For example, although baby boomer employees may be more family-oriented than prior generations, they seemingly prefer to keep work and life more separate than Generation X, Y, and Z employees (Beutell & Wittig-Berman, 2008). Understanding those preferences is crucial for gaining a better understanding of work dynamics both within and across generations.

When considering the baby boomer generation as an important subset of employees, it is relevant to note the considerable changes this generation has experienced that have impacted typical work expectations and priorities. Specifically, boomers were "raised in an era of social turmoil and changing sex roles with women entering the workforce and men experiencing pressure to be more family-oriented" (Beutell & Wittig-Berman, 2008, p. 509). Interestingly, while baby boomers may value regular work schedules wherein work serves as an anchor in their lives (Beutell & Wittig-Berman, 2008) and most do not use all their vacation days, boomers prefer to mostly disconnect from work while away (AARP Research, 2018).

2.2 Baby Boomer Postretirement Leisure Well-Being

In general, after age 50, most individuals have enhanced well-being and positive emotions (Stone et al., 2010) and baby boomers typically are better educated, have greater discretionary income, and have better health compared to previous generations (Patterson & Pegg, 2009; Sperazza & Banerjee, 2010). Trying to forecast how the baby boomer generation will increasingly impact the tourism and leisure industry is a growing focus (Cochran et al., 2009). Sperazza and Banerjee (2010) detailed, "No longer can it be assumed that bingo, church services, and van rides to view spring flowers will represent the collective leisure interests of baby boomers in retirement" (p. 197). Trends indicate baby boomers may be more focused on active, intellectual, and health-related leisure activities, particularly those activities that give meaning to their postretirement lives (IJspeert & Hernandez-Maskivker, 2020; Sperazza & Banerjee, 2010).

The leisure and tourism industries have shown greater interest in marketing toward the baby boomer generation because of the sheer size of the segment, the increased discretionary income in comparison to prior generations, the interest in more active lifestyles, and the increased free time that comes with retirement (IJspeert & Hernandez-Maskivker, 2020; Patterson & Pegg, 2009; Sperazza & Banerjee, 2010). Moreover, in relation to the size of the baby boomer generation, it is important for practitioners to understand that there is a greater heterogeneity and diversity in the baby boomer generation, and it is paramount to continue to work to understand this generation due to its impact on facilities, programs, services, and health (Kim et al., 2015; Sperazza & Banerjee, 2010).

2.3 Job Design and Crafting

Job design has a long history of utilization within organizational structures as it expands the capacity for organizations to coordinate their workflow and thereby enhance the performance of employees and the overall organization (e.g., enhanced job satisfaction, creativity, employee well-being, and organizational citizenship behaviors; Oldham & Fried, 2016). A job design is the structure of tasks and relationships therein that is assigned to a specific employee (i.e., subordinate) by a manager (i.e., superior; Berg et al., 2013; Oldham & Fried, 2016). Thus, the manager or supervisor holds a critical role in one's job design as they designate and coordinate the tasks that are to be carried out by their subordinates (Tims et al., 2016; Wrzesniewski & Dutton, 2001). In this way, job design theory is a top-down approach to management in that the manager dictates the tasks and roles to those below them within the organizational hierarchy. Yet, modern approaches to job designs have begun to emphasize the subordinate employee and their autonomy to improve organizational performance.

One such expansion of job designs is that of job crafting, which denotes employee initiative and proactiveness (Berg et al., 2013; Tims et al., 2016; Wrzesniewski & Dutton, 2001). Job crafting involves physical and cognitive alterations that employees create in relation to their task and relational boundaries (Wrzesniewski & Dutton, 2001), which represents a bottom-up approach whereby employees themselves change their task and relational boundaries (Berg et al., 2013; Wrzesniewski & Dutton, 2001). The emphasis on the subordinate employee altering their task and relational boundaries further contrasts job crafting from traditional job design perspectives as the attitudinal and motivational responses from job tasks are a result of the employee changing their job, as opposed to these responses being a result of the job itself (Wrzesniewski & Dutton, 2001). Job crafting is consequently not a passive action nor a concept that is handed down to an employee from their manager. Instead, job crafting requires an employee to independently commence the actions necessary to alter their task and/or relational boundaries and by doing so modify their work tasks to accentuate their own values, interests, and strengths (Berg et al., 2013; Tims et al., 2016; Wrzesniewski & Dutton, 2001). The outcomes of active job crafting among employees include employee growth and organizational and individual performance (Berg et al., 2010; Berg et al., 2013; Slemp & Vella-Brodrick, 2014; Wrzesniewski & Dutton, 2001).

Job crafting contains three perspectives: task, relational, and cognitive crafting (Berg et al., 2013; Wrzesniewski & Dutton, 2001). Task crafting is the act of an employee changing the task boundaries of their job. This includes amending the degree, scope, or form of their work tasks by adding, subtracting, or taking on more tasks than what is initially posted within their formal job description. Relational crafting is the undertaking of relationship management in that job crafters revise the quality and/or quantity of their interactions with fellow staff members. The last technique is cognitive crafting, which details how job crafters manipulate their psychological perceptions of their jobs and relationships. This allows job crafters to view their work tasks and coworkers in a positive manner rather than a negative non-productive viewpoint.

3 Conceptual Model

In light of the aforementioned opportunities to improve the work-related experiences of baby boomers, we propose a conceptual model to demonstrate how innovations to job designs that enable job crafting can produce a competitive advantage for an organization. The model relies on the willingness of managers to provide their employees with the necessary autonomy to take command of their job task, relational, and cognitive boundaries. Without such independence, baby boomers would be unable to leverage their unique knowledge and skillsets via job crafting to

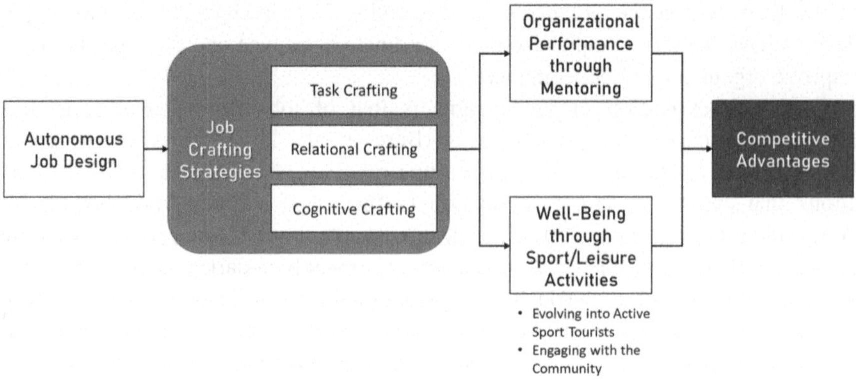

Fig. 1 Conceptual model. *Note*: Authors' own

enhance an organization's ability to compete with other firms. For a competitive advantage to be realized, we posit that when baby boomers are able to actively participate in job crafting two opportunities will arise in the form of mentoring less experienced workers and enrichments to their well-being through active sport tourism and more broadly other sport/leisure activities (Fig. 1).

3.1 Autonomous Job Designs for Job Crafting Among Baby Boomers

Job designs are the task and relationship structures for specific jobs as defined by a manager for an employee (Oldham & Fried, 2016). This top-down approach provides needed coordination for organizations at they compete with other firms in their environment; however, there are opportunities for organizations to surpass their competition with job designs, known as job crafting, that empower employees to utilize their own human capital to innovate the manner by which their job is completed (Berg et al., 2013; Tims et al., 2016; Wrzesniewski & Dutton, 2001). For the proposed model to function, managers need to endorse job designs that promote active job crafting among baby boomer employees in order to realize professional growth within their work experiences (Berg et al., 2013; Wrzesniewski & Dutton, 2001). Although some managers may be wary of permitting employees to have the latitude to control how their job tasks and relationships are coordinated, baby boomers represent a unique constituency group. Baby boomers are likely to be some of the most experienced employees in an organization, which not only signifies that baby boomers would be capable of job crafting, but that managers may have more confidence to authorize baby boomers to craft their jobs given their vast experience. As such, we put forth that job designs which enable baby boomers to participate in job crafting are not only likely to produce greater innovations amongst the workforce but are also a realistic proposition in that managers are more likely to trust the more experienced baby boomers to successfully craft their jobs.

3.2 Organizational Performance Through Mentoring

As noted above, job crafting consists of three elements: task, relational, and cognitive crafting (Berg et al., 2013; Wrzesniewski & Dutton, 2001). We propose that all three elements can uniquely contribute to a baby boomer's ability to transition to a mentorship role within their work capacity. First, the task crafting element of the model represents the most tangible link to an improved performance or competitive advantage. Baby boomers who participate in task crafting can utilize their skills and knowledge of the firm and/or industry to provide efficient task completion strategies (Berg et al., 2013; Wrzesniewski & Dutton, 2001), but more so baby boomers could also modify their tasks so that their task completion strategies include a mentorship element. These task alterations could include opportunities for job shadowing, professional lunches, and an official mentorship program whereby baby boomers are matched with new employees to pass along the unique knowledge they have gained during their time in the industry or organization.

The utilization of task crafting is significant as it moves beyond standard employee manuals and highly formalized mentorship initiatives. Instead, baby boomers would be able to use their own experiences and knowledge to best inform future generations of workers by coordinating and completing their tasks with the efficiencies they have learned. Put differently, human knowledge could be passed along that could not be transferred via an employee manual. Thus, baby boomers who use job crafting to alter their tasks to include a mentorship perspective are likely to provide future employees with knowledge that may have otherwise been lost when a baby boomer moves on to retirement.

Second, relational crafting among baby boomers is put forth as a key element in the social fabric of the baby boomer-new employee dyad, as molding positive relationships with less experienced employees would enable the transfer of knowledge and innovations pertaining to task crafting. Baby boomers who partake in relational crafting are also likely to see improved efficiencies as they would be able to manage their relationships by way of increased communication with key stakeholders as well as shielding themselves from unnecessary social interactions (Berg et al., 2013; Wrzesniewski & Dutton, 2001). Specific to the model, building trust and comradery between baby boomers and new employees despite potential generational differences could pose challenges. Yet, efforts by both groups to enable relating to one another could allow for enhanced understandings and conviction that each group means well.

Despite these potential challenges, baby boomers who are able to manage their relationships to prioritize their interactions with new employees could garner the requisite trust to facilitate a meaningful relationship with their mentee, and new employees who value and appreciate the wisdom and knowledge of their mentor could equally build trust for a meaningful relationship based on the management of their relationship. When trust is established, baby boomer employees could then freely share their innovations and lessons they have learned while completing a job task, and the new employee would be a willing learner and absorb critical information regarding job task efficacy. Overall, building rewarding relationships between a baby boomer and new employee would empower the sharing of task management between one another.

Third, cognitive crafting is an essential element of the mentorship relationship as it represents the acceptance of a baby boomer to provide mentorship to a new employee. By reframing how they view the meaning and tasks of their jobs (Berg et al., 2013; Wrzesniewski & Dutton, 2001), baby boomers can use cognitive crafting to embrace a new role for their organizations. More so, incorporating the role of mentor into their cognitive repertoire can serve as a way to give back to their organization. When baby boomers accept a mentorship role, they provide a lasting and meaningful contribution to their organization. These contributions could be a source of pride for baby boomers while they see their innovations and advancements to their organization continue after they have formally left the organization. However, in order to facilitate relational crafting's trust and task crafting exchange of ideas and knowledge, a baby boomer would need to be accepting of a mentorship role and thus reframe the way they view their job to that of a mentor. Thus, all three elements of job crafting are critical components to ensure that baby boomers can provide superior mentorship to new employees.

3.3 Well-Being Through Participating in Sport and Leisure Activities

Baby boomer employees who utilize job crafting principles are expected to show an increased likelihood of exhibiting improved leisure activity patterns outside of work, especially for activities involving sport and leisure. Mainly through task crafting, these employees can adopt more flexible work schedules and forms of work, which also enables them to augment their time for recreation. With more free time to spend and fewer family obligations, the new retirement cohort group of baby boomers has developed an increasing interest in participating in new sport and leisure activities (IJspeert & Hernandez-Maskivker, 2020). Correspondingly, many tourism scholars have maintained that the cohort of baby boomers engaging with tourism has significantly grown and has been described as a prime example of a niche market (e.g., Mahika, 2011; Patterson, 2012). Sport tourism, in particular, is classified into three types: sport event tourism, active sport tourism, and nostalgia sport tourism (Gibson, 1998). Among these, active sport tourism has elicited attention from many baby boomers, who pursue an adventurous lifestyle and want social interactions.

Because baby boomers tend to be more health-conscious individuals, many of them look for more physically challenging and self-fulfilling experiences within their leisure time. The main motivations for active sports participation among this population are "fun and enjoyment," the "beauty of nature," "social" factors, and "health" (IJspeert & Hernandez-Maskivker, 2020). By occupying themselves with "adrenaline-driven" sport activities (e.g., surfing, skydiving), baby boomer employees can augment both their physical and social well-being. Furthermore, the richer feeling of experiences obtained by learning new skills and being involved in adventurous sport activities may best satisfy their functional and subjective needs, thereby ultimately enriching their lives (Patterson & Pegg, 2009). In summation, we anticipate that baby boomer employees who effectively and efficiently use job crafting strategies can evolve into active sport tourists on their days off and that these active sports would count as one of the leisure options that they can avail themselves of after retirement.

Similar to becoming active sport tourists, baby boomer employees' engagement with the community is highly associated with job crafting principles. As previously indicated, in an organization that permits and encourages employees to craft their jobs, employees are afforded more flexible work schedules through task crafting and opportunities to reconsider their current professional social interactions. Although baby boomer employees are accustomed to performing their jobs in a hierarchical structure in workplaces, it may be a good time to evaluate the quality and quantity of their interactions with their colleagues. Rather than feeling a sense of futility in life after retirement, they can find ways to satisfy their psychological and social needs prior to retirement by crafting tasks and reforming social lives at work. Engaging with the community has been considered as one of the most accessible and sustainable options for baby boomer employees.

For seniors, one of the most common and popular sport and leisure activities is community-based sport participation. The leisure programs provided by a community encompass a wide variety of sports, hobbies, arts, and outdoor recreation activities (Sperazza & Banerjee, 2010), and many senior individuals choose to participate in group sports. According to data from the US Census, baby boomers considerably demand high-tech fitness centers, active recreational group classes, diverse cultural programs, and extensive walking trails in their communities (Cochran et al., 2009). Another path through which seniors can involve themselves with the community is to volunteer for local sporting events. As a socially rewarding experience within a physically active environment, volunteering influences improvements in seniors' physical health, mental health, and quality of life (McDonald et al., 2013; Warburton et al., 2007). Through task and relational crafting, baby boomers can acquire increasing opportunities to enlist in sporting events (e.g., 5 K and 10 K races, community tennis tournaments, collegiate sports) and carry on engaging with their local communities after retirement. Interacting with sport participants and helping others enables them to be a part of their communities and maintain their active lifestyles (Pettigrew et al., 2015).

3.4 Generating a Competitive Advantage with Baby Boomer Job Crafters

The model concludes with two pathways to a competitive advantage for organizations through baby boomer employees who are empowered to actively participate in job crafting. The first path is through mentorship provided by baby boomer employees for new employees. When baby boomers welcome the role of mentor, build a relationship with a mentee, and provide them with their unique knowledge of their innovations and improvements to task efficiences, it is likely to result in the cultivation of a knowledgeable and advanced workforce to take over for the baby boomer generation. Thus, those organizations who promote a job design that enables the autonomy for baby boomers to participate in job crafting are likely to see a more prepared and informed generation of workers to continue the efforts to remain competitive. More so, fostering such an environment could provide a unique advantage over rival organizations that do not provide opportunities for experienced workers to share their knowledge of task efficiencies and completion strategies to new employees. Another potential benefit of creating a space for job crafting within organizations is that the new generation may be emboldened to participate in job crafting as they would have first-hand knowledge of job crafting in practice (Berg et al., 2013; Wrzesniewski & Dutton, 2001). In all, job crafting could be a powerful tool for organizations to retain the talents and learned skills of their retiring employee population.

Another mechanism for a competitive advantage is via the enhanced well-being of baby boomer employees. Scholars have long supported the relationship between employee well-being and organizational performance (Kooij et al., 2013; Nielsen et al., 2017). The current model contributes to this line of research by proposing that baby boomer employees who are either active sport tourists or are able to craft their jobs in a manner that provides additional opportunities for sport and leisure, which then produces enhanced well-being and thusly a competitive advantage. Organizations that allow for innovations to job designs that permit more opportunities for sport and leisure could realize improvements to their organizational performance because of the well-being of their employees. In this way, the model represents a nexus between sport/leisure and management strategies by tying job crafting with employee sport and leisure opportunities with building a competitive advantage from internal human resource practices.

4 Conclusion

In innovative work environments, organizations have attempted to use various strategies for facilitating employee psychological well-being, which ultimately achieves competitive advantages. We proposed job crafting as a promising technique for advancing employee welfare. In particular, we discussed how different job crafting strategies can help baby boomer employees achieve success at work and beyond, and for their organizations to realize a competitive advantage. In workplaces, task and cognitive crafting principles can be expected to help baby boomer employees enhance their perspectives of meaningfulness in their work and avoid unnecessary social interactions. These principles can also aid them in improving their work productivity. With regard to beyond-work settings, we explored the possibilities of baby boomers' evolution into active sport tourists, community-based sport participants, and volunteers in local community sporting events. Through these new and innovative experiences, baby boomer employees who are close to retirement may feel that they can carry on making meaningful contributions to their current workplaces and the communities to which they belong. More so, these contributions can set up the organization to remain competitive once the baby boomer generation – and their industry knowledge – has left the workforce. In conclusion, we expect the positive advancements achieved through job crafting principles (e.g., a desired sense of autonomy, independence, a sense of self-worth, fulfillment) to synergistically augment baby boomers' overall health and quality of life in the contemporary dynamic working environment.

References

AARP Research. (2018). 2019 Boomer travel trends. https://www.aarp.org/content/dam/aarp/research/surveys_statistics/life-leisure/2018/2019-boomer-travel-trends.doi.10.26419-2Fres.00263.001.pdf.

Berg, J. M., Dutton, J. E., & Wrzesniewski, A. (2013). Job crafting and meaningful work. In B. J. Dik, Z. S. Byrne, & M. F. Steger (Eds.), *Purpose and meaning in the workplace* (pp. 81–104). American Psychological Association.

Berg, J. M., Grant, A. M., & Johnson, V. (2010). When callings are calling: Crafting work and leisure in pursuit of unanswered occupational callings. *Organizational Science, 21*(5), 973–994.

Beutell, N. J., & Wittig-Berman, U. (2008). Work-family conflict and work-family synergy for generation X, baby boomers, and matures: Generational differences, predictors, and satisfaction outcomes. *Journal of Managerial Psychology, 23*(5), 507–523.

Buonocore, F., Russo, M., & Ferrara, M. (2015). Work-family conflict and job insecurity: Are workers from different generations experiencing true differences? *Community, Work & Family, 18*(3), 299–316.

Cochran, L. J., Rothschadl, A. M., & Rudick, J. L. (2009). *Leisure programming for baby boomers*. Human Kinetics.

DeVaney, S. A. (1995). Retirement preparation of older and younger baby boomers. *Journal of Financial Counseling and Planning, 6*, 25–33.

Gibson, H. J. (1998). Sport tourism: A critical analysis of research. *Sport Management Review, 1*(1), 45–76.

IJspeert, R., & Hernandez-Maskivker, G. (2020). Active sport tourists: Millennials vs baby boomers. *Journal of Tourism, Heritage & Services Marketing, 6*(2), 12–20.

Kim, Y. W., Fidgeon, P., & Kim, J. (2015). Analyzing the leisure activities of the baby boomers and the generation of liberation: Evidence from South Korea. *Journal of Tourism and Cultural Change, 13*(2), 132–148.

Kooij, D. T., Guest, D. E., Clinton, M., Knight, T., Jansen, P. G., & Dikkers, J. S. (2013). How the impact of HR practices on employee well-being and performance changes with age. *Human Resource Management Journal, 23*(1), 18–35.
Macunovich, D. J. (2000). The baby boomers. In D. Ekerdt (Ed.), *Macmillan encyclopedia of aging*. Columbia University.
Mahika, E. C. (2011). Current trends in tourist motivation. *Cactus Tourism Journal, 2*(2), 15–24.
Mäkikangas, A., Kinnunen, U., Feldt, T., & Schaufeli, W. (2016). The longitudinal development of employee well-being: A systematic review. *Work & Stress, 30*, 1–25.
McDonald, T. W., Chown, E. L., Tabb, J. E., Schaeffer, A. K., & Howard, E. K. (2013). The impact of volunteering on seniors' health and quality of life: An assessment of the retired and senior volunteer program. *Psychology, 4*(3A), 283–290.
Nielsen, K., Nielsen, M. B., Ogbonnaya, C., Känsälä, M., Saari, E., & Isaksson, K. (2017). Workplace resources to improve both employee well-being and performance: A systematic review and meta-analysis. *Work & Stress, 31*(2), 101–120.
O'Bannon, G. (2001). Managing our future: The generation X factor. *Public Personnel Management, 30*(1), 95–110.
Oldham, G. R., & Fried, Y. (2016). Job design research and theory: Past, present, and future. *Organizational Behavior and Human Decision Processes, 136*, 20–35.
Patterson, I. (2012). Baby boomer travel market is on the increase. *Journal of Tourism and Hospitality, 1*(5), 232–243.
Patterson, I., & Pegg, S. (2009). Serious leisure and people with intellectual disabilities: Benefits and opportunities. *Leisure Studies, 28*(4), 387–402.
Pettigrew, S., Jongenelis, M., Newton, R. U., Warburton, J., & Jackson, B. (2015). Research protocol for a randomized controlled trial of the health effects of volunteering for seniors. *Health and Quality of Life Outcomes, 13*(1), 1–8.
Reh. (2019). *The employee life cycle: Hire, inspire, admire, retire (HIAR)*. https://www.thebalancecareers.com/hire-inspire-admire-retire-2276048.
Scheiber, S., & Zacher, H. (2013). A lifespan perspective on emotion regulation, stress, and well-being in the workplace. *Research in Occupational Stress and Well Being, 11*, 163–193.
Slemp, G. R., & Vella-Brodrick, D. A. (2014). Optimising employee mental health: The relationship between intrinsic need satisfaction, job crafting, and employee well-being. *Journal of Happiness Studies, 15*, 957–997.
Sperazza, L. J., & Banerjee, P. (2010). Baby boomers and seniors: Understanding their leisure values enhances programs. *Activities, Adaptation & Aging, 34*(3), 196–215.
Stone, A. A., Schwartz, J. E., Broderick, J. E., & Deaton, A. (2010). A snapshot of the age distribution of psychological well-being in the United States. *Proceedings of the National Academy of Sciences, 107*(22), 9985–9990.
Tims, M., Derks, D., & Bakker, A. B. (2016). Job crafting and its relationships with person–job fit and meaningfulness: A three-wave study. *Journal of Vocational Behavior, 92*, 44–53.
Transamerica Center for Retirement Studies. (2020). *Retirement security: A compendium of findings about U.S. workers*. https://transamericacenter.org/docs/default-source/retirement-survey-of-workers/tcrs2020_sr_20th_annual_compendium_of_workers_report.pdf
U.S. Department of Health and Human Services Centers for Disease Control and Prevention Strategic and Proactive Communication Branch. (2021). *Audience insights: Communicating to boomers 1946–1962*. https://www.cdc.gov/healthcommunication/pdf/audience/audienceinsight_boomers.pdf.
Warburton, J., Paynter, J., & Petriwskyj, A. (2007). Volunteering as a productive aging activity: Incentives and barriers to volunteering by Australian seniors. *Journal of Applied Gerontology, 26*(4), 333–354.
World Economic Forum. (2020). *The future of jobs report 2020*. http://www3.weforum.org/docs/WEF_Future_of_Jobs_2020.pdf
Wrzesniewski, A., & Dutton, J. E. (2001). Crafting a job: Revisioning employees as active crafters of their work. *Academy of Management Review, 26*(2), 179–201.

Minjung Kim is an assistant professor of Sport Management in the Department of Health and Kinesiology at Texas A&M University. She completed her Bachelor's and Master's degrees in Sport and Leisure Studies from Yonsei University, Seoul, Korea. She then received her PhD in Sport Management at Florida State University. Her research efforts endeavor to understand what sport organizations can do to ensure their stakeholders' well-being. Dr. Kim has devoted her efforts to studying positive organizational behavior in sport, sport consumer well-being, and sport business analytics. Her work has been published in leading journals in the field of sport management, including Journal of Sport Management, Sport Management Review, and European Sport Management Quarterly.

Brent D. Oja is an assistant professor of Sport Management in the College of Physical Activity and Sport Sciences at West Virginia University. He received a Bachelor of Arts degree in History and a Bachelor of Science degree in Sport Studies (Emphasis in Sport Management) from the University of Minnesota. He completed his MS (Sport Management) at West Virginia University and his PhD (Sport Management) from the University of Kansas. His research line is grounded within the positive organizational behavior paradigm and is designed to enhance sport employees' skillsets, well-being, and psychological capacities to cultivate a sustainable competitive advantage for sport organizations. His work has been published in journals such as Journal of Sport Management, Sport Management Review, European Sport Management Quarterly, Leisure Sciences, and Managing Sport and Leisure.

Claire C. Zvosec is an assistant professor of Sport Management in the School of Kinesiology at Louisiana State University. She received a BS in Psychology and a BS in Spanish from Washington University in St. Louis. She then completed her MS and PhD in Sport Management from the University of Kansas. Her research interests primarily rely on examining the financial underpinnings of athletics department decision-making and athletics department marketability. In doing such research, Dr. Zvosec often utilizes various theories and conceptual frameworks from organizational behavior, sociological aspects of sport, and the higher education setting. As a secondary research interest, Dr. Zvosec examines the realm of sport officiating. Her work has been published in Sport Management Review, European Sport Management Quarterly, Journal of Global Sport Management, and Managing Sport and Leisure.

Chul Won Lee is a professor of Sports Industry Studies at Yonsei University. He completed his bachelor's and master's degrees in the Department of Physical Education, Yonsei University. Later, he received his PhD in Leisure Studies at the Ohio State University. He is interested in the characteristics of successful leisure organizations and companies. He worked as the former president of the Korean Society of Leisure, Recreation and Park. Currently, he is the president of the Korean Society for Leisure Sciences. His work has been published in the Journal of Coastal Research, Leisure/Loisir, and the International Journal of Qualitative Studies on Health and Well-being.

Aligning Strategic MSME Entrepreneurship to Local Government Policy: A Case Study of a Tourism Village in Bogor Indonesia

Nining Latianingsih, Iis Mariam, Christina L. Rudatin, Petrus Usmanij, and Vanessa Ratten

Abstract The Indonesian Government regulation direction in alleviating the economic added value in 2020–2024 focuses on strengthening MSME entrepreneurship, which includes cooperatives and small and medium enterprise (SME) centers. The strategy of strengthening MSME entrepreneurship implemented is through increasing business partnership between MSMEs and medium to large companies, increasing business capacity and funding access, increasing capacity, range and innovation of cooperatives, increasing business opportunity and startups, and increasing added value of social businesses. The research problem in this chapter focuses on MSME strategic policy of MSME for local community empowerment of tourism village. This chapter employs a descriptive-qualitative method. The result reveals that the strategic development of MSME in tourism village in West Java has been successful in organizing the development of tourist village activities in accordance with the characteristics of the main attractions and its surrounding environment, in maintaining its competitiveness, and in improving local tourism services. In this study, the research examines Kampung Sawah in Cilember village, Cisarua district, Bogor regency as a case study of a tourist village. With the issuance of the central government policy set forth in PP No. 7 year 2021, which contains the Ease, Protection, and Empowerment of Cooperatives and MSMEs derived from Law No. 11 of 2020 Cipta Kerja can unite MSMEs in many sectors. The release of this policy on MSMEs can be a steppingstone in order to support the development of cooperatives and MSMEs in Indonesia.

N. Latianingsih · I. Mariam · C. L. Rudatin
Politek Negeri Jakarta, Jakarta, Indonesia
e-mail: nining.latianingsih@bisnis.pnj.ac.id

P. Usmanij (✉)
La Trobe University, Melbourne, Australia
e-mail: p.usmanij@latrobe.edu.au

V. Ratten
Department of Management, Sport and Tourism, La Trobe Business School, La Trobe University, Melbourne, VIC, Australia
e-mail: v.ratten@latrobe.edu.au

J. Leitão, V. Ratten (eds.), *Strategic Innovation*, Contributions to Management Science, https://doi.org/10.1007/978-3-030-87112-3_3

1 Introduction

The number of entrepreneurs in Indonesia is still below the ideal ratio and only reaches 2% of the population of Indonesia. The ideal ratio is 4%, which will certainly boost the national economic growth (Widarti, 2019). The Indonesian government regulations to empower MSME (Micro, Small and Medium Enterprise) and increase the role of cooperatives are essential, considering about 99.99% of the total business units throughout Indonesia are MSMEs. Additionally, MSMEs have absorbed 87% of the workforce in the business world in 2018 and the MSME sector contributes 61.07% of total GDP in 2018 (Kulsum, 2020).

The government regulation direction in alleviating the economic added value in 2020–2024 focuses on strengthening MSME entrepreneurship, which includes cooperatives and SME (Small and Medium Enterprise) centers (Moerdijat, 2020). The strategy of strengthening MSME entrepreneurship implemented is through increasing business partnership between MSMEs and medium to large companies, increasing business capacity and funding access, increasing capacity, range and innovation of cooperatives, increasing business opportunity and startups, and increasing added value of social businesses. The entrepreneurship development and MSMEs, including cooperative and micro-and-small industrial center, are directed in accordance with the regional potential and are intended for supporting the specific economic region, industrial estates, tourism areas, national priority rural areas as well as the most lagging outer region, and integrated with the infrastructure development (Moerdijat, 2020).

A major challenge of entrepreneurship began in early 2020 during the Covid-19 pandemic outbreak, which impact exceeded SARS in 2002–2003. However, the economic recovery in some countries is predicted to drive improvement in global economic growth in 2020 (Supriyanto, 2020). As reported by the Coordinating Ministry for Economic Affairs of Indonesia (Menko Perekonomian, 2021), the Indonesian economy has indicated a positive growth around 5% due to improvement in poverty, unemployment, inflation, stability, volatility of the Indonesian Rupiah, and the Indonesian Stock Exchange in May 2021. The Indonesian Economic Recovery Program has been proven successful. The balance of trade and the export-import have also indicated a positive growth. The Coordinating Minister of Economic Affairs reported 2.19% trade surplus, economic growth increase of 51.94%, and import increase of 29.93%. The social indicator of the Indonesian economy has moved toward positive outcome as signified by the decrease of unemployment during the Covid-19 pandemic from 7.0% to 6.26% by August 2020 (Menko Perekonomian, 2021).

The research problem in this chapter focuses on MSME strategic policy of MSME for local community empowerment of tourism village. This chapter employs a descriptive-qualitative method. The result reveals that the strategic development of MSME in tourism village in West Java has been successful in organizing the development of tourist village activities in accordance with the characteristics of the main attractions and its surrounding environment, in maintaining its competitiveness, and in improving local tourism services.

2 Literature Review

Tourism is an activity carried out by tourists to a tourist destination outside of daily life and residential environment to make a temporary layover from home, which is driven by some needs without intending to earn income but based on the need to obtain pleasure, as well as accompanied by enjoying a variety of entertainment that can unwind and produce travel experiences and hospitality services (Wahyudi, 2021). One becomes a tourist when one leaves home while free of primary obligations. The activities one engages in then usually are not carried on in isolation. The duties of those who serve the tourist also have been referred to as tourism or (in modern society) the tourist industry (Nash, 1981).

The approach of tourism development is based on the local community's ability to engage in the development of tourism itself. Roads that place the community as an integral part of tourism products and understanding that tourism products are a process of social engineering is at the core of community-based development, the embodiment of community empowerment through the development of economic activities to support any tourism potential that grows in the environment (Adikampana, 2017). The character of rural communities that are resistant to adversity, for example, is the capital for the birth of village entrepreneurs. Village economic entities, such as MSMEs, cooperatives, and village-owned enterprises namely BUMDES must be actively involved in accelerating community empowerment in improving their welfare. The ability to stimulate the dynamics of potential-based economic entrepreneurs and local wisdom through business units to be managed to meet global quality must be done by strengthening the capacity of community communities in a sustainable manner (diskopukmJogya website, 2020).

At the same time, the Indonesian tourist villages are popping up in every district and city (or country town) which seems to have become a trend in accordance with their potential and excellence. Furthermore, there is a tourist village established by investors. Unfortunately, government policies governing the existence of tourist villages and their support such as MSME entrepreneurship or cooperatives are still lacking even at the national level. The management of tourist village does not yet have uniformity, so government policy governing everything about tourist villages in Indonesia is still badly needed.

It has been one year since the Covid 19 pandemic impacted almost all aspects of life globally including health, economic, social, and other aspects. One of the affected aspects is the tourism sector, especially tourist villages. Tourist trips are almost stopped internationally even there are flight cancellations and tourism plans (Hoque et al., 2020). Chinazzi et al. (2020) and Hoque et al. (2020) stated that travel restrictions are in place and apply globally primarily to curb and stop the spread of the virus. The World Economic Culture Forum (WEF, 2020) notes the tourism industry currently accounts for 10% of Global Gross Domestic Product since this industry has a big impact on growth, employment, and livelihoods.

There are two types of management that can be done to manage the tourism village, namely (i) structured type (*enclave*), where the tourist location is separated from the local population so that the negative impacts can be controlled, and the land used is usually not very large and (ii) open type (*spontaneus*), which blends with the local people both tourist activity, space and life patterns with the local community. The community is very much involved in the activities of the tourist village.

A number of obstacles in the implementation of tourism management policies, including limitations of human resources, low coordination, and similarity of perception between local government organizations (OPD), whereas the aspect of coordination is essential in the efforts to encourage the increase of tourist visits (Hernawan & Pratidina, 2015).

The authors observed 23 legal foundations that are the basis for implementing MSME policy in Indonesia, which can be seen in Appendix 1. The issuance of the Work Creation Law (or also known as Undang-undang Cipta Kerja) also impacted the existence of MSMEs in the provision of three facilities to MSMEs to start their business in the country. The step is regulated in the government regulation (known as Peraturan Pemerintah or PP) No. 7 year 2021 concerning Ease, Protection, and Empowerment of Cooperatives and MSMEs. This regulation is a derivative rule of Law No. 11 year 2020 on Copyright Work (Yusuf, 2021).

The government-ratified regulation of PP No.7 year 2021 provides three facilities and supports from the central government and local government as the following: First, the ease of legality process in terms of the establishment of limited liability companies (or also known as PT or Perseroan Terbatas) for SMEs, the registration for Business Identification Number (BIN) as a sole license for SMEs, the fostering the fulfillment of product standards from the government, and the exemption of licensing fees for SMEs. Only the BIN is required to fulfil the legality requirements and the registration process takes between 2 and 3 hours. Second, the ease of production and government financing for MSMEs' capital funding, the provision of raw materials, and the production processes in improving the quality of SMEs' human resources. Only the BIN is required by the MSMEs for the financing application and then access funding from the bank. So far, by presenting a BIN, MSMEs can access up to IDR ten million or equivalent to AUD 1000.00. They can also apply for ban credit through the mechanism of the SME credit. In relation to products, the government through PP 7/2021 has provided guarantees in state spending obliging to take from MSMEs at least 40%. Thus, ministerial institutions and state-owned enterprises are now prioritizing at least 40% spending dedicated for MSMEs. Third is the ease of marketing and post-production with the allocation of 30% of commercial land, shopping places, and infrastructure for MSMEs and then the allocation of at least 40% of government procurement of goods/services for SME's products. This way will boost the SME's market to be better.

The existence of the village and the participation of the community is a very important thing in the life of the state of the Republic of Indonesia. In the sovereign system of the government, local (district) government is referred to as a self-government, and villages are referred to as self-governing communities. The city from a historical point of view is an autonomous community older than the province or country. Therefore, it is natural for the government to give an independent position to the village in a democratic system.

However, since the beginning of the year the Covid-19 virus has not only attacked humans but also public health, the economic and social aspect of the world with all problems arising from chain effects. For tourism business, this is a devastating blow that resulted in them being forced to house almost 90% of employees who depend heavily on tourism. Today the tourism world is significantly weakened and has suffered a very drastic decline. The experiments imposed by the Indonesian government in defending the tourism sector from the negative impact of COVID-19 is by providing incentives to the tourism industry and offering discounts to tourists, but in fact it does not have a constructive impact for now.

The development of tourism village as one of the tourism objects should be followed up in line with the shift in tourism patterns today that are more appreciative of the environment. This fact has triggered awareness of environmentally sound tourism development that considers sustainable utilization of resources for future generations. Travel has been halted with travel bans, closures, lockdowns, and various other forms of travel restrictions. These restrictions have triggered a global economic crisis affecting all sectors. Several tourism events and activities have also been cancelled or postponed/suspended including major sporting and cultural tourism events as well as major exhibitions and conferences.

The United Nations World Tourism Organization (WTO, 2020) states that the COVID-19 outbreak presents the tourism sector with major and growing challenges that will require international leadership in order for tourism to be included as a priority in future recovery efforts. The tourism industry is associated with several key sectors in society including transportation (aviation, cruise ships as well as roads and railways); hospitality and accommodation; culture, sports, and recreation, etc. The World Economic Forum (WEF, 2020) notes that the tourism industry currently accounts for 10% of global GDP (Gross Domestic Product). Therefore, the industry has a huge impact on growth, employment, and livelihoods. The World Travel and Tourism Council (quoted in the WEF, 2020) estimates that up to 50 million jobs related to the travel and tourism sectors are at global risk accounting for a 12–14% reduction in employment. Some island economies and tourist destinations rely almost exclusively on the tourism sector for job creation and economic growth (Dinarto et al., 2020). In addition, travel and recreation are associated with several socio-psychological and educational benefits. Tourism activities, especially tourist villages, have begun to squirm again, especially occurring at the level of MSME entrepreneurship as the supporting capacity of tourist villages.

3 Research Methodology

In this study, the research examines Kampung Sawah in Cilember village, Cisarua district, Bogor regency as a case study of a tourist village. Case studies are the main type of research for the fields of social sciences and management. According to Yin (1994), case study methods are already used in research in the realms of business and organization, education, child development, adolescents, and families, international issues, evaluation, technological development, and social issues. The author hopes that by adopting a case study method on Kampung Sawah can open an initial discourse for research on strategic alignment of local government policies toward MSMEs in the field of tourism development through tourism villages.

There are 15 tourism village managers in Cilember rice field village who participated in the study. The study employed a sociological and empirical normative approach by collecting data not only from the literature but also by means of focus group discussion in the field and polls through Google form. While field research is carried out via communication with the community observed as the perpetrator of tourism activities in Kampung Sawah tourist villages. In addition, the field research is also juridically and sociologically related to the legal context and the participation of local governments, especially rural governments through community empowerment.

There were several interviews conducted on several speakers such as Assistant Deputy for Sustainable Tourism Development of the Ministry of Maritime Affairs and Investment, Head of The Office of Cooperatives and MSMEs, Head of the Cultural and Tourism Office, and Chairman of the Association of Indonesian Business Women of Bogor Regency through several media, such as on a talk show on local radio station namely Teman (or Tegar Beriman) at 95.3 FM. Additionally, the talk show covers preparing various programs, stimulus including taxation in order to reduce the burden of tourism industry operators.

In this study, the authors specifically also tried to describe the socialization of tourism for of the rice field farmers to obtain an idea of the nature or characteristics of a symptom that occurs in the community in developing tourism as a local government program to empower the local people during the Covid-19 pandemic.

In obtaining good qualitative data, the authors conducted field research and directly observed the community. Research tools are interviews, questionnaires, and data/information gathered from related agencies. Data collection techniques are carried out by means of surveys conducted through direct visits to the Kampung Sawah village, by approaching the tourist village through its chairman and the tourism office that potentially has access to data in its entirety. Data analysis is conducted qualitatively in accordance with the type of data studied.

The national entrepreneurial ecosystem is perceived by both Indonesian entrepreneurs and practitioners. This is supported by the results of Gem Survey in 2018 (Gunadi, 2018) which shows the overall aspect of Indonesia above the global average, including the aspects of physical infrastructure that still need to be improved.

4 Results and Discussion

As a startup, this study uses a management model of Kampung Sawah tourism village located in Cilember village, Cisarua Subdistrict, Bogor Regency, conducted through community empowerment as reflected in the residents' attitude in particular those who were complacent during the Covid-19 pandemic. Data obtained from the study in relation to MSMEs conducted in the tourist village of Kampung Sawah tourism village revealed that the MSME types discovered in the research field are homestays, typical food, photography services, cooperatives, wood flowers and ecovillage cooperatives, handicrafts and arts. A summary of the data can be found in Appendix 2. Kampung Sawah tourism village has aligned itself with the policy of MSMEs in Bogor Regency Government by making it easier for MSMEs to operate. This is consistent with other tourism villages in other regions in Indonesia. A summary of the profile of Kampung Sawah tourism village is outlined below.

Kampung Sawah tourism village was established since 2015 under the category of village, was called tourism village and was a member of the forum for tourism development network namely the Bogor Regency Tourism Village Forum. This tourism village support was obtained in 2019 from the Bogor District Tourism Culture Office that helped in improving the human resources of the tourism village management. Then, another support was obtained from Bunda Mulya University in 2019 in improving the knowledge of homestay governance participants of the State University of Jakarta and the Jakarta State Polytechnic.

The implementation and the socialization of the MSME Policy in Bogor Regency have started since 2016. The purpose of this initiative is for MSMEs in Bogor Regency to obtain facilitation in the 2016 MSME Policy. The desired result is the improvement of understanding on the MSME rules and policy which supports the second priority of improving the competitiveness of the local community economy. Starting from 2020 until the time of the Central Government and Bogor Regency Government in West Java make various efforts in empowering SMEs and strengthen the tourism sector with various programs and stimulus to survive the Covid-19 pandemic.

MSMEs are encouraged by various efforts. Furthermore, the government tries to embrace all MSMEs in Bogor district to jointly bridge the MSME actors so that they can meet their consumers with various digital media, so that they do not deteriorate. The government launched a proud national movement namely "made in Indonesia" as the spirit of nationalism that was built to advance domestic products. This is the Policy of the Central Government in developing the overall MSME activities.

The Bogor Regency Government supports and expects MSMEs to survive during the pandemic as well as with the central government's policy on the movement to advance domestic products. There are about 1.3 million MSMEs already on boarding on digital platforms. In addition, the Bogor district government tries to help access to MSME capital funding. One of them is by establishing communication with the set of state banks and finally launched a digital credit program for MSMEs. There is approximately IDR 4.2 trillion channeled to this initiative.

Table 1 List of MSMEs and their products

No	Business name	Product brand
1	Cakes	d_laquw
2	Lele Gastro Kriuk	gastro.quik
3	Roti Durian Cibo	abibakery17
4	Snack Kering	barliansyah_snack
5	Madu Detox	imagorawhoney
6	Minuman Markisa Bogor	suryanti_sugandi
7	Sambel Kurma	intanpratiwi.official
8	Tas Rajut Nenny Collection	nennyiwapijabar
9	Sandal Kulit	ghanaf.project
10	Aneka Jam Custom	jamdinding_klokkloku

MSMEs that are interested in taking out loans from state banks through digital platforms alone can do so via online. Therefore, good communication needs to be built from various lines in order to provide easiness to MSMEs.

The head of the Office of Cooperatives and MSMEs of Bogor Regency stated that Bogor district is among the areas affected by Covid 19 where there are 1569 Bogor district MSMEs that need help from both the local government and the central government in the form of strengthening their operations so that they can be more independent in the midst of the pandemic. There are several programs that are set to be launched such as training programs for MSMEs to adapt quickly to digital platforms.

In addition, the Office of Cooperatives and MSMEs Bogor district has a MSME coaching program in the form of business consulting clinics which provides a direct assistance by involving stakeholders. This activity includes stages of socialization, MSME problem diagnosis, including monitoring management problems, marketing, and others. All of those supports are coming from the central government in the form of policies that can be implemented in the related areas.

The breakthrough implemented by the cultural office and virtual cooperatives is in producing creative products that are recognized nationally such as a collaboration with the Indonesian Association of Women Entrepreneurs and the MSME Office which involved a selection of creative economy. This virtual activity opens up breakthrough activities that open opportunities for MSMEs to participate in a competition for the promoting themselves and tourism in conjunction with tourism objects including tourist villages, hotel venues in cooperation with the Indonesian Hotel Entrepreneurs Association. These stimulus programs can help the MSME actors of Bogor Regency to survive during the Covid-19 Pandemic.

One of the policies of the Bogor Regency Government is to provide incentives to ten selected MSMEs in this region and to invite them to come to Regency Hall for having run their business in line with the main government program namely "Pancakarsa." The implementation of Pancakarsa is to mobilize cooperatives and MSMEs. Table 1 contains a list of ten selected MSME actors who were invited to come to Regency Hall.

Through this program, the Bogor Regency relies on MSMEs as one of the economic restorer sectors in the region due to the COVID-19 pandemic. In order to revive the MSME sector in Bogor Regency, there are several strategic steps implemented by the local government, including by inviting MSMEs to implement digital marketing. The Bogor District UMKM Office has conducted technical guidance and virtual seminars where MSMEs participate. Other efforts are SME bazaar activities both online and offline in collaboration with several malls in Bogor with the theme of expressing the importance of SME survival in the midst of the Covid-19 pandemic. Another program is that the Bogor Regency Government has facilitated MSMEs through store rental programs. Of the 40 new subdistricts, 29 of them that have got store rental program facilities so that MSMEs can run their businesses. Therefore, digital-based business strategy is very important to be implemented, considering that there are still many MSMEs in Bogor district that reached 707 thousand MSMEs (Rama, 2021). MSME actors at the time of the Covid-19 pandemic are also producing goods according to current conditions such as masks, handwash sinks, hand sanitizers, and others that are marketed online to be more optimal in their marketing and buying and selling transactions.

5 Conclusion

The policy implemented to manage MSMEs in Bogor district is in accordance with the current conditions of the Covid-19 outbreak. Kampung Sawah tourist village is ready to become one of the international tourist destinations in Bogor. This is evidenced by the existence of several activities carried out, among others, jamboree activities to the sixth Tourism Village Association Bogor. The availability of a number of homestays in Kampung Sawah for visitors, homestays facilities there are at least 48 home stays provided by tourist villagers and has become part of the business of Cilember tourist village community.

With the issuance of the central government policy set forth in PP No. 7 year 2021, which contains the Ease, Protection, and Empowerment of Cooperatives and MSMEs (KUMKM) derived from Law No. 11 of 2020 Cipta Kerja can unite MSMEs in many sectors. The release of this policy on MSMEs can be a steppingstone in order to support the development of cooperatives and MSMEs in Indonesia.

Appendices

Appendix 1: 23 landasan hukum yang menjadi dasar pelaksanaan kebijakan UMKM di Indonesia

1. Undang-Undang Nomor 11 Tahun 2020 tentang UU Cipta Kerja/Omni Buslaw.
2. UU 9/1995 tentang Usaha Kecil.
3. UU 20/2008 tentang Usaha Mikro, Kecil, dan Menengah.
4. Undang-Undang Nomor 6 Tahun 2014, tentang Desa.
5. Perpres 12/2021 merupakan salah satu peraturan pelaksana dari UU Cipta Kerja.
6. Peraturan Pemerintah Nomor 5 Tahun 2021 tentang Penyelenggaraan Perizinan Berusaha Berbasis Risiko.
7. Peraturan Pemerintah Nomor 6 Tahun 2021 tentang Penyelenggaraan Perizinan Berusaha di Daerah.
8. Peraturan Pemerintah Nomor 7 Tahun 2021 tentang Kemudahan, Perlindungan, dan Pemberdayaan Koperasi dan Usaha Mikro, Kecil, dan Menengah.
9. Peraturan Pemerintah Nomor 8 Tahun 2021 tentang Modal Dasar Perseroan serta Pendaftaran Pendirian, Perubahan, dan Pembubaran Perseroan Yang Memenuhi Kriteria Untuk Usaha Mikro dan Kecil.
10. Peraturan Pemerintah Nomor 9 Tahun 2021 tentang Perlakuan Perpajakan Untuk Mendukung Kemudahan Berusaha.
11. Peraturan Pemerintah Nomor 11 Tahun 2021 tentang Badan Usaha Milik Desa.
12. Peraturan Pemerintah Nomor 35 Tahun 2021 tentang Perjanjian Kerja Waktu Tertentu, Alih Daya, Waktu Kerja dan Waktu Istirahat, dan Pemutusan Hubungan Kerja.
13. Peraturan Pemerintah Nomor 39 Tahun 2021 tentang Penyelenggaraan Bidang Jaminan Produk Halal.
14. Peraturan Pemerintah Nomor 44 Tahun 2021 tentang Pelaksanaan Larangan Praktek Monopoli dan Persaingan Usaha Tidak Sehat.
15. Peraturan Presiden Nomor 10 Tahun 2021 tentang Bidang Usaha Penanaman Modal.
16. Peraturan Menteri Desa, Pembangunan Daerah Tertinggal, dan Transmigrasi Nomor 11 Tahun 2019, tentang Prioritas Penggunaan Dana Desa Tahun 2020.
17. Peraturan Menteri Desa, Pembangunan Daerah Tertinggal, dan Transmigrasi Nomor 16 Tahun 2019, tentang Musyawarah Desa.
18. Peraturan Menteri Desa, Pembangunan Daerah Tertinggal, dan Transmigrasi Nomor 17 Tahun 2019, tentang Pedoman Umum Pembangunan dan Pemberdayaan Masyarakat Desa.
19. Peraturan Menteri Desa, Pembangunan Daerah Tertinggal, dan Transmigrasi Nomor 18 Tahun 2019, tentang Pedoman Umum Pendampingan Masyarakat Desa.
20. Undang-Undang Nomor 22 Tahun 1999 tentang Pemerintahan Daerah.
21. Undang-Undang Nomor 25 Tahun 1999 tentang Perimbangan Keuangan antara Pemerintah Pusat dan Pemerintah Daerah.

22. Peraturan Pemerintah (PP) Nomor 7 Tahun 2021 tentang Kemudahan, Perlindungan, dan Pemberdayaan Koperasi dan UMKM.
23. Peraturan Menteri Koperasi dan UKM (Permenkop UKM) No. 2/2021 tentang Pedoman Umum Penyaluran BPUM.

Appendix 2: Data and Information Collected About Kampung Sawah Tourist Village

Table 2 The potentials and attractions of Kampung Sawah Tourist Village

Potentials	Type of tourism	Attractions
(i) Natural beauty	Rice fields and rivers	Nandur and Gupak at the rice fields and river tubing
(ii) Cultural uniqueness	Traditional martial arts "Pencak Silat"	Jaipongan dance and dancing tutorial
(iii) Handicrafts	Wood flower, recycle products	Open workshops of the handicrafts production
(iv) Culinary	Traditional snacks	Factory visit
(v) Other potential	Photography	Selfie

Table 3 Groups and organizations associated with Kampung Sawah Tourist Village

Group and organization (G&O) names	Prior to becoming a tourist village		After becoming a tourist village	
	Number of G&O	Number of Manpower	Number of G&O	Number ofmManpower
Lembaga Desa Wisata	0	0	1	20
Kelompok Pemandu Wisata	0	0	3	8
Kelompok Sanggar Kerajinan	3	8	6	50
Kelompok Seni Budaya	0	0	3	20
Kelompok Makanan Khas	2	4	3	12
Kelompok Homestay	1	48	1	48
Kelompok Jasa Fotografi	1	2	3	8
Kelompok Sarana Pendukung Wisata Lainnya:				
– Kopersi Desa Wisata	0	0	1	23
– Koperasi Bunga Kayu	0	0	1	25
– Ecovillage	1	6	1	12
TOTAL	**8**	**68**	**22**	**226**

Table 4 Manpower in the Kampung Sawah tourism village by education and gender

	Male					Female				
Name of G&O	PS	SS	SC	B	M	PS	SS	SC	B	M
Pengurus Desa Wisata		2	10					2		
Kelompok Pemandu Wisata		2	3	1				2		
Kelompok Sanggar Kerajinan	18	5	5			20	2			
Kelompok Seni Budaya		5	6			2	4	3		
Kelompok Kuliner		2				2	4	4		
Kelompok Homestay	4	5	3			18	10	8		
Kelompok Sarana Pendukung Wisata Lainnya:										
– Koperasi Desa Wisata	2	6	10	2		1	1	1		
Total	24	27	37	3		43	21	20		
Grand total	91 male + 84 female = 175 or 52% male and 48% female									

References

Adikampana, I. M. (2017). *Pariwisata berbasis Masyarakat*. Retrieved May 21, 2021, from https://simdos.unud.ac.id/uploads/file_pendidikan_1_dir/2380508977a611bbadb6e562e19690b8.pdf

Chinazzi, M., Davis, J. T., Ajelli, M., Gioannini, C., Litvinova, M., Merler, S., Piontti, A.P., Mu, K., Rossi, L., Sun, K., & Viboud, C. (2020). The effect of travel restrictions on the spread of the 2019 novel coronavirus (COVID-19) outbreak. *Science*. https://doi.org/10.1126/science.aba9757.

Dinarto, D., Wanto, A., & dan Sebastian, L.C. (2020). *Keamanan Kesehatan Global–COVID-19: Dampak pada Sektor Pariwisata Bintan*. Komentar RSIS, 033-20.

Diskopukpm DIY. (2020). *Tatakelola Pelaksanaan Desa Preneur*. Retrieved May 20, 2021, from https://diskopukm.jogjaprov.go.id/files/20200728159592271 1_SK%20Tatakelola%20Pelaksanaan%20DESA%20PRENEUR.pdf

Gunadi, D. (2018). *Kebijakan Pengembangan Kewirausahaan oleh Bappenas*. Retrieved May 20, 2021, from https://smeru.or.id/sites/default/files/events/ahmad_dading_gunadi_-_kebijakan_pengembangan_kewirausahaan_oleh_bappenas.pdf

Hernawan, D., & dan Pratidina, G. (2015). Model Implementasi Kebijakan Pengembangan Pariwisata dalam Meningkatkan Destinasi Pariwisata di Kabupaten Bogor. *Jurnal Sosial Humaniora, 6*(2). Retrieved May 24, 2021, from https://ojs.unida.ac.id/JSH/article/view/504/pdf

Hoque, A., Shikha, F. A., Hasanat, M. W., Arif, I., & Hamid, A. B. A. (2020). The effect of coronavirus (COVID-19) in the tourism industry in China. *Asian Journal of Multidisciplinary Studies, 3*(1), 1–7.

Kulsum, K. U. (2020). Retrieved May 23, 2021, from https://kompaspedia.kompas.id/baca/paparan-topik/perkembangan-kebijakan-pemerintah-terhadap-umkm-di-indonesia

Menteri Koordinator Bidang Perekonomian (Menko Perekonomian). (2021). *Airlangga Hartarto Biro Pers, Media, dan Informasi Sekretariat Presiden*. Retrieved May 24, 2021, from https://www.presidenri.go.id

Moerdijat, L. (2020). *Kebijakan Peningkatan Nilai Tambah Ekonomi dalam tahun 2020–2024*. Retrieved May 24, 2021, from https://www.lestarimoerdijat.com/pustakalestari/read/2019/08/13/661/Kebijakan-Peningkatan-Nilai-Tambah-Ekonomi-dalam-tahun-2020-2024

Nash, D. (1981, October). Tourism as an anthropological subject. *Current Anthropology, 22*(5), 461–481.
Rama, H. (2021) Inilah strategi Dinas Koperasi dan UKM kabupaten Bogor bantu Pelaku Usaha saat Pandemi covid 19. *Dinas UMKM Kabupaten Bogor*. Retrieved May 20, 202, from https://wartakota.tribunnews.com/2021/04/17/inilah-strategi-dinas-koperasi-dan-ukm-kabupaten-bogor-bantu-pelaku-usaha-saat-pandemi-covid-19
Supriyanto, B. (2020). Retrieved May 20, 2021, from https://ekonomi.bisnis.com/read/20200427/9/1233454/dampak-pandemi-covid
The World Economic Forum. (2020). *This is how coronavirus could affect the travel and tourism industry*. Retrieved April 26, 2021, from https://www.weforum.org/agenda/2020/03/world-travel-coronavirus-covid19-jobs-pandemic-tourism-aviation/
The World Trade Organisation. (2020). *COVID-19: Putting people first—Tourism and COVID-19*. Retrieved April 28, 2021, from https://www.unwto.org/tourism-covid-19
Wahyudi, I. (2021). Retrieved May 25, 2021, from https://cvinspireconsulting.com/konsep-pengembangan-pariwisata/.
Widarti, P. (2019). Retrieved May 22, 2021, from https://ekonomi.bisnis.com/read/20191001/9/1154153/rasio-jumlah-wirausahawan-di-indonesia-baru-2-persen-idealnya-4-persen
Yin, R. (1994). *Applications of case study research*. Sage.
Yusuf, I. S. (2021). 3 Kemudahan UMKM setelah terbitnya PP 7/2021. https://industri.kontan.co.id/news/ini-3-kemudahan-umkmsetalah-terbitnya-pp-72021 as viewed on 28th May 2021.

Nining Latianingsih is a lecturer and researcher of the Politeknik Negeri Jakarta, Indonesia.

Iis Mariam is a lecturer and researcher of the Politeknik Negeri Jakarta, Indonesia.

Christina L. Rudatin is a lecturer and researcher of the Politeknik Negeri Jakarta, Indonesia.

Petrus Usmanij is a researcher of La Trobe University, Australia.

Vanessa Ratten is a researcher of La Trobe University, Australia.

Exploring Entrepreneurial Diversity: A Fascination or Frustration?

Chinthaka Aluthgama-Baduge and Duminda Rajasinghe

Abstract This chapter critically discusses the importance of acknowledging diversity within entrepreneurship and some strategies to facilitate the richness of the phenomenon. It helps researchers and practitioners to understand the importance and benefits of having different but equally valid world views about the phenomenon, which is vital for entrepreneurship research to progress further. We acknowledge that there are already some established arguments to support inclusiveness within the current context of entrepreneurship research. The aim here is to strengthen these arguments with a brief literature rationale, which is informed by our research experience. One of the key advantages of acknowledging heterogeneity is that it can help scholars to convert any frustrations that is caused by not having common understanding to a fascination to embrace the wholeness of the phenomenon. Our understanding of how to appreciate diversity and inclusion is limited; as a solution, we encourage critical debates among multiple actors of entrepreneurship and urge to widen research adopting more innovative and creative approaches.

1 Introduction

This chapter aims to discuss the importance of diversity in entrepreneurship to help the field to move forward progressively. In our view, appreciation of diversity is vital to develop a holistic understanding of the phenomenon. Developing such understanding, for example, can facilitate governments, policy makers, and funding bodies to tailor support that they extend for both established and nascent entrepreneurs.

For this chapter, we position entrepreneurship as a multifaceted, complex social construct. Therefore, it is contextually embedded and subjective (see Rajasinghe

C. Aluthgama-Baduge (✉)
Derby Business School, University of Derby, Derby, UK
e-mail: c.aluthgama@derby.ac.uk

D. Rajasinghe
Nottingham Business School, Nottingham Trent University, Nottingham, UK

J. Leitão, V. Ratten (eds.), *Strategic Innovation*, Contributions to Management Science, https://doi.org/10.1007/978-3-030-87112-3_4

et al., 2021). This leads us to argue that it is vital to appreciate the diversity which should be encouraged by challenging current predispositions and dominant views. Otherwise, our understanding of the phenomenon can be limited by dominant paradigms (Berglund & Johansson, 2007; Rajasinghe et al., 2021) and may mute the complexities within the field. Thus, we emphasize the importance of appreciating diversity and discuss how this can facilitate creativity and innovation.

According to Davidsson (2004, 2016, p. 1), "one of the fascinations [of researching entrepreneurship] is the richness of the phenomenon which leads to one of the greatest frustrations, namely the lack of common understanding of what precisely entrepreneurship is." It seems to us that society at large is still driven in search of near impossible, "a common understanding." In our view, frustration emphasized by Davidsson is a result of deeply rooted predispositions of the phenomenon and different world views of diverse stakeholders of entrepreneurship. Once these mental models and world views are challenged and questioned, the diversity within the field can be fascinating for entrepreneurship scholars, practitioners, and other stakeholders. This is vital for the phenomenon to move forward without restricting it into a mechanistic discipline (Rajasinghe et al., 2021; Rajasinghe & Mansour, 2019). We acknowledge that numerous researchers and practitioners have been establishing theories and practices that embrace diversity. However, many (see Hlady-Rispal & Jouison-Laffitte, 2014; Marlow, 2020) continue to affirm that the field is still positivist dominant which can restrict our understanding of entrepreneurship and entrepreneurial activity.

2 Nature of Entrepreneurship

Entrepreneurship is subjected to multiple interpretations (Aluthgama-Baduge, 2017; Blundel et al., 2018). For example, some authors attempt to define entrepreneurship by incorporating traits (Chell, 2013) and psychological aspects (Gartner, 2012; Tang, 2020) of entrepreneurs into their definitions. Furthermore, governments and policy makers explore to understand entrepreneurship through metrics such as economic growth, technology clusters, and job creation (Block et al., 2017). There is a public discourse which encourages the view that entrepreneurship resides within individuals, for example, Sir Richard Branson, Sir Alan Sugar, and Sir James Dyson (Block et al., 2017; Bridge, 2017). Moreover, entrepreneurship is described differently through various social, cultural, and geographical lenses (Baker & Welter, 2020). For instance, in China, the success of entrepreneurship is closely linked with "Guanxi," the social networks that underpin the practice of entrepreneurship (Burt & Burzynska, 2017). In conjunction with risk-taking and experimentation, "a culture of failure (. . .) appears to be prevalent in Silicon Valley" (Gold, 2017, p. 119), USA. Therefore, failure appears as a key element of entrepreneurship in this context, whereas entrepreneurial endeavor is predominantly perceived as a value creation and individual activity in places such as Denmark (Reffstrup & Christiansen, 2017).

We also noticed some common themes within entrepreneurship literature – for instance, newness (e.g., product, process, organization) (Gartner, 1988; Lumpkin & Dess, 1996); profit-making (Kirzner, 1973); recognising, creating and exploiting opportunities (Rae, 2015). In addition, themes such as creating new combinations (Schumpeter, 1934, 2017) and managing turnaround in an existing organization (Panicker & Manimala, 2015) are also relatively popular. More recent themes in the field include creating value for others (see Lackéus, 2020) and social value co-creation (see Ratten, 2020). Entrepreneurship is also researched from different perspectives, such as economics and management (Block et al., 2017); arts (Paulsen et al., 2020); and in various disciplines from health care (Haase & Franco, 2020) to engineering, and design (Mäkimurto-Koivumaa & Belt, 2016). Research is also being carried out in different contexts varying from academia (Schaeffer & Matt, 2016), family business (Jones & Li, 2017), diverse ethnic groups (Henry et al., 2018), refugees (Refai et al., 2018), natives, and immigrants (Brzozowski et al., 2018). Therefore, there is evidence of diversity in definitions, themes, and scholarly efforts to acknowledge the subjective nature of the phenomenon. However, majority appears to be influenced by "public prominence of innovative, high-growth, technology-based, and venture capital-backed ventures" (Welter et al., 2017, p. 313) which seems to have influenced practitioner and research agendas within the field.

3 Why Is Acknowledging Diversity Important?

The diversity present with entrepreneurship is an opportunity for us to know about the phenomenon deeply and to develop more relevant and applicable knowledge (Welter et al., 2016). Our position of entrepreneurship that it is a social activity informed by humanism (Rajasinghe & Mansour, 2019) helps us to argue that entrepreneurship is predominantly grounded within culturally and contextually informed experiences of various actors (e.g., entrepreneurs, intrapreneurs, venture capitalists, and scholars) who reside in entrepreneurial ecosystems (Stam, 2016). However, "much of our research continues the highly skewed quest to develop our understanding of entrepreneurship by studying a tiny group of outliers, while frequently ignoring the vast bulk and diversity" (Welter et al., 2017, pp. 312–313) of what is actually happening in everyday entrepreneurial activities. This appears to have restricted our understanding of the phenomenon.

Less attention placed upon understanding contextual influences on entrepreneurial process can also be observed. For example, sufficient emphasis has not been placed on cross-cultural and transnationally networked nature of entrepreneurship and innovation (Sun, 2020; Williams et al., 2020). "Focusing on such linkages not only would uncover the complex ways that actors mobilize a range of resources and traverse social and geographic spaces (as they travel physically and virtually) but would further foreground the changing nature of space itself" (Fraiberg, 2021, p. 177). Similarly, identities, behaviors and actions of entrepreneurs, individual consciousness, perceptions, attitudes, and environmental and socio-cultural factors should be captured to develop a comprehensive understanding of the phenomenon (see Anderson & Gaddefors, 2017; Berglund, 2015; Raco & Tanod, 2014). Given the "demand for creativity and judgement in the face of unclear goals and uncertainty" (Rajasinghe et al., 2021, p. 867), it is also vital to understand the complex interplay between individuals, social and environmental factors (Joo et al., 2013) within entrepreneurial eco-systems which may revitalize the wholeness of the field.

This idea can be appealing to researchers who acknowledge the subjective nature of entrepreneurship (Brannback & Carsrud, 2016; Gaddefors & Anderson, 2017). To our understanding, acknowledging diversity from scholarly perspective is an indirect endorsement of different realities that exist including positivist paradigm. Thus, our urge for active acceptance of diversity within entrepreneurship should not be seen as an effort to discard any world views but as an endeavor to appreciate them all equally to develop a deeper understanding. This lays a foundation for entrepreneurship stakeholders to see the phenomenon beyond their own frame of reference.

Therefore, we invite stakeholders of entrepreneurship to be more open for diversity and to promote different avenues of knowing so the field progresses further to achieve its true potential. This may reduce the risk of restricting our understanding of the phenomenon by the limited world views that we currently possess as researchers and practitioners.

4 Strategies to Appreciate Diversity

We are yet to develop a comprehensive understanding of how the field should approach appreciating diversity. We re-emphasize that the critical entrepreneurship scholarly communities and practitioners should continue to explore the possibilities and the challenges of ensuring diversity. Based on our experience of research and practitioner engagement, we discuss three such strategies that may help generating further debates.

4.1 Wider Research to Develop Subjective Knowledge

It is vital to challenge the socially accepted predispositions of entrepreneurship that limit our understanding (Berglund & Johansson, 2007; Fraiberg, 2021) as they appear to mask complications and ambiguities rooted within the phenomenon (Fraiberg, 2021; McKelvey, 2004; Steyaert & Katz, 2004). Therefore, wider research to develop subjective knowledge embedded in various contexts (Fuller-Love & Akiode, 2020; Welter et al., 2016) by appreciating "inclusivity, diversity, and pluralism in research perspectives and approaches" (Leitch et al., 2010, p. 79) should continue rather than restricting our understanding to few different variables (Rajasinghe et al., 2021). We endorse the idea of Welter et al. (2017, p. 318) that "there is no one type of entrepreneurship. No one best way. No ideal context. No ideal type of entrepreneur. Differences matter, and, if we actually believe this, then, we need to be looking for where, when, and why those differences matter most. And we need to pay attention to our language: does it extend to such variety, differences and heterogeneity?" Therefore, encouraging critical debates, questioning our ontological and epistemological assumptions, social, religious and cultural belief systems assist us to develop different but equally valid understanding of the phenomenon.

4.2 Innovative Research Approaches to Deepen Understanding of Uniqueness

We emphasize the importance of exploring individual and collective experience and understanding of wider stakeholders of entrepreneurship considering that entrepreneurship is grounded in the experience of multiple stakeholders (Packard, 2017; Rajasinghe et al., 2021; Stam, 2016). This allows scholars to fully appreciate the richness of the contextually embedded unique experiences which may not be sufficiently acknowledged through dominant positivist approaches or by relying on few popular qualitative frameworks (Raco & Tanod, 2014; Van Burg et al., 2020) "overlooking the breadth of approaches qualitative research has to offer" (Van Burg et al., 2020, p. 2). To address these challenges, scholars should "enable different forms of analysis and offer the potential for novel theorising of entrepreneurship process" (Van Burg et al., 2020, p. 2) through innovative research approaches and perspectives. However, it appears that our attention to such innovative approaches is relatively insufficient to meet the current knowledge demands within the field (Rajasinghe et al., 2021; Van Burg et al., 2020).

4.3 Facilitating Knowledge Co-Creation

There is encouraging evidence of growth of studies that focus on developing required understanding for policy, practice and research but the society continues to search for universal truths by muting the complexities present within entrepreneurship (Marlow, 2020; McDonald et al., 2015). This is not solely an issue with research but also our perspectival directedness towards more generalizable knowledge (Anderson & Gaddefors, 2017) and practice. Thus, the field needs adopting contemporary approaches to knowledge production, for example, by facilitating co-creation of knowledge (Aluthgama-Baduge, 2017), i.e., joint production of knowledge between practitioners, researchers, policy makers, and other actors (OECD, 2021). This is crucial particularly in the contexts such as entrepreneurship "where collaboration between multiple stakeholders matters and can also help prepare for societal transitions to more sustainable, inclusive and resilient futures" (OECD, 2021, p. 6). It is also vital to understand the role of context in knowledge production (Baker & Welter, 2020) and question "whom should our research serve?" or the purpose of our entrepreneurial practice. This is timely given that "we have become rather self-centred in the development of our research" (Welter et al., 2017, p. 317) and practice, narrowing down our themes to fit into criteria to gain tenure or to celebrate the wealthy and successful (Welter et al., 2017) by depriving opportunities of many unknown individuals, groups, and organizations who could facilitate us to understand the phenomenon deeply.

5 Benefits of Exploring and Appreciating Diversity

We reiterate that the gaps highlighted above should be addressed by creating space for diverse stories of entrepreneurs to emerge thereby facilitating deeper understanding of the practice of entrepreneurship, for example, how it is practiced, interpreted, and perceived in various contexts (Welter et al., 2017). These different lenses may include commercial, social, and natural lenses (Bacq & Janssen, 2011; Dobson and McLuskie, 2020) or entrepreneurship during times of crisis such as Covid-19 (Ratten, 2020). Openness to these differences within entrepreneurship leads us to understand the iterative and inherently open process of entrepreneurship which ranges from, ideation, exploration of opportunities, creativity and innovation, growth, result-orientation, success, and failures.

For example, if we look at entrepreneurship from creativity perspective, we can argue that the creativity is a vital element of the phenomenon. This is evident when we look at Amabile's (1988) notion of creativity as the generation of useful and novel ideas or some others' interpretations that it involves generation of workable original solutions to complex ill-defined problems (Lubart, 2001). Woodman et al. (1993, p. 293) position creativity as a "creation of new product, service, idea procedure or process" by actors within a complex social system. Novelty, complexity, and providing valuable solutions continue to appear as key themes within the creativity literature (see Joo et al., 2013; Zhang & Zhou, 2014). These to our understanding echo well with the notion of more holistic entrepreneurship. Therefore, we urge readers to consider that entrepreneurship and creativity are set of complicated interdependencies rather than isolated discoveries (see Joo et al., 2013) and respect these complexities of the phenomenon. This is for us is appreciation of diversity which seems to create a platform to be more creative and innovative.

Promoting studies that appreciate diversity also underpins conceptualizing messy paths of entrepreneurship and how initial ideas evolve over a period of time through multiple interactions of social actors (Baker & Nelson, 2005; Nayak & Chia, 2011). The more diverse the new knowledge generated in a region, the higher the probability for a greater volume of entrepreneurship. Similarly, an inclusive approach to entrepreneurship forms the basis for economic agents to perceive and value potential market opportunities differently (Qian et al., 2012) and to enhance economic performance (Verheul & Van Stel, 2010). This can help challenge the notion that entrepreneurship is an intentionally planned linear trajectory (Steyaert, 2007).

Above all, the appreciation of diversity lays a foundation for entrepreneurship stakeholders to explore wider ontological and epistemological positions, thereby not solely relying on measurable outcomes and statistically generalizable knowledge. Such attempts to rely on positivist expectations often appear to lead to one of the greatest frustrations but we see the possibility of converting such frustration into "one of the fascinations of researching (. . .) and understanding entrepreneurship" (Davidsson, 2016, p. 1) by acknowledging the richness and the contextual nature of the construct. We also believe that fascination generated by appreciating richness leads entrepreneurs to be free thinkers rather than relying on one world view thereby creating opportunities to be more creative and effective in their entrepreneurial engagements. It can facilitate practitioners to empathize and comprehend the stories of other social actors, and also policy makers to understand the need for tailoring support structures within the contexts that they operate.

6 Conclusion

This chapter emphasizes the need for accepting diversity in entrepreneurship research and practice. Diversity can be frustrating for many who cannot enjoy the complexity within the field. This frustration may be a result of our predispositions or due to the structures and the cultures that we belong to or associate with. We invite readers to question their world views (ontological and epistemological positions of entrepreneurship) and strive to be more inclusive in research approaches, practice, and policy initiatives by placing more emphasis on areas such as ethnicity, religion, sexual orientation, age, gender, cultural, information and personality diversity. Facilitating a fuller appreciation of entrepreneurial diversity can advance our understanding of the disparate ways that entrepreneurship can help in times of crisis situations such as Covid-19.

We are obsessed by the diversity and firmly believe that it is a vital ingredient of growth and sustainability. Thus, our aim was to discuss and re-emphasize the importance of diversity in entrepreneurship to help the field to move forward progressively. This may help us to be more fascinated by the heterogeneity and richness of the phenomenon.

References

Aluthgama-Baduge, C. J. (2017). *Educating for enterprise: Exploring the role of the teacher. An interpretative phenomenological analysis* [PhD thesis]. Abertay University.

Amabile, T. M. (1988). A model of creativity and innovation in organisations. In B. M. Staw & L. L. Cummings (Eds.), *Research in organisational behaviour* (pp. 123–167). JAI Press.

Anderson, A. R., & Gaddefors, J. (2017). Is entrepreneurship research out of context? *Journal of Asia Entrepreneurship and Sustainability, 13*(4), 3–9.

Bacq, S., & Janssen, F. (2011). The multiple faces of social entrepreneurship: A review of definitional issues based on geographic and thematic criteria. *Entrepreneurship and Regional Development, 23*(5–6), 376–403.

Baker, T., & Nelson, R. (2005). Creating something from nothing: Resource construction through entrepreneurial bricolage. *Administrative Science Quarterly, 50*, 329–366.

Baker, T., & Welter, F. (2020). *Contextualizing entrepreneurship theory*. Routledge.

Berglund, H. (2015). Between cognition and discourse: Phenomenology and the study of entrepreneurship. *International Journal of Entrepreneurial Behavior and Research, 21*(3), 472–488.

Berglund, K., & Johansson, A. W. (2007). Constructions of entrepreneurship: A discourse analysis of academic publications. *Journal of Enterprising Communities: People and Places in the Global Economy, 01*(1), 77–102.

Block, J. H., Fisch, C. O., & van Praag, M. (2017). The Schumpeterian entrepreneur: A review of the empirical evidence on the antecedents, behaviour and consequences of innovative entrepreneurship. *Industry and Innovation, 24*(1), 61–95.

Blundel, R., Lockett, N., & Wang, C. (2018). *Exploring entrepreneurship* (2nd ed.). Sage.

Brannback, M., & Carsrud, A. L. (2016). Understanding entrepreneurial cognitions through the lenses of context. In F. Welter & W. B. Gartner (Eds.), *A research agenda for entrepreneurship and context* (pp. 16–27). Edward Elgar.

Bridge, S. (2017). *The search for entrepreneurship: Finding more questions than answers*. Routledge.

Brzozowski, J., Cucculelli, M., & Surdej, A. (2018). Exploring transnational entrepreneurship. Immigrant entrepreneurs and foreign-born returnees in the Italian ICT sector. *Journal of Small Business and Entrepreneurship, 35*(5), 413–431.

Burt, R. S., & Burzynska, K. (2017). Chinese entrepreneurs, social networks, and *Guanxi*. *Management and Organization Review, 13*(3), 221–260.

Chell, E. (2013). Review of skill and the entrepreneurial process. *International Journal of Entrepreneurial Behaviour and Research, 19*(01), 6–31.

Davidsson, P, (2004). *Researching entrepreneurship*. Springer Science + Business Media.

Davidsson, P. (2016). *Researching entrepreneurship: Conceptualization and design* (2nd ed.). Springer.

Dobson, S., & McLuskie, P. (2020). Performative entrepreneurship: Identity, behaviour and place in adventure sports enterprise. *International Entrepreneurship and Management Journal, 16*(3), 879–895.

Fraiberg, S. (2021). Introduction to special issue on innovation and entrepreneurship communication in the context of globalization. *Journal of Business and Technical Communication, 35*(2), 175–184.

Fuller-Love, N., & Akiode, M. (2020). Transnational entrepreneurs dynamics in entrepreneurial ecosystems: A critical review. *Journal of Entrepreneurship and Innovation in Emerging Economies, 06*(1), 41–66.

Gaddefors, J., & Anderson, A. (2017). Entrepreneursheep and context: When entrepreneurship is greater than entrepreneurs. *International Journal of Entrepreneurial Behaviour and Research, 23*(2), 267–278.

Gartner, W. B. (1988). Who is an entrepreneur' is the wrong question. *American Small Business Journal, 12*(4), 1–31.

Gartner, W. B. (2012). Psychology, entrepreneurship, and the 'critical mess'. In J. R. Baum, M. Frese & R. A. Baron (Eds.), *The psychology of entrepreneurship* (pp. 325–334). Psychology Press.

Gold, B. (2017). *Silicon valley start-ups and corporate innovation: Approaches to resolve the innovator's dilemma*. Springer Gabler.

Haase, H., & Franco, M. (2020). Leadership and collective entrepreneurship: Evidence from the health care sector. *Innovation: The European Journal of Social Science Research, 33*(3), 368–385.

Henry, E. Y., Dana, L., & Murphy, P. J. (2018). Telling their own stories: Māori entrepreneurship in the mainstream screen industry. *Entrepreneurship and Regional Development, 30*(1-2), 118–145.

Hlady-Rispal, M., & Jouison-Laffitte, E. (2014). Qualitative research methods and epistemological frameworks: A review of publication trends in entrepreneurship. *Journal of Small Business Management, 54*(4), 594–614.

Jones, O., & Li, H. (2017). Effectual entrepreneuring: A sensemaking in a family-based start-up. *Entrepreneurship & Regional Development, 29*(5-6), 67–499.

Joo, B., McLean, G., & Yang, B. (2013). Creativity and human resource development: An integrative literature review and a conceptual framework for future research. *Human Resource Development Review, 12*(4), 390–421.

Kirzner, I. M. (1973). *Competition and entrepreneurship*. The University of Chicago Press.

Lackéus, M. (2020). Comparing the impact of three different experiential approaches to entrepreneurship in education. *International Journal of Entrepreneurial Behaviour and Research, 26*, 5937–5971.

Leitch, C. M., Hill, F. M., & Harrison, R. T. (2010). The philosophy and practice of interpretivist research in entrepreneurship: Quality validity and trust. *Organizational Research Methods, 13*(1), 67–84.

Lubart, T. I. (2001). Models of the creative process: Past, present and future. *Creativity Research Journal, 13*(3-4), 295–308.

Lumpkin, G. T., & Dess, G. G. (1996). Clarifying the entrepreneurial orientation construct and linking it to performance. *Academy of Management Review, 21*(1), 135–172.

Mäkimurto-Koivumaa, I., & Belt, P. (2016). About, for, in or through entrepreneurship in engineering education. *European Journal of Engineering Education, 41*(5), 512–529.

Marlow, S. (2020). Gender and entrepreneurship: Past achievements and future possibilities. *International Journal of Gender and Entrepreneurship, 12*(1), 39–52.

McDonald, S., Gan, B. C., Fraser, S. S., Oke, A., & Anderson, A. R. (2015). A review of research methods in entrepreneurship 1985-2013. *International Journal of Entrepreneurial Behavior & Research, 21*(3), 291–315.

McKelvey, B. (2004). Toward a complexity science of entrepreneurship. *Journal of Business Venturing, 19*(3), 313–341.

Nayak, A., & Chia, R. (2011). Thinking becoming. Process philosophy and organization studies. *Philosophy and Organization Theory Research in the Sociology of Organizations, 32*, 281–309.

OECD. (2021). *Knowledge co-creation in the 21st century: A cross-country experience-based policy report* (OECD Science, Technology and Industry Policy Papers No. 115). OECD Publishing. Retrieved June 20, 2021, from https://doi.org/10.1787/c067606f-en

Packard, M. D. (2017). Where did interpretivism go in the theory of entrepreneurship? *Journal of Business Venturing, 32*(5), 536–549.

Panicker, S., & Manimala, M. J. (2015). Successful turnarounds: The role of appropriate entrepreneurial strategies. *Journal of Strategy and Management, 8*(1), 21–40.

Paulsen, R. J., Alper, N., & Wassall, G. (2020). Arts majors as entrepreneurs and innovators. *Small Business Economics*. https://doi.org/10.1007/s11187-020-00416-x.

Qian, H., Acs, Z. J., & Stough, R. R. (2012). Regional systems of entrepreneurship: The nexus of human capital, knowledge and new firm formation. *Journal of Economic Geography, 13*(4), 559–587.

Raco, J. R., & Tanod, R. H. M. (2014). The phenomenological method in entrepreneurship. *International Journal of Entrepreneurship and Small Business, 22*(3), 276–285.

Rae, D. (2015). *Opportunity-centered entrepreneurship*. Red Globe Press.

Rajasinghe, D., Aluthgama-Baduge, C., & Mulholland, G. (2021). Researching entrepreneurship: An approach to develop subjective understanding. *International Journal of Entrepreneurial Behavior & Research, 27*(4), 866–883.

Rajasinghe, D., & Mansour, H. F. (2019). Coaching as an entrepreneurship learning and development tool. In G. Mulholland & J. Turner (Eds.), *Enterprising education in UK higher education: Challenges for theory and practice* (pp. 51–69). Routledge.
Ratten, V. (2020). Coronavirus (covid-19) and entrepreneurship: Changing life and work landscape. *Journal of Small Business & Entrepreneurship, 32*(5), 503–516.
Refai, D., Haloub, R., & Lever, J. (2018). Contextualizing entrepreneurial identity among Syrian refugees in Jordan: The emergence of destabilised habitus? *International Journal of Entrepreneurship and Innovation, 19*(04), 250–260.
Reffstrup, T., & Christiansen, S. K. (2017). *Nordic Entrepreneurship Islands: Status and potential mapping and forecasting entrepreneurship education on seven selected Nordic Islands*. Nordic Council Ministers.
Schaeffer, V., & Matt, M. (2016). Development of academic entrepreneurship in a non-mature context: The role of the university as a hub-organisation. *Entrepreneurship & Regional Development, 28*(9-10), 724–745.
Schumpeter, J. A. (1934). *The theory of economic development: An inquiry into profits, capital, credit, interest, and the business cycle*. Harvard University Press.
Schumpeter, J. A. (2017). *Essays on entrepreneurs, innovations, business cycles and the evolution of capitalism*. .
Stam, E. (2016). Theorising entrepreneurship in context. In F. Welter & W. B. Gartner (Eds.), *A research agenda for entrepreneurship and context* (pp. 93–108). Edward Elgar.
Steyaert, C. (2007). Entrepreneuring' as a conceptual attractor. A review of process theories in 20 years of entrepreneurship studies. *Entrepreneurship and Regional Development, 19*, 453–477.
Steyaert, C., & Katz, J. (2004). Reclaiming the space of entrepreneurship in society: Geographical, discursive and social dimensions. *Entrepreneurship & Regional Development, 16*(3), 179–196.
Sun, H. (2020). *Global social media design: Bridging differences across cultures*. Oxford University Press.
Tang, J. (2020). Psychological capital and entrepreneurship sustainability. *Frontiers in Psychology, 11*(866), 01–07.
Van Burg, E., Cornelissen, J., Stam, W., & Jack, S. (2020). Advancing qualitative entrepreneurship research: Leveraging methodological plurality for achieving scholarly impact. *Entrepreneurship: Theory and Practice*. https://doi.org/10.1177/1042258720943051
Verheul, I., & Van Stel, A. J. (2010). Entrepreneurial diversity and economic growth. In J. Bonnet, D. Garcia, & H. van Auken (Eds.), *The entrepreneurial society; How to fill the gap between knowledge and innovation* (pp. 17–36). Edward Elgar.
Welter, F., Baker, T., Audretsch, D. B., & Gartner, W. B. (2017). Everyday entrepreneurship—A call for entrepreneurship research to embrace entrepreneurial diversity. *Entrepreneurship Theory and Practice, 41*(3), 311–321.
Welter, F., Gartner, W. B., & Wright, M. (2016). The context of contextualizing contexts. In F. Welter & W. B. Gartner (Eds.), *A research agenda for entrepreneurship and context* (pp. 1–15). Edward Elgar.
Williams, S. D., Ammetller, G., Rodríguez-Ardura, I., & Li, X. (2020). Narratives of international women entrepreneurs: An exploratory case study of identity negotiation in technology startups. *IEEE Transactions on Professional Communication, 63*(1), 39–51.
Woodman, R. W., Sawyer, J. E., & Griffin, R. W. (1993). Toward a theory of organisational creativity. *Academy of Management Review, 18*(2), 293–321.
Zhang, X., & Zhou, J. (2014). Empowering leadership, uncertainty avoidance, trust, and employee creativity: Interaction effects and a mediating mechanism. *Organisational Behaviour and Human Decision, 124*(2), 150–164.

Chinthaka J. Aluthgama-Baduge, PhD, is working as a lecturer in Enterprise and Entrepreneurship at Derby Business School, University of Derby, UK. His key research interest areas are entrepreneur development and education practices, and entrepreneurship, especially social entrepreneurship and innovation. Design thinking and knowledge exchange between university and industry are his other research interest areas. He has studied design thinking at the School of Entrepreneurial Design Thinking of University of Koblenz-Landau, Germany. He holds a master's degree in Leadership and Management from York St John University, UK. He is a Fellow of Advance HE (FHEA), UK.

Duminda Rajasinghe, PhD is a senior lecturer in Human Resource Management and Organisational Behaviour. He is an experienced academic with industry experience in HRM. Prior to Nottingham Trent University, he worked for, Northampton, Salford and York Business Schools. Duminda's current research interest lies in adult learning, coaching, leadership development, and entrepreneurship. He holds a PhD from Leeds Business School, Masters from York Business School and BSc in Computing and Information Systems from London Metropolitan University, UK. He is a fellow of Advance HE, UK (FHEA).

Financial Constraints to Innovative Activities Revealed Barriers Versus Deterring Barriers: Evidence from Turkey

Hülya Ünlü, Erhan Çankal, and Ahmet Kibar Çetin

Abstract In this chapter, we examine the hampering factors on innovation, which are financial obstacles. Hampering factors have two possible effects on firms' decision to introduce innovation, namely, revealed and deterring obstacles. The nature and degree of the perception of financial obstacles to innovation is investigated by firm-level data from Turkish CIS 2006 and CIS 2010. The estimations are done by using ordered probit models. According to our findings, categorizing firms by their size and foreign ownership is useful for the consideration of financial obstacles. The assessments of barriers are important for the firms who engage in five or more innovative activities. Innovatively active firms in CIS 2006 are more likely to face financial barriers to innovation than firms in CIS 2010. Highly innovatively active firms are more likely to assess barriers as highly important.

1 Introduction

During the last century, economies have prioritized increasing productivity, ensuring continuity in quality and finding new ways to meet the needs of individuals. However, the innovation they adopt in order to achieve this goal, from knowledge to the final product/service, is a long order and costly.

This Chapter is derived from Ph.D. dissertation entitled "Financial Constraints to Innovation Activities: Revealed Barriers versus Deterring Barriers", by Hülya ÜNLÜ, under the supervision of Dr. Erhan ÇANKAL in the Department of Banking and Finance at Yildirim Beyazit University Ankara/Turkey in 2016.

H. Ünlü (✉)
Department of Economics, Cankiri Karatekin University, Çankırı, Turkey
e-mail: hunlu@karatekin.edu.tr

E. Çankal
Department of Finance and Banking, Ankara Yildirim Beyazit University, Ankara, Turkey

A. K. Çetin
Department of Economics, Ankara Haci Bayram Veli University, Ankara, Turkey

J. Leitão, V. Ratten (eds.), *Strategic Innovation*, Contributions to Management Science, https://doi.org/10.1007/978-3-030-87112-3_5

It is known that the innovative activities are difficult to be financed because of their specific characteristics: main composition of the investments are intangible assets and returns that are expected from innovation investments are highly uncertain (Campello et al., 2010; Carpenter et al., 1998; Carpenter & Petersen, 2002; Lee et al., 2015; Mazzucato, 2013). Innovative firms have been investigated for various aspects. Many researchers showed the determinants of being innovative, cyclical effect on the being innovative and effect of barriers on innovative firms (Amara et al., 2004; Blanchard et al., 2013; D'Este et al., 2012; Iammarino et al., 2009). However, both being innovative, and facing barriers are wide concepts, that should be investigated in more detailed way.

According to the researchers, the completion and sustainability of the innovation process depends on the presence of some talents in the relevant companies (Almeida et al., 2013; D'Este et al., 2012; Guariglia & Liu, 2014; Iammarino et al., 2009). Lack of or partial possession of these capabilities can lead to various barriers to innovative activities (Canepa & Stoneman, 2008; Mohnen et al., 2008; Tiwari et al., 2007).

Some studies are focused on potentially innovative firms (D'Este et al., 2008, 2010, 2012, 2014; Hölzl & Janger, 2014). These studies investigated the barriers faced by innovation-intensive firms and examined the effects of firm-specific characteristics on the perception of barriers for developed countries. Developing countries are less studied (de-Oliveira & Rodil-Marzábal, 2019; De Fuentes et al., 2020; Santiago et al., 2017). However, very few studies have been conducted for Turkey (Çetin et al., 2017; De Fuentes et al., 2020). Barriers are explored in various dimensions, and special attention is paid to financial constraints on R&D spending by firms in OECD countries (Alvarez & Crespi, 2015; Hall, 2002; Hall & Lerner, 2010; Himmelberg & Petersen, 1994; Mulkay et al., 2001). The financial barriers faced by Turkish firms and the transformation of this innovation barriers vis-à-vis innovation intensity have not been examined previously.

It is important to define and highlight the different types of enterprises according to their innovation status and perception of obstacles. A successful innovation process for the enterprises depends on several elements, among which is the financing innovation investments. Enterprises engaging in innovation process perceive difficulties in accesses to finance or costs of the investments as "innovation barriers." According to their impact on innovative activities, innovation barriers are divided into two main categories, namely, **revealed barriers** and **deterring barriers** (D'Este et al., 2012). Although enterprises are affected negatively by revealed barriers, the effects are not strong enough to terminate the innovation process. Deterring barriers, however, are strong enough to prevent the enterprises from engaging in innovative process.

The goal of this chapter is to examine the assessment of introducing innovation and the perception of financial obstacles, whether firms are affected badly but not enough to terminate the innovation process or to prevent the enterprises from engaging in innovative activities. To investigate this relationship, we developed a direct measure of perception of financial obstacles, which takes into account whether a firm has perceived problems as "lack of available finance within the firm," "lack of available finance from other organizations," and "high direct innovation costs." In order to control each perception level of financial barriers, both the revealed and deterred firms have been investigated using the ordered probit model, which allows control of the correlation among financial barriers. The empirical analysis is based on the data from waves of the Turkish Community Innovation Survey (CIS), which are cross-section data, for periods of 2004–2006 and 2008–2010 (we label CIS 2006 and CIS 2010). One may also consider the effect of crises on financial barriers to innovation. Our datasets can be thought as economic boom wave and wave of economic crisis.

In the literature it is seen that each paper has its definition of innovators and non-innovators. Our study needs special care about the definition of innovators and non-innovators. It is important to define and highlight the different types of enterprises according to their innovation status. There are several reasons to have specific definitions; first in this study, as we mentioned before, we use the Community Innovation Survey, which has the information related to innovative activities of enterprises, and we are investigating the definition of the innovation concept, which is based on the Oslo Manual [(second edition from 1997 and third edition from 2005). That is why we stick with the definition of OECD/Eurostat (2005)]. Second, we believe that obstacles' perception is closely related to the engagement in innovative activities (Marin et al., 2014). Third, and most importantly, we investigate the "revealed and deterring financial barriers." The interpretations of the financial impediments on the innovation differ according to the perceived effect by entrepreneurs (D'Este et al., 2012). An important point, which is not to be missed out, is filtering out non-innovation-related firms from our sample. It needs to be considered in order to correct a sample selection bias (D'Este et al., 2008, 2010; Mohnen et al., 2008; Savignac, 2008).

This chapter provides a comprehensive analysis of the fundings involved in supporting innovation efforts in firms. This will help decision-makers in designing policies and in monitoring the implementations. In the case of Turkey, the effect of barriers manifests itself in two different ways: deterring barriers and revealed barriers. Our empirical findings are very much in line with the conclusions by D'Este et al. (2008, 2010, 2012) regarding the barrier perception of those participating in innovative activities. We have shown that the assessments of barriers are important for the firms who engage in five or more innovative activities. There is a common pattern among three types of financial constraints. This result is consistent with our expectation of revealed barriers. Innovatively active firms in CIS 2006 are more likely to face financial barriers to innovation than firms in CIS 2010. Highly innovatively active firms are more likely to consider barriers as highly important. If we compare two datasets, then one may say that the revealed effect is higher in CIS 2006 and, on the other hand, lower in CIS 2010.

The rest of the chapter is organized as follows: Sect. 2 analyzes the literature related to financial constraints to innovation. Section 3 describes the data and the econometric methodology. Section 4 shows our main empirical results. Finally, Sect. 5 presents the main conclusions.

2 Financing Constraints to Innovation

Arrow (1962) emphasized the importance of the financing of innovation, where firms are more prone to face credit rationing. Innovation projects show different characteristics. As we mentioned before innovation projects are highly uncertain, intangible, and asymmetrical in nature. Additionally, innovation projects are heterogeneous and accumulative. Innovative activities are different in each firm. It depends on the willingness and other undetermined conditions of the firms. It is seen that companies adopt different approaches to innovation. While there are firms that are not at all interested in innovation, there are firms that focus on only one type of innovation, as well as those that focus their entire concentration on all types of innovation. Bond et al. (2003) demonstrated that being uncertain and the intangible nature of innovation increase firms' cost of funding and/or limit their borrowing opportunities. That is why innovative firms are more prone to facing financial obstacles. Some authors argued that the existence of financing opportunities for all firms undermines the assumptions of the perfect capital markets (Kamien and Schwartz 1972, 1978). On the contrary, recent researches revealed that the investment decisions for both firms and financiers are different in many ways because of market imperfections and problems arising from asymmetric information.

According to Fazzari et al. (1988):

> …investment may depend on financial factors, such as the availability of internal finance, access to new debt or equity finance, or the functioning of particular credit markets. (p. 141)

Kaplan and Zingales (1997) suggested that any firm facing a wedge between internal and external fundings is likely to be financially constrained. When the firm is more financially constrained, the widening of the gap between the internal and external funds is a kind of bilateral effect. Hall (2002) stated that the gap between external and internal funds is not the only constraint expected to limit the funding capabilities of firms and indicated that any firm that faces a wedge between internal and external funds is likely to be financially constrained. It is a kind of a two-sided effect that the wedge between internal and external funds increase, when the firm is more financially constrained. Bond et al. (2003) defined financial constraints as a result of a cost premium for external sources of finance. This cost premium may reflect asymmetric information and conflicts of interest among shareholders, managers, and suppliers of external financing.

Early studies focused on the relationships between R&D investments and the financial factors. The more the project is found to be sensitive to the financial factors, the more the project is financially constrained. Himmelberg and Petersen (1994) examined the small and high-tech firms in the USA. Their findings revealed that there is a significant effect of internal funds on R&D investments. Mulkay et al. (2001) have a similar study to Himmelberg and Petersen (1994). Mulkay et al. (2001) studied a sample of US and French manufacturing firms and found a large impact of cash flow on R&D investments. Bond et al. (2003) examined the cash flow sensitivity of R&D investments and fixed asset investments. They indicated that financial constraints are more significant in British than in German firms who are engaged in R&D.

Canepa and Stoneman (2008) studied the role of financial factors in innovation. Particularly they have examined how these constraints vary across firm sizes and sectors. They used CIS2 and CIS3 data and analyzed them in the UK. In the analysis, they used an ordinal logistic model and found that high-tech firms are more prone to facing financial obstacles than low-tech firms. According to their results, size is also an important matter, in that small-sized firms are more affected by financial obstacles than large-sized firms.

Mohnen et al. (2008) investigated the financial constraint effects on the firms' decision to have an innovation project. They have examined the innovation projects' situation, whether they are abandoned, prematurely stopped, seriously slowed down, or not started. By this way they analyzed the degree of obstacles. They used a probit model in which the sample was taken from CIS3.5 for the Netherlands. They found an important and vast negative effect of obstacle on innovative activities. While most of the studies investigated the link between financial disabilities and innovative input or output, Almeida et al. (2013) investigated whether there is a relationship between financial obstacles and innovative efficiency in their work. Innovative efficiency is related to future profitability of innovation. They found that financially constrained firms are more efficiently innovative. According to them, "Tighter constraints (*less* slack) thus lead to *more* productive and value-enhancing innovation" (p. 2). According to Guariglia and Liu (2014), most of the outside investors are unwilling to fund innovation investments that are extremely uncertain.

According to Arundel (1997) to D'Este et al. (2014), the existing literature proved that the degree of intensity to be innovative and the perception of obstacles are connected to each other. Iammarino et al. (2009) used two groups of firms in their study. According to their study, innovators (introducing innovations) and non-innovators perceived innovation barriers differently. In addition, researchers found that firms who are more prone to experiencing greater barriers are also more likely to innovate successfully (Arundel 1997 and Iammarino et al. 2009). Baldwin and Lin (2002) and Tourigny and Le (2004) both found that the more the firm has an incentive to innovation, the more the firm faces greater barriers. Our hypothesis is derived from this point of view. We suggest that being innovatively active brings many problems. High costs of developing innovation and lack of access to both internal and external finances are only some of the measurable financial problems (survey-based direct measures are an example). These firms' willingness to innovate is not lost, even if they face higher impact than barriers. For this reason, these companies are faced with revealed barriers. On the other hand, previously successful companies see their success as sufficient, and discouraged companies lose their tendency to innovate because they feel the barriers. The barriers perceived by this group of companies are deterred barriers. The literature for Turkish businesses is lacking at this point: there is a need to show how firm characteristics differ in perception of financial barriers for innovatively active firms, discouraged firms, and previously successful innovators.

The literature also investigates the effect of firm characteristics. We will give a brief literature to guide our findings. Malerba (2005) suggested that relevant sources of knowledge, stakeholders, and innovative activities are going to be different across sectors. Their incentive to be innovatively active and the perception of the financial obstacles differ between sectors (Baldwin & Lin, 2002; Tourigny & Le, 2004). Carpenter and Petersen (2002) emphasized that high-tech firms are more prone to facing financial barriers because of the nature of innovation investments, which have high uncertainty, greater information asymmetry, less collateral, and long-run projects.

According to Hipp et al. (2000), firm size has effects on the success of innovation. They suggest that larger firms have different business activities; for this reason there are more areas where firms can be innovative. Larger firms have also an advantage in terms of the available sources for innovation, and there is less risk of failure compared with smaller firms. The size of firm and its effects are a bit complicated. While larger firms have a superior advantage, smaller firms tend to be more flexible on the decision-making procedures in the introduction of innovations. According to De Brentani (1995), smaller firms are more excited about introducing innovations. Most of the papers used firm size as a determinant of innovation (Ettlie & Rubenstein, 1987). Early authors accepted the monopoly power of large firms on innovation. Schumpeter (1942) is one of them, and he suggested that risk-taking is an important feature for innovation. However, Scherer (1992) indicated that the more flexible the management structures, the less bureaucracy, and less inertia makes smaller firms more innovative than larger firms.

Schmidt and Rammer (2007) suggested that a firm that belongs to a group of firms and a firm that is not part of a group have totally different innovation strategies. This may be because the headquarter of a group of firms assigns a specific task to a given firm. If a firm belongs to a group and if the headquarter has an incentive to innovate, then it becomes more probably aware of the need of funds. It is easy for them to use their abilities of funding an innovation project for a given firm. Literature suggest that there is a link between innovation and multinational companies (MNCs) (Papanastassiou, 1999; Patel, 1995; Balcet & Evangelista, 2004; Frenz et al., 2005; Frenz & Ietto-Gillies, 2004). Castellani and Zanfei (2003) suggested that foreign-owned firms are in general more productive than domestic firms. The most important advantage of the affiliation of MNCs is that they can learn from the diverse local environments, which support a contagion effect of innovativeness on the locations where they operate. Finally MNCs not only spread the knowledge within the company but also to the countries where the organizations are located (Frenz & Ietto-Gillies, 2004). Pires et al. (2008) stated that the increasing number of foreign-owned firms has an effect on the efficiency of innovation processes. We expect the parent companies of foreign companies to introduce capital opportunities at a lower cost and bring more cash to the firm by selling products in international markets. To sum up foreign-owned firms are less likely to face financial obstacles (D'Este et al., 2014; Desai et al., 2007; Hanson et al., 2005). The advantage of being a multinational firm is having an easy access to resources, assets, and knowledge by using the partner firms' networks, at both the global and regional levels (Dachs & Ebersberger,

2009; Dachs et al., 2008). We introduced human capital intensity variable as another independent variable (number of employees with PhD degree). Skilled personnel are important to solve clients' innovative problems; moreover, they are a creative part of firms' own innovation process. Human capital is also linked to the promotion of innovation (He & Wong, 2009) and the number of highly skilled workers in a firm is related to its absorptive capacity (Cohen & Levinthal, 1989, 1990). Tsang (2000) suggested that innovation and the complexity of the technique behind the innovation force the firms to understand and use external knowledge in their innovation processes. Although the use of external knowledge is necessary for firms, Hottenrott and Peters (2012) suggested that an enterprise with a high level of human capital is more likely to be unprotected against financial constraints. Intangible assets worsen the information asymmetry problems in the market for having an external capital (Lahr & Mina, 2013). Export intensity is also included as a control variable, and the correlation between the perception of financial obstacles and export intensity is expected to be positive. He and Wong (2009) suggested that a firm who is an exporter has a chance to leverage its experience within a foreign country's customers in a demanding market to present innovative solutions to clients in foreign markets. For this reason an exporter firm expects higher returns from its innovation efforts due to its wide market reach. This also creates financing opportunities for a firm with overseas market access and increases its incentive to innovate because of its wide market reach (Boso et al., 2013; Şeker, 2012).

3 Data and Methodology

3.1 Data Source

The empirical analysis is based on the data from waves of the Turkish CIS, which are cross-section data, for the periods of 2004–2006 and 2008–2010 (we label them CIS 2006 and CIS 2010). The Turkish Community Innovation Survey is collected by the Turkish Statistical Institute. The CIS micro data can be accessed in the Safe Centre (SC) in Ankara. The Turkish CIS data is based on a stratified random sample (A 30 stratum for economic activity and three groups of firm sizes (10–49, 50–249, and 250+) are taken to consider sample sizes.). CIS 2006 was stratified by NACE revision 1.1, and CIS 2010 was stratified by NACE revision 2. NACE is a Statistical Classification of Economic Activities in the European Community. The dataset represents the sector and at the same time the firm size of the whole population of Turkish firms, which have more than ten employees.

CIS has made use of a rich and direct source of a detailed description of innovation and innovative activities, other firm characteristics and factors influencing innovative activity. First and most importantly, the data provides detailed information on the financial hampering factors, "such as lack of available finance within the firm," "lack of available finance from other organizations," and "high direct innovation costs." Second, it allows to see the level of perception of barriers

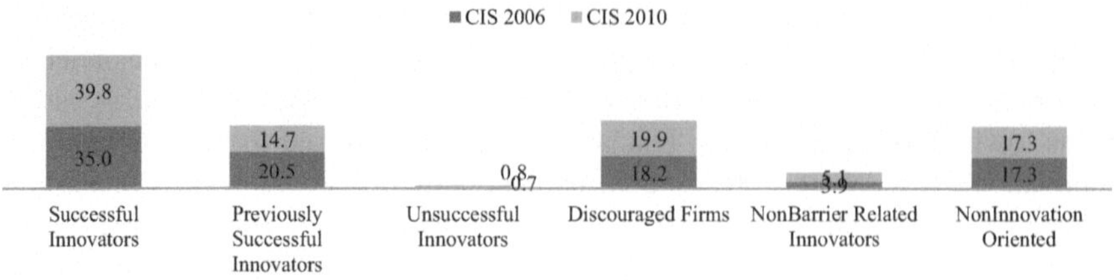

Fig. 1 Types of Innovators, CIS 2006 versus CIS 2010. Source: Author's own

when the tendency of companies to innovate differs; wants to innovate but not being able to, participation in innovative activities, and successful introduction of a new product/process innovation. The advantage of using CIS data is that it allows us to use a direct measure of the key variables rather than using indirect proxies in analysis. The most interesting part of the CIS survey in this study concerns the financial factors that hinder innovation. In line with the questions asked to companies that responded to the surveys at different times in Fig. 1, we first wanted to show whether the behavior of companies that want to innovate is affected differently by financial factors. In this way, unlike previous studies, it will be possible to see both the revealed and deterred effects of obstacles.

In CIS 2012, CIS 2014, and CIS 2016, the questionnaires are different from those of CIS 2006 and CIS 2010, and firms are not asked about barriers if they answer the question of whether they would introduce any innovation with "yes." In CIS 2018, questions related to innovative activities do not exist. Similarly in CIS 2008, questions related to barriers do not exist. In CIS 2006 and CIS 2010, each firm in the sample was asked to indicate that the financial factors that prevent the firm from making an innovation decision have high, medium, low or no effect. The important point is that all firms were asked to respond to this question without looking at introducing or not introducing any innovation.[1] We believe that the perception of obstacles needs to be interpreted at each perception level. This is why we prefer to use the ordered probit model in our analysis. Contrarily, most of the previous papers considered that a medium or high effect implies that the firm intends to innovate and is constrained (Canepa & Stoneman, 2008; D'Este et al., 2012). This approach might result in some biases, because the given answers are so sensitive for firms. A firm may state that it underestimates the impact of the barrier, but in reality, this effect can have a strong enough deterrent effect on the decision to innovate. We estimated our model using the entire original sample of 5767 businesses in CIS 2010 and 2172 firms in CIS 2006. Following D'Este et al. (2010), we have excluded primary sectors (agriculture and mining) from our sample (147 firms in CIS 2006 and 223 firms in CIS 2010).

[1] Same structure does not exist on other waves of the CIS questionnaire.

3.2 *Relevant Sample: Types of Innovators and Non-innovators*

To give a detailed information, we categorize firms into subsamples. Figure 1 presents the types of firm according to innovation positions. We examine firms under two main groups: "Innovators and Non-innovators." Each group is different in itself.

Non-innovators are non-innovation-oriented firms, non-barrier-related non-innovators, and discouraged firms. The **non-innovation-oriented firms**, which are excluded from our sample, are not innovatively active, have not introduced any kind of product or process innovation, and have not faced any barriers. Another group of non-innovators are the **non-barrier-related non-innovators**. Similarly the non-innovation-oriented firms, which are not innovatively active firms, have not introduced any kind of product or process innovations and are different from the previous group of firms. For these firms, the reason for being a non-innovator is that there is no demand at the market for introducing innovation. On the other hand, there exists a special case of non-innovators, which needs to be examined. The **discouraged firms** can be defined as firms that have not found a chance to innovate or be innovatively active because they are facing financial obstacles. It is seen from Fig. 1 that non-innovation-oriented firms and non-barrier-related firms consist of almost 21% of the samples of CIS 2006 and 22% of the samples of CIS 2010. The common similarity between non-innovation-oriented firms and non-barrier-related non-innovators is that they are not willing to innovate. Such an unwillingness is not related to facing any financial barriers. We are only interested in financial barriers; we have not examined the relationship between the decision to innovate and any other types of barriers. The pure effect of financial barriers is demonstrated in the study. Discouraged firms are the most important subsamples of this study, which account for around 19% of the total sample in both waves (Fig. 1).

Determining innovators is quiet challenging. In the first group of innovators, the **successful innovators** are determined as having innovation as an output. More precisely, an enterprise is defined as a successful innovator if the firm has done at least one of the following innovations (during the given time period): (i) the firm introduced a new or significantly improved good/service, (ii) the firm introduced a new or significantly improved process that is used for producing a good/service, (iii) the firm introduced a new or significantly improved logistics and delivery methods for supplies, and (iv) the firm produced products or introduced new or significantly improved supporting activities for any of its processes. We are also interested in **previously successful innovators**, which need to be analyzed in depth and differentiated from non-innovators. A previously successful innovator has not done any innovation (output) but has claimed that it has during the previous time period. **Unsuccessful innovators** are the ones who did not introduce any kind of product or process innovation while engaging in at least one of the innovative activities. The success of introducing innovations changes over time. As presented in Fig. 1, while the successful innovators account for 35% of the whole sample in CIS 2006, they

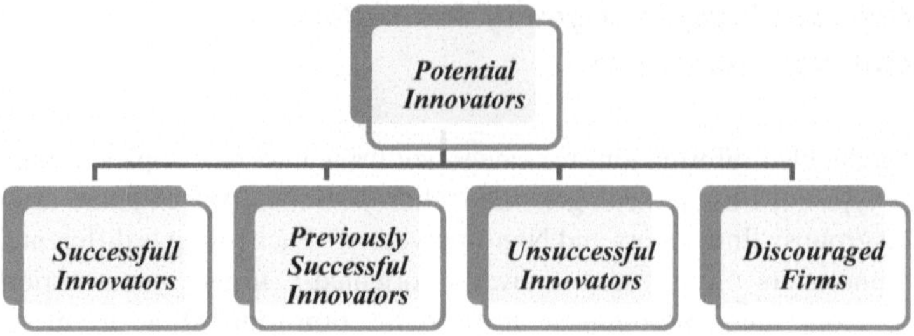

Fig. 2 Determination of potential innovators

account for 40% of the whole sample in CIS 2010. This shows that Turkish companies are getting better at introducing innovation when compared with the previous wave of CIS data. Unsuccessful innovators do not seem to change over time and stay at the same level, and they account for 1% of the whole sample. Our findings show that the previously successful innovators account for 20% of the overall sample in CIS 2006 and 15% of the overall sample in CIS 2010. It is seen that a 6% difference exists between CIS 2006 and CIS 2010. One can see that the position of these firms is changed from being previously successful innovators to successful innovators. Again there is a surprising result. While the firms are becoming more successful over time, the ratio of discouraged firms in CIS 2010 is higher than that of firms in CIS 2006. This is why we are interested in drawing an inference between the revealed and deterring effects of obstacles on innovation decisions.

After distinguishing the subsamples, *relevant samples* can be called **potential innovators** (Fig. 2). Potential innovators are the ones who are willing to innovate; the keyword here is willingness. There are several ways to determine the willingness of the firms to do innovation, such as having an innovation output, engaging in at least one of the innovative activities, or having a previous innovation output. But there is still a group of firms who are misjudged in the context of potential innovators, which are categorized as discouraged firms. These firms are thought of as non-innovators most of the time. At first sight this group seems to be non-innovators, but at a deeper look, one can see that these firms are a special case of potential innovators. They have willingness to do innovation, but they are deterred of introducing an innovation or even engaging in innovative activities. Our study is different from other studies at this point. We have several subsamples that provide an opportunity to offer more information about the determinants of both revealed and deterred barriers to the policymakers.

Our analyses reveal that a relevant sample composition could be as follows:

Innovatively active firms: These firms are the ones who claimed to engage in at least one of the innovative activities. The overall response rate of these firms who claimed to be innovatively active in CIS 2006 was only 46% of the whole sample of potential innovators (Fig. 3). After excluding the missing data and possible duplication problems, the sample size was 730 firms. For CIS 2010, the overall response rate of those firms who claimed to be innovatively active was around 53% of the

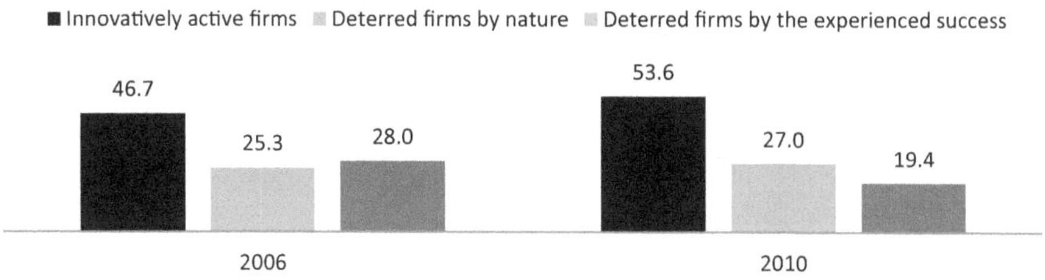

Fig. 3 Composition of Potential Innovators, CIS 2006 versus CIS 2010

whole sample of potential innovators (Fig. 3). After excluding the missing data and possible duplication problems, the sample size was 2276 firms.

Deterred firms by nature: These innovative are the ones who claimed that they were not innovatively active but had willingness to be innovatively active. Unfortunately financial disability was the reason for their failure to introduce any kind of innovation and/or to engage in any innovative activities. In the previous section, we referred to these firms as discouraged firms, which accounted for only 25% of the whole sample of potential innovators in CIS 2006 and 27% of the whole sample of potential innovators in CIS 2010 (Fig. 3). After excluding the missing data, the sample sizes were 396 firms in CIS 2006 and 1147 in CIS 2010.

Deterred firms by the experienced success: These firms are the ones who claimed to have innovation outputs during the previous time period. They also did not have any kind of innovation outputs during the related time period. As we differentiated previously successful innovators from successful innovators by determining whether they introduced any kind of innovation output, we found a special case of an innovator who could not carry on the introduction of any kind of innovation output. Now the important question that comes to our mind is that are they engaged in any kind of innovative activity or are they deterred from any kind of innovative activity? Our investigation has quite surprising findings. We found that according to the result of both time periods (CIS 2006 and 2010), Turkish firms did not engage in any kind of innovative activity or spend on R&D investments if they claimed that they introduced innovation output before the interested time period. It was found that the theory of "success brings success" does not hold in the case of previously successful innovators. These groups of firms account for only 28% of the whole sample of potential innovators in CIS 2006 and 19% of the whole sample of potential innovators in CIS 2010 (Fig. 2). After excluding the missing data, the sample sizes are 438 firms in CIS 2006 and 826 in CIS 2010.

3.3 *Determination of Variables and Descriptive Statistics*

3.3.1 Dependent Variables

The CIS questionnaire has a special module in which the respondents are asked the following: "During the three years 2008 to 2010, how important were the following

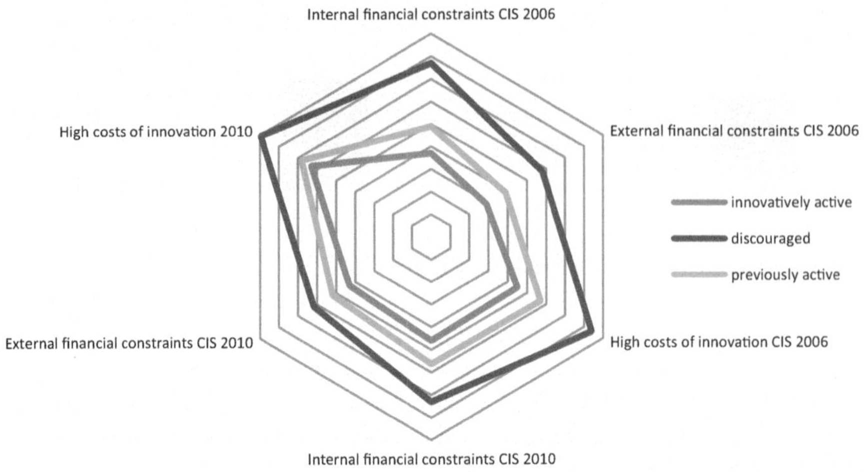

Fig. 4 Barriers to innovation: revealed vs. deterring

factors in preventing your enterprise from innovating or in hampering your innovation activities?" The degree of importance of the financial factors is our main concern (Fig. 4):

- Lack of funds within your enterprise or group **(internal finance)**
- Lack of finance from sources outside your enterprise **(external finance)**
- Innovation costs too high **(high costs)**

There is a natural order of the degree of importance of each category. The ordinal variables are regenerated to take the following values: factor not experienced (1), low (2), medium (3), and high (4).

3.3.2 Independent Variables

The responses from the survey allow us to measure the degree of engagement in innovative activities. The engagement in innovative activity is measured by binary variables. Binary variables are coded 1 for each variable, **Zero-active** if a firm does not engage in any of the activities, **Low-active** if a firm engages in one or two activities, **Medium-active** if a firm engages in three or four activities, and **High-active** if a firm engages in five or more activities. A non-linear relationship between engagement in innovative activity and perception of obstacles is expected. There is a threshold before a positive relation occurs between the perception of obstacle and engagement in innovative activity. Under this threshold the relation is expected to be negative (D'Este et al., 2010, 2012).

Sector dummies are created according to the NACE revisions of the related sample collection periods.[2] If the firm belongs to any main sector, it takes the value of 1 and 0 otherwise. **Sizes** of the firms are categorized into four: small, medium, large, and highly large. Binary variables are coded 1 for each variable if the total number of the firm's employees is between 10 and 49 (*small*), between 50 and 249 (*medium*), between 250 and 999 (*large*), over 1000 (*highly large*), and 0 otherwise. Our hypothesis is that the size has an effect on the perceptions of the obstacles on decision to innovate. Larger firms are more protected against obstacles (Blanchard et al., 2013; Cohen & Klepper, 1996; D'Este et al., 2014; Katila & Shane, 2005). If the firm is part of an enterprise group, the binary variable takes the value of 1 and 0 otherwise. The possibility of facing financial barriers is less likely to happen in the case of a corporate group. **Foreign-owned firms** are determined by looking at the ratio of capital owner. If the foreign partner has more than 50% of the existing capital, then the binary variable takes the value of 1 and 0 otherwise. The human capital variable is determined by the number of employees who have a PhD degree. **Receiving Public Financial Support** is constructed as a set of binary variables. Each of the binary variables takes the value of 1 if the firm claims that it received that specific public support, 0 otherwise. According to the question, there are three possible public supports: Support from local or regional authorities (**funloc**), support from central government (including central government agencies or ministries) (**fungov**), and support from the European Union (**funeu**). **Market Internationalization** is determined by the question "In which geographic markets did your enterprise sell goods and/or services during the three years 2008–2010?" We generated an ordinal variable to measure the distance of the markets where the enterprise sell goods and/or services. If the firm gives the answer of yes to the following options then the dummy variables takes the value 1 and 0 otherwise.

- Local/regional within [your country] **(local)**
- National (other regions of [your country]) **(national)**
- Other European Union or associated countries **(EU)**
- All other countries **(other)**

3.4 *Econometric Model: The Ordered Probit Model*

Building on the literature and theoretical background of financing innovation investments given above, we confirm that **internal financing** of innovation for firms are important, whereas **external financing** is critical. There exists another important issue, which, in this case, is referred to in the survey as **high costs**. The investigation of whether these factors have possibly two types of important effects on the decision to innovate, namely, revealed and deterring effects, is performed using the ordered

[2] See also Hatzichronoglou (1997).

probit model. The dependent variable is sometimes perceived to be different from a binary variable or from a continuous variable. It is possible to examine a dependent variable that has more than two possible outcomes. If the possible outcomes of dependent variable, y, has a natural ordered outcomes, then an ordered probit model can be used for estimation. A good example of a categorical variable could be that respondents are asked to report a particular category, in our case financial obstacle status that is categorized into no effect (1), low effect (2), medium effect (3), and high effect (4). The order of the categories is given in the parentheses; it is obvious that there is natural ordering. The ordered probit model is an extension of the binary probit model (Jones, 2007).

If y is an ordered response, as we suggested above, then we cannot say that the indicators of outcomes are no longer arbitrary. We cannot say that the difference between the high and medium effects of obstacles is twice as important as the difference between the no effect and low effect.

The dependent variable, y, now takes the values $\{0, 1, 2, 3, 4, \ldots J\}$ for integer J in an ordered response. Like the binary models, the ordered probit models can be derived from a latent variable model. It is again needed to have an error term that is distributed as standard normal.

$$y^* = X'\beta + e, e \mid X \sim \text{Normal } (0, 1)$$

where $X'\beta$ is an index function, x is a $K \times 1$ regressor vector (this time it does not contain a constant), and β is a K×1 vector of unknown parameters. The threshold parameters can be expressed as $\alpha_1 < \alpha_2 < \alpha_3 < \ldots < \alpha_{j.}$(In the case of binary variable, the threshold point is "0"; if the latent variable takes higher than the "0," y takes the value of 1):

$$
\begin{aligned}
y &= 0 \text{ if } \ y^* < \alpha_1 \\
y &= 1 \text{ if } \alpha_1 < y^* \leq \alpha_2 \\
&\vdots \\
y &= J \text{ if } y^* > \alpha_j
\end{aligned}
$$

While it is known that the error term has a standard normal distribution, one can derive the conditional distribution of y given X

$$
\begin{aligned}
P(y = 0|X) &= P(y^* \leq \alpha_1|X) = P(X'\beta + e \leq \alpha_1|X) = \phi(\alpha_1 - X'\beta) \\
P(y = 1|X) &= P(\alpha_1 < y^* \leq \alpha_2|X) = \phi(\alpha_2 - X'\,\beta) - \phi(\alpha_1 - X'\beta)
\end{aligned}
$$

..

..

$$P\left(y = J - 1 \middle| X\right) = P\left(\alpha_{j-1} < y^* \le \alpha_j \middle| X\right) = \phi\left(\alpha_j - X\beta\right) - \phi\left(\alpha_{j-1} - X\beta\right)$$
$$P(y = J|X) = P(y^* > \alpha_J|X) = 1 - \phi\left(\alpha_j - X'\beta\right)$$

When $J = 1$, it is same as the binary probit model.

As we determined the probabilities of each outcome above, it is important to mention that unlike the binary probit models, the signs of the "interior" marginal effects are unknown and cannot be completely determined by the sign of the betas of the regression models. For this reason we have investigated the probabilities of possible 4 outcomes by using the ***mfx*** STATA command. The mfx command allows us to estimate the marginal effect of a variable in a discrete choice model that depends on the values taken by each of the covariates.

We have three dependent variables which have the form of ordinary nature. Each of the dependent variables take the value $\{1, 2, 3, 4\}$ if the respondent gives the answer high degree of importance, dependent variables take the value 4, if the answer is medium degree of importance dependent variables take the value 3, if the answer is low degree of importance dependent variable take the value 2, and if the answer is that firm is not effected then dependent variables take the value 1. Our dependent variables are internal financial obstacle (IFo), external financial obstacle (EFo), and high costs (HCo), where "o" means the ordered nature.

Our models can be written as follows:

Model 1

$$y_{IFo}{}^* = X'\beta + e, e \mid x \sim Normal\ (0, 1)$$

$$y_{IFo} = \begin{cases} 1\ if\ y^*_{IFo} < \alpha_1 \\ 2\ if\ \alpha_1 < y^*_{IFo} \le \alpha_2 \\ 3\ if\ \alpha_2 < y^*_{IFo} \le \alpha_3 \\ 4\ if\ \alpha_3 < y^*_{IFo} \end{cases}$$

Model 2

$$y_{EFo}{}^* = W'\theta + \varepsilon, \varepsilon \mid x \sim Normal\ (0, 1)$$

$$y_{EFo} = \begin{cases} 1\ if\ y^*_{EFo} < \varphi_1 \\ 2\ if\ \varphi_1 < y^*_{EFo} \le \varphi_2 \\ 3\ if\ \varphi_2 < y^*_{EFo} \le \varphi_3 \\ 4\ if\ \varphi_3 < y^*_{EFo} \end{cases}$$

Model 3

$$y_{HCo}{}^{*} = Z'\gamma + \epsilon, \epsilon \mid x \sim Normal\,(0, 1)$$

$$y_{HCo} = \begin{cases} 1 \text{ } if \text{ } y^{*}_{HCo} < \delta_1 \\ 2 \text{ } if \text{ } \delta_1 < y^{*}_{HCo} \leq \delta_2 \\ 3 \text{ } if \text{ } \delta_2 < y^{*}_{HCo} \leq \delta_3 \\ 4 \text{ } if \text{ } \delta_3 < y^{*}_{HCo} \end{cases}$$

4 Results

The estimation on the subsamples of different types of firms by deterred and revealed firms was carried out to explore the firm characteristics and engagement in innovative activities that predict the best financial obstacles of firms. It is given that financial obstacle is a polychotomous dependent variable with a natural order. Each table in this chapter shows the results of ordered probit model (OPM) estimations of the financing barriers for both CIS 2006 and CIS 2010. We report the estimated probability that a firm describes financing as a major obstacle depending on the characteristics of firms. Each column of the table represents the probability of assessing internal financing barriers as highly important. Because of the possible heterogeneity problem, it is preferred to use sector dummies as independent variables; hence robust estimation results are found.[3]

Table 1 shows the results for the importance that innovatively active, discouraged and formerly active firms place on internal financial barriers. The results for the importance that innovatively active, discouraged and formerly active firms place on internal financial barriers. For the revealed group of firms, the relationship between assessment of internal financial disabilities and engagement in innovative activities is statistically significant and positive. The probability of assessing high importance to internal financial disabilities is increasing in the case of CIS 2006; contrarily, there is a U-shaped relationship in the case of CIS 2010. The important point that takes our attention is that during the previous time period, firms have changed their way of looking at assessment of internal financial barriers. There is a lower assessment of internal financial barriers for firms who engaged in innovative activities in CIS 2010.

In the case of both CIS 2006 and CIS 2010, being a small and medium-sized firm increases the importance of internal financial barriers to innovation for innovatively active firms in both cases. This is exactly what we expected to find. While we expected to have results of large firms who are protected against internal financial obstacles, for CIS 2010, things are quite different. Large-sized firms perceive lack of internal finance as highly important. However, a firm that is part of a large group is better positioned against internal financial obstacles. This shows that partner

[3] STATA collin command used for collinearity estimation (Ender, 2010).

Table 1 Ordered probit model results for internal financial obstacles: probabilities of barrier assessed as highly important

	2006				2010		
	Revealed	Deterring			Revealed	Deterring	
Variables	(1) Inn. Active Firms	(2) Pre. succ inn.	(3) Dis. firms	Variables	(4) Inn. active firms	(5) Pre. succ. inn.	(6) Dis. firms
Low-active	0.064*			Low-active	0.054**		
	(0.037)				(0.024)		
Medium-active	0.110***			Medium-active	0.050**		
	(0.033)				(0.023)		
High-active	0.147***			High-active	0.065***		
	(0.043)				(0.022)		
Small	0.223***	0.157***	0.324***	Small	0.196***	0.333***	0.130
	(0.042)	(0.047)	(0.092)		(0.028)	(0.082)	(0.081)
Medium	0.199***	0.131*	0.390***	Medium	0.120***	0.411***	0.062
	(0.051)	(0.078)	(0.103)		(0.032)	(0.143)	(0.092)
Large	0.049	0.004	0.276**	Large	0.061**	0.290*	0.034
	(0.045)	(0.067)	(0.117)		(0.028)	(0.149)	(0.093)
Part of a group	−0.061**	−0.118***	0.001	Part of a group	−0.072***	−0.129***	−0.163***
	(0.025)	(0.030)	(0.096)		(0.015)	(0.029)	(0.043)
Local market	0.039	0.086**	−0.024	Local market	0.013	−0.006	0.072
	(0.026)	(0.036)	(0.056)		(0.014)	(0.029)	(0.074)
National market	0.010	0.057	−0.039	National market	−0.013	0.009	−0.042
	(0.028)	(0.036)	(0.056)		(0.017)	(0.029)	(0.030)
EU markets	0.019	0.005	−0.090	EU market	0.001	0.032	−0.042
	(0.027)	(0.039)	(0.060)		(0.017)	(0.033)	(0.031)
Other markets	−0.002	0.008	0.001	Other markets	0.010	−0.060**	−0.001
	(0.029)	(0.040)	(0.070)		(0.017)	(0.030)	(0.036)

(continued)

Table 1 (continued)

Variables	2006			Variables	2010		
	Revealed	Deterring			Revealed	Deterring	
	(1) Inn. Active Firms	(2) Pre. succ inn.	(3) Dis. firms		(4) Inn. active firms	(5) Pre. succ. inn.	(6) Dis. firms
Public support local	0.115			Public support local	0.028		−0.062*
	(0.103)				(0.036)		(0.032)
Public support national	0.019			Public support national	0.050***		−0.293***
	(0.028)				(0.016)		(0.015)
Public support EU	0.121			Public support EU	−0.084**		0.622***
	(0.076)				(0.034)		(0.014)
Foreign	−0.099***	−0.070	−0.029	Foreign	0.012	−0.133***	−0.382***
	(0.026)	(0.050)	(0.138)		(0.023)	(0.039)	(0.014)
				Dr	−0.003	−0.011	−0.017
					(0.002)	(0.018)	(0.024)
				Encouragement	−0.001	−0.002	−0.009
					(0.003)	(0.006)	(0.007)
Observations	730	438	396	Observations	2276	826	1147

Standard errors in parentheses
***$p < 0.01$, **$p < 0.05$, *$p < 0.1$

cooperation is more likely to offer internal finance opportunities to the firm. It was found that selling goods in national or EU markets implies either an advantage or a disadvantage in overcoming revealed internal financial barriers. One of the independent variables exist only in CIS 2010, which is Human capital. It is not found any significant relationships between highly educated work force and assessment of financial barriers. We found statistically significant and negative relationships between EU grants and assessment of internal financial barriers. The result suggests that if a firm highly innovatively active then it perceives barrier highly important.

For the deterring groups of firms, in columns 3 and 5, medium-sized firms report significantly higher financial obstacles than small ones. In columns 3 and 5, the coefficients of large firms are statistically significant. However, a firm that is part of a large group is better positioned against internal financial obstacles. This shows that partner cooperation is more likely to offer internal finance opportunities to the firm. It was found that selling goods in other than EU markets implies either an advantage for overcoming deterring effects (previously successful innovators (PSIs) and deterred firms (DFs)) of internal financial barriers in CIS 2010.

The probabilities in column 1 of Table 2 show that foreign-owned firms report significantly lower external financial obstacles, and those in column 4 of Table 2 indicate that firms affiliated with a group and foreign-owned firms report significantly lower external financial obstacles. A firm that is part of a large group is better positioned against external financial obstacles. This shows that partner cooperation is more likely to be able to find external finance opportunities for previously successful firms in CIS 2006. For CIS 2010, the results are quite different; not only previously successful firms but also discouraged firms are more advantaged for a being part of a corporate. Even though being a part of a group protects firms against external financial barriers, it would not be enough for not deterred from innovation. This time our findings do not support the “learning by doing” effect on the probability of assessing external financial difficulties. There is not any significant relationship between highly educated work force and assessment of financial barriers as highly important. We also find that there is a significant and negative relationship between foreign ownership and assessment of financial barriers as highly important. Previously successful firms are more advantaged for being part of a corporate than the innovatively active firms. Even if protected against internal financial barriers, it would not be enough to be not deterred from innovation. However, it was found that selling goods in any of the markets implies either an advantage or a disadvantage in overcoming deterring or revealed internal financial barriers. Only in CIS 2010, EU grants and local grants are statistically significant for the deterred firms that are overcoming external financing barriers.

The probabilities in columns 1 and 4 of Table 3 indicate that the firms affiliated with a group and foreign-owned firms report different results. Firms that are part of large groups feel significantly less impacted by higher innovation costs in CIS 2010. In the case of both CIS 2006 and CIS 2010, being a small and medium-sized firm increases the importance of high costs of innovation for innovatively active firms. Additionally, the same relationship exists between large firms and the importance of high costs of innovation in CIS 2010. No significant relationship between highly

Table 2 Ordered probit model results of external financial obstacles: probabilities of barrier assessed as highly important

	2006				2010		
	Revealed	Deterring			Revealed	Deterring	
Variables	Inn. active firms	Pre. succ inn.	Dis. firms	Variables	Inn. active firms	Pre. succ. Inn.	Dis. firms
Low-active	0.021			Low-active	0.030		
	(0.025)				(0.022)		
Medium-active	0.064***			Medium-active	0.029		
	(0.024)				(0.021)		
High-active	0.077**			High-active	0.053***		
	(0.031)				(0.021)		
Small	0.112***	0.086**	0.190**	Small	0.187***	0.211***	0.025
	(0.030)	(0.038)	(0.093)		(0.029)	(0.068)	(0.096)
Medium	0.089**	0.071	0.176	Medium	0.114***	0.266**	−0.052
	(0.036)	(0.059)	(0.128)		(0.033)	(0.113)	(0.093)
Large	−0.019	−0.020	0.192	Large	0.070**	0.187*	−0.003
	(0.026)	(0.045)	(0.137)		(0.030)	(0.112)	(0.101)
Part of a group	−0.024	−0.084***	−0.014	Part of a group	−0.065***	−0.137***	−0.059
	(0.018)	(0.021)	(0.083)		(0.015)	(0.024)	(0.041)
Local market	0.029	0.035	−0.001	Local market	0.013	−0.012	−0.005
	(0.019)	(0.027)	(0.049)		(0.014)	(0.027)	(0.026)
National market	−0.003	0.005	−0.037	National market	−0.009	0.011	0.012
	(0.020)	(0.027)	(0.049)		(0.016)	(0.027)	(0.026)
EU markets	0.021	0.032	0.014	EU market	0.008	0.004	−0.012
	(0.021)	(0.031)	(0.054)		(0.016)	(0.029)	(0.031)
Other markets	−0.021	−0.001	−0.050	Other markets	0.016	−0.044	−0.034
	(0.021)	(0.031)	(0.057)		(0.016)	(0.028)	(0.029)
Public support local	0.015			Public support local	0.010		−0.174***
	(0.055)				(0.034)		(0.015)

Public support national	0.021			Public support national	0.037**		0.723***
	(0.021)				(0.015)		(0.013)
Public support EU	0.068			Public support EU	−0.048		−0.281***
	(0.057)				(0.039)		(0.013)
Foreign	−0.086***	−0.037	−0.203***	Foreign	−0.041**	−0.144***	0.076
	(0.015)	(0.039)	(0.064)		(0.020)	(0.027)	(0.064)
				Dr	−0.002	−0.009	−0.007
					(0.002)	(0.016)	(0.016)
				Encouragement	0.005*	0.002	−0.002
					(0.003)	(0.006)	(0.006)
Observations	730	438	396	Observations	2276	826	1147

Standard errors in parentheses
$^{***}p < 0.01$, $^{**}p < 0.05$, $^{*}p < 0.1$

Table 3 Ordered probit model results of high costs of innovation: probabilities of barrier assessed as highly important

	2006				2010		
	Revealed	Deterring			Revealed	Deterring	
Variables	Inn. active firms	Pre. succ. inn.	Dis. firms	Variables	Inn. active firms	Pre. succ. inn.	Dis. firms
Low-active	0.058			Low-active	0.026		
	(0.043)				(0.030)		
Medium-active	0.100***			Medium-active	0.087***		
	(0.038)				(0.029)		
High-active	0.106**			High-active	0.097***		
	(0.047)				(0.028)		
Small	0.164***	0.136**	0.124	Small	0.193***	0.332***	−0.077
	(0.045)	(0.067)	(0.092)		(0.035)	(0.106)	(0.122)
Medium	0.131***	0.049	0.140	Medium	0.091**	0.289**	−0.127
	(0.050)	(0.084)	(0.097)		(0.037)	(0.125)	(0.128)
Large	−0.040	−0.064	0.063	Large	0.060*	0.226*	−0.133
	(0.044)	(0.082)	(0.104)		(0.034)	(0.130)	(0.130)
Part of a group	−0.032	−0.129**	0.103	Part of a group	−0.051**	−0.137***	−0.092
	(0.033)	(0.051)	(0.112)		(0.022)	(0.044)	(0.077)
Local market	0.009	0.045	−0.034	Local market	−0.001	0.001	0.001
	(0.032)	(0.050)	(0.059)		(0.019)	(0.036)	(0.033)
National market	−0.040	0.055	−0.075	National market	−0.064***	−0.004	0.012
	(0.038)	(0.052)	(0.060)		(0.023)	(0.037)	(0.033)
EU markets	0.041	0.081	0.084	EU market	−0.003	0.074*	0.090**
	(0.033)	(0.054)	(0.063)		(0.022)	(0.041)	(0.039)
Other markets	0.004	−0.017		Other markets	0.045**	−0.028	−0.006
	(0.034)	(0.052)			(0.022)	(0.042)	(0.037)
Public support local	0.001			Public support local	0.027		0.444***
	(0.102)				(0.051)		(0.015)

Public support national	0.047			Public support national	0.067***		0.442***
	(0.035)				(0.021)		(0.015)
Public support EU	0.071			Public support EU	−0.040		0.000
	(0.080)				(0.054)		(0.090)
Foreign	−0.117***	−0.182***	−0.336**	Foreign	−0.040	−0.200***	−0.092
	(0.035)	(0.062)	(0.137)		(0.029)	(0.056)	(0.077)
				Dr	−0.005*	−0.038*	−0.007
					(0.003)	(0.022)	(0.013)
				Encouragement	0.002	0.005	0.002
					(0.004)	(0.008)	(0.007)
Observations	730	438	396	Observations	2276	826	1147

Standard errors in parentheses
$^{***}p < 0.01$, $^{**}p < 0.05$, $^{*}p < 0.1$

educated work force and assessment of financial barriers as highly important has been reported. However, it was found that selling goods in national markets implies either an advantage in overcoming revealed barriers in CIS 2010. The results in columns 1 and 4 of Table 3 show significant difference between high-tech and med high-tech firms. As we expected, a firm that is in a higher-tech sector is more constrained in its innovative activities.

5 Conclusion

The goal of this chapter was to examine the nature and the degree of the perception of financial obstacles to innovation using firm-level data from Turkish CIS 2006 and CIS 2010. While it is known that innovation is a key factor for taking advantage over the competitive markets, it does not mean that all firms are skilled, talented, and financially appropriate for introducing innovation. This study puts forward three main contributions.

First of all, it distinguishes different firm groups in accordance with the effects of financial barriers on the decision to innovate. The first group of firms is potential innovators; these firms have an intention to innovate but still face financial barriers that do not prevent them from engaging in innovative activities; revealed barriers. These firms claim to be innovatively active and in CIS 2006 only 46% of the whole sample is potential innovators similarly, around 53% of the whole sample is potential innovators in CIS 2010. The second and third groups of firms have a common feature when they are faced with financial barriers; they are prevented from undertaking any innovative activities (deterring barriers). Our study is different from other studies (i.e., D'Este et al., 2014; Pellegrino, 2014) at this point. It is important to look deeply to the groups of firms that are faced with deterring barriers. **Deterred firms by the experienced success** are only 28% of the whole sample of potential innovators in CIS 2006 and 19% of the whole sample of potential innovators in CIS 2010, and **Deterred firms by nature** are only 25% of the whole sample of potential innovators in CIS 2006 and 27% of the whole sample of potential innovators in CIS 2010. Considering several subsamples gives an opportunity to offer more information about the determinants of both revealed and deterred barriers to the policymakers as well as managers of the firms. Second, the nature of the subject requires the use of micro-level data as well as a comparative analysis. For this reason, we used two specific time periods of the Turkish economy: periods of economic downturn and boom. The Turkish example provides evidence that firms have perceptions of both deterring and revealed effects of financial obstacles to innovation. The high engagement of innovative activities has made a statistically significant impact on the revealed financial barriers for innovatively active firms. Third, high costs of innovation barrier were ranked higher for both time periods and for all groups of firms by the respondents of the surveys. In particular, discouraged firms who have not found a chance to innovate or be innovatively active because of financial obstacles seem to assign more importance to all of the financial obstacles independent of time.

To determine which certain firm characteristics alleviate deterring and revealed obstacles, we examined our main hypotheses: "the firm characteristics predict the perception of financial obstacles differently for innovatively active firms, discouraged firms and previously successful innovators" and "The firm is more likely to face higher revealed barriers when the firm has a higher engagement in innovative activities." These hypotheses were tested by using ordered probit models. Our findings are parallel with those of Beck et al. (2006). In particular categorizing firms by their size and foreign ownership is useful for the consideration of financial obstacles. Our results suggest that multinational companies overcome financial obstacles, and large firms are perceiving obstacles lower than small and medium-sized firms. With regard to the findings of Canepa and Stoneman (2008) and Carpenter and Petersen (2002), high-tech firms are showing a pattern of having difficulties on accessing internal–external finance, and they found high cost of innovation to be a barrier. Differently from D'Este et al. (2014), we have not found any significant effect of human capital.

Our empirical findings are very much in line with the conclusions of D'Este et al. (2008, 2012, 2010) about the relationships between engagement in innovative activities and assessment of the barriers. We have shown that the assessments of barriers are important for the firms who engage in five or more innovative activities. There is a common pattern among three types of financial constraints. This result is consistent with our expectation of revealed barriers. Innovatively active firms in CIS 2006 are more likely to face financial barriers to innovation than firms in CIS 2010. Highly innovatively active firms are more likely to assess barriers as highly important. If we compare two datasets, then one may say that the revealed effect is higher in CIS 2006 but lower in CIS 2010. This means that innovatively active firms are using the revealed effect, which can be called as the learning-by-doing effect for their own advantage. With this result we also proved our reasons for dividing whole samples into three groups. It is possible to conclude that a decrease in the probability of assessing financial barriers may be a result of both the management and policy's success in Turkey.

One may also consider the effect of crises on financial barriers to innovation. Our datasets can be thought of as economic boom wave and wave of economic crisis. During the completion of the questionnaire, the growth rate in Turkey was around 7% on an average of three years in a yearly basis, whereas during the crisis period, it was around 2%. Larger firms are oversensitive to crisis periods. Being innovative as a hedge against the effects of the crisis creates a good advantage for companies. Our results also suggest that during the crisis period, the firm characteristics that predict the best financial obstacles of a firm are changed. This may also help both policymakers and mangers think about the weaknesses of firms. Innovatively active firms lose their advantage on overcoming financial obstacles when they are large and foreign-owned. It was also observed that being a part of a group was an advantage during the crisis period for firms.

References

Almeida, H., Hsu, P.-H., & Li, D. (2013). *Less is more: Financial constraints and innovative efficiency*. SSRN 1831786. https://papers.ssrn.com/sol3/papers.cfm?abstract_id=1831786

Alvarez, R., & Crespi, G. A. (2015). Heterogeneous effects of financial constraints on innovation : Evidence from Chile. *Science and Public Policy, 42*(5), 1–14. https://doi.org/10.1093/scipol/scu091

Amara, N., Landry, R., Becheikh, N., & Ouimet, M. (2004). Radical innovations in traditional manufacturing industries. In *Druid summer Conference, Industrial dynamics, innovation and development.*

Arrow, K. J. (1962). Economic welfare and the allocation of resources for invention. In *The rate and direction of inventive activity: Economic and social factors* (pp. 609–626). Princeton University Press.

Arundel, A. (1997). Enterprise strategies and barriers to innovation. *Innovation Measurement and Policies, 50*, 101–108.

Balcet, G., & Evangelista, R. (2004). *Global technology: Innovative strategies of multinational affiliates in Italy.*

Baldwin, J., & Lin, Z. (2002). Impediments to advanced technology adoption for Canadian manufacturers. *Research Policy, 31*(1), 1–18. https://doi.org/10.1016/S0048-7333(01)00110-X

Beck, T., Demirgüç-Kunt, A., Laeven, L., & Maksimovic, V. (2006). The determinants of financing obstacles. *Journal of International Money and Finance, 25*(6), 932–952.

Blanchard, P., Huiban, J. P., Musolesi, A., & Sevestre, P. (2013). Where there is a will, there is a way? Assessing the impact of obstacles to innovation. *Industrial and Corporate Change, 22*(3), 679–710. https://doi.org/10.1093/icc/dts027

Bond, S., Harhoff, D., & Reenen, J. Van. (2003). *Investment, R & D and financial constraints in Britain and Germany Stephen Bond, Dietmar Harhoff and John Van Reenen (December).*

Boso, N., Story, V. M., & Cadogan, J. W. (2013). Entrepreneurial orientation, market orientation, network ties, and performance: Study of entrepreneurial firms in a developing economy. *Journal of Business Venturing, 28*(6), 708–727.

Campello, M., Graham, J. R., & Harvey, C. R. (2010). The real effects of financial constraints: Evidence from a financial crisis. *Journal of Financial Economics, 97*(3), 470–487. https://doi.org/10.1016/j.jfineco.2010.02.009

Canepa, A., & Stoneman, P. (2008). Financial constraints to innovation in the UK: Evidence from CIS2 and CIS3. *Oxford Economic Papers, 60*(4), 711–730. https://doi.org/10.1093/oep/gpm044

Carpenter, R. E., Fazzari, S. M., & Petersen, B. C. (1998). Financing constraints and inventory investment: A comparative study with high-frequency panel data. *The Review of Economics and Statistics, 80*(4), 513–519. https://doi.org/10.1162/003465398557799

Carpenter, R. E., & Petersen, B. C. (2002). Capital market imperfections, high-tech investment, and new equity financing. *The Economic Journal, 112*(477), F54–F72.

Castellani, D., & Zanfei, A. (2003). Technology gaps, absorptive capacity and the impact of inward investments on productivity of European firms. *Economics of Innovation and New Technology, 12*(6), 555–576.

Çetin, A. K., Dölarslan, E. Ş., Yakışık, H., & Ünlü, H. (2017). Sanayi ve hizmet sektörlerinde inovasyon bariyerleri. *Journal of Social and Humanities Sciences Research, 4*(5), 940–955.

Cohen, W. M., & Klepper, S. (1996). A reprise of size and R & D. *The Economic Journal, 106* (437), 925–951. https://doi.org/10.2307/2235365

Cohen, W. M., & Levinthal, D. A. (1989). Innovation and learning: The two faces of R & D. *The Economic Journal, 99*(397), 569–596.

Cohen, W. M., & Levinthal, D. A. (1990). Absorptive capacity: A new perspective on learning and innovation. *Administrative Science Quarterly, 35*(1), 128–152. https://www.jstor.org/stable/2393553

D'Este, P., Iammarino, S., Savona, M., & Von Tunzelmann, N. (2008). *What hampers innovation? Evidence from the UK CIS4. SPRU Electronic Working Paper Series Paper*. http://www.sussex.ac.uk/spru/

D'Este, P., Iammarino, S., Savona, M., & Von Tunzelmann, N. (2012). What hampers innovation? Revealed barriers versus deterring barriers. *Research Policy, 41*(2), 482–488. https://doi.org/10.1016/j.respol.2011.09.008

D'Este, P., Rentocchini, F., & Vega-Jurado, J. (2010). Lowering barriers to engage in innovation: Evidence from the Spanish innovation Survey. In *International Schumpeter Society Conference 2010* (pp. 1–25).

D'Este, P., Rentocchini, F., & Vega-Jurado, J. (2014). The role of human Capital in Lowering the barriers to engaging in innovation: Evidence from the Spanish innovation survey. *Industry and Innovation, 21*(1), 1–19. https://doi.org/10.1080/13662716.2014.879252

Dachs, B., & Ebersberger, B. (2009). Does foreign ownership matter for the innovative activities of enterprises ? *International Economics and Economic Policy, 6*(1), 41–57. https://doi.org/10.1007/s10368-009-0126-3

Dachs, B., Ebersberger, B., & Lööf, H. (2008). The innovative performance of foreign-owned enterprises in small open economies. *The Journal of Technology Transfer, 33*, 393–406. https://doi.org/10.1007/s10961-007-9058-7

de-Oliveira, F., & Rodil-Marzábal, Ó. (2019). Structural characteristics and organizational determinants as obstacles to innovation in small developing countries. *Technological Forecasting and Social Change, 140*, 306–314. https://doi.org/. https://doi.org/10.1016/j.techfore.2018.12.021

De Brentani, U. (1995). Firm size: Implications for achieving success in new industrial services. *Journal of Marketing Management, 11*(1–3), 207–225.

De Fuentes, C., Santiago, F., & Temel, S. (2020). Perception of innovation barriers by successful and unsuccessful innovators in emerging economies. *The Journal of Technology Transfer, 45*(4), 1283–1307. https://doi.org/10.1007/s10961-018-9706-0

Desai, M. A., Foley, C. F., & Forbes, K. J. (2007). Financial constraints and growth: Multinational and local firm responses to currency depreciations. *The Review of Financial Studies, 21*(6), 2857–2888. https://doi.org/10.1093/rfs/hhm017

Ender, P. B. (2010). *Collin: Collinearity diagnostics*. Institute for Digital Research and Education, University of California. http://www.ats.ucla.edu/stat/stata/ado/analysis/default.htm

Ettlie, J. E., & Rubenstein, A. H. (1987). Firm size and product innovation. *Journal of Product Innovation Management, 4*(2), 89–108.

Fazzari, S. M., Hubbard, R. G., Petersen, B. C., Blinder, A. S., & Poterba, J. M. (1988). Financing constraints and corporate investment. *Brookings Papers on Economic Activity, 1988*(1), 141–206. https://doi.org/10.2307/2534426

Frenz, M., Girardone, C., & Ietto-Gillies, G. (2005). Multinationality matters in innovation: The case of the UK financial services. *Industry & Innovation, 12*(1), 65–92.

Frenz, M., & Ietto-Gillies, G. (2004). The impact of multinationality on the propensity to innovate: An analysis of the UK Community Innovation Survey 3. In *Schumpeter Conference. Milan.*

Guariglia, A., & Liu, P. (2014). To what extent do financing constraints affect Chinese firms' innovation activities? *International Review of Financial Analysis, 36*, 223–240. https://doi.org/10.1016/j.irfa.2014.01.005

Hall, B. H. (2002). *The financing of research and development* (NBER Working Paper Series No. 8773). Cambridge.

Hall, B. H., & Lerner, J. (2010). The financing of R & D and innovation. *Handbook of the Economics of Innovation, 1*(1 C), 609–639. https://doi.org/10.1016/S0169-7218(10)01014-2

Hatzichronoglou, T. (1997). *Revision of the high-technology sector and product classification*. OECD STI Working papers GD (97) 216.

Hanson, G. H., Mataloni, R., & Slaughter, M. (2005). Vertical production networks in multinational firms. *The Review of Economics and Statistics, 87*(4), 664–678.

He, Z.-L., & Wong, P.-K. (2009). Knowledge interaction with manufacturing clients and innovation of knowledge-intensive business services firms. *Innovations, 11*(3), 264–278. https://doi.org/10.5172/impp.11.3.264

Himmelberg, C. P., & Petersen, B. C. (1994). R & D and internal finance: A panel study of small firms in high-tech industries. *The Review of Economics and Statistics, 76*(1), 38–51. http://www.jstor.org/stable/2109824

Hipp, C., Tether, B. S., & Miles, I. (2000). The incidence and effects of innovation in services: Evidence from Germany. *International Journal of Innovation Management, 4*(04), 417–453.

Hölzl, W., & Janger, J. (2014). Distance to the frontier and the perception of innovation barriers across European countries. *Research Policy, 43*(4), 707–725. https://doi.org/10.1016/j.respol.2013.10.001

Hottenrott, H., & Peters, B. (2012). *Innovative capability and financing constraints for innovation more money, more innovation?* (ZEW Discussion Paper from No. 09–081). http://ftp.zew.de/pub/zew-docs/dp/dp09081.pdf.

Iammarino, S., Sanna-Randaccio, F., & Savona, M. (2009). The perception of obstacles to innovation. Foreign multinationals and domestic firms in Italy. *Revue d ' Économie Industrielle, 125*. Retrieved from http://rei.revues.org/3953

Jones, A. (2007). *Applied econometrics for health economists: A practical guide* (2nd ed.). CRC Press. https://doi.org/10.1201/9781785230141

Kamien, M. I., & Schwartz, N. L. (1972). A direct approach to choice under uncertainty. *Management Science, 18*(8), B-470.

Kamien, M. I., & Schwartz, N. L. (1978). Self-financing of an R and D project. *The American Economic Review, 68*(3), 252–261. http://www.jstor.org/stable/1805258

Kaplan, S. N., & Zingales, L. (1997). Do investment-cash flow sensitivities provide useful measures of financing constraints? *The Quarterly Journal of Economics, 112*(1), 169–215.

Katila, R., & Shane, S. (2005). When does lack of resources make new firms innovative? *Academy of Management Journal, 48*(5), 814–829.

Lahr, H., & Mina, A. (2013). Dynamic financial constraints and innovation : Evidence from the UK Innovation Surveys. *4th European Conference on Corporate R&D and Innovation*, (September), 35.

Lee, N., Sameen, H., & Cowling, M. (2015). Access to finance for innovative SMEs since the financial crisis. *Research Policy, 44*(2), 370–380. https://doi.org/. https://doi.org/10.1016/j.respol.2014.09.008

Malerba, F. (2005). Sectoral systems: How and why innovation differs across sectors. In J. Fagerberg, D. C. Mowery, & R. R. Nelson (Eds.), *The oxford handbook of innovation* (pp. 380–406). Oxford University Press.

Marin, G., Marzucchi, A., Zoboli, R., Marin, G., Marzucchi, A., & Zoboli, R. (2014). *SMEs and barriers to eco-innovation in EU: A diverse palette of greens SMEs and barriers to eco-innovation in EU*. A Diverse Palette of Greens.

Mazzucato, M. (2013). Financing innovation: Creative destruction vs. destructive creation. *Industrial and Corporate Change, 22*(4), 851–867. https://doi.org/10.1093/icc/dtt025

Mohnen, P., Palm, F. C., Van der Loeff, S. S., & Tiwari, A. (2008). Financial constraints and other obstacles: Are they a threat to innovation activity? *De Economist, 156*(2), 201–214. https://doi.org/10.1007/s10645-008-9089-y

Mulkay, B., Hall, B. H., & Mairesse, J. (2001). Firm level investment and R&D in France and the United States: A comparison. In D. Bundesbank (Ed.), *Investing today for the world of tomorrow*. Springer. https://doi.org/10.1007/978-3-642-56601-1_19

OECD/Eurostat. (2005). *Oslo manual: Guidelines for collecting and interpreting innovation data* (The measurement of scientific and technological activities) (3rd ed.). OECD Publishing.

Papanastassiou, M. (1999). Technology and production strategies of multinational enterprise (MNE) subsidiaries in Europe. *International Business Review, 8*(2), 213–232.

Patel, P. (1995). Pattern of technological activity: Their measurement and interpretation. In *Handbook of the economics innovation and technological change*.

Pellegrino, G. (2014). *Essays on determinants and effects of barriers to innovation.*
Pires, C. P., Sarkar, S., & Carvalho, L. (2008). Innovation in services – How different from manufacturing? *The Service Industries Journal, 28*(10), 1339–1356. https://doi.org/10.1080/02642060802317812
Santiago, F., De Fuentes, C., Dutrénit, G., & Gras, N. (2017). What hinders innovation performance of services and manufacturing firms in Mexico ? *Economics of Innovation and New Technology, 26*(3), 247–268. https://doi.org/10.1080/10438599.2016.1181297
Savignac, F. (2008). Impact of financial constraints on innovation: What can be learned from a direct measure? *Economics of Innovation and New Technology, 17*(6), 553–569. https://doi.org/10.1080/10438590701538432
Scherer, F. M. (1992). Schumpeter and plausible capitalism. *Journal of Economic Literature, 30*(3), 1416–1433. https://www.jstor.org/stable/2728064
Schmidt, T., & Rammer, C. (2007). *Non-technological and technological innovation: Strange bedfellows?* (ZEW Discussion Papers No. 07–052). Zentrum für Europäische Wirtschaftsforschung (ZEW). http://hdl.handle.net/10419/24623
Schumpeter, J. A. (1942). *Capitalism, socialism, democracy*. Harper.
Şeker, M. (2012). Importing, exporting, and innovation in developing countries. *Review of International Economics, 20*(2), 299–314.
Tiwari, A., Mohnen, P., Palm, F. C., & van der Schim Loeff, S. (2007). Financial constraint and R&D investment: Evidence from CIS. *Working Paper Series MERIT* (31), 1–45.
Tourigny, D., & Le, C. D. (2004). Economics of innovation and new technology impediments to innovation faced by Canadian manufacturing firms. *Economics of Innovation and New Technology, 13*(3), 217–250. https://doi.org/10.1080/10438590410001628387
Tsang, E. W. K. (2000). Transaction cost and resource-based explanations of joint ventures: A comparison and synthesis. *Organization Studies, 21*(1), 215–242. https://doi.org/10.1177/0170840600211004

Hülya Ünlü holds a PhD in Banking and Finance from the Yildirim Beyazit University in Ankara, Turkey. Currently, she is an assistant professor of Economics at the Cankiri Karatekin University, Turkey. She has an MSc in Financial Economics and Econometrics from the University of Essex, UK. Her research interests are Economics of Innovation and Technology, Financial Econometrics, and Applied Microeconometrics.

Erhan Çankal is an associate professor in the Department of Finance and Banking at Ankara Yildirim Beyazit University. His areas of expertise include Financial Economics, Financial Econometrics, Applied Microeconometrics, and Political Economy. Dr. Çankal's works have been published in various international journals and books.

Ahmet Kibat Çetin is a professor of Economics at Ankara Haci Bayram Veli University. His research focuses on Macroeconomics. Recently, he is working on Economics of Innovation and Technology.

Entrepreneurship, Education, and Athletes: Entrepreneurship Within European Dual Career Programmes

Louis Moustakas, Lisa Kalina, Antonio Sánchez-Pato, Elena Conde, and Håkon Ege

Abstract Balancing competitive sport and post-athletic career development is an inherently challenging endeavour for European athletes. In response, numerous countries and sport federations have developed dual career support policies and programmes. These programmes have principally focused on connecting athletes with education or employment opportunities or developing more general life skills. There has also been a growing focus on entrepreneurship's potential as a dual career pathway. University and advocacy work has called for the integration of entrepreneurship, and many pan-European projects have emerged on the topic. Nonetheless, entrepreneurship is mostly absent from dual career policies and programmes. This absence is especially notable given the potential of entrepreneurship as both an economic driver and a viable pathway for athletes. Using extensive findings generated from the SENTA project, this chapter, therefore, argues for the relevance of entrepreneurship within the context of athlete dual careers. In particular, we highlight how athletes may be uniquely well-positioned to thrive as entrepreneurs and how entrepreneurship can actively contribute to economic growth. Correspondingly, we suggest numerous solutions to better recognise and integrate entrepreneurship with dual career programmes, ranging from educational offers to post-career support. Finally, we conclude by proposing future avenues for research and discussion around this topic.

L. Moustakas (✉) · L. Kalina
Institute for European Sport Development and Leisure Studies, German Sport University, Cologne, Germany
e-mail: L.Moustakas@dshs-koeln.de

A. Sánchez-Pato · E. Conde
Facultad de Deporte, Catholic University of Murcia, Murcia, Spain

H. Ege
FURIM Institut, Oslo, Norway

J. Leitão, V. Ratten (eds.), *Strategic Innovation*, Contributions to Management Science, https://doi.org/10.1007/978-3-030-87112-3_6

1 Introduction

The notion of a dual career for athletes involves engagement in both sports and work-related activities, such as employment, education, or training (European Commission, 2012). Athletic careers are relatively short, and most athletes do not make enough money to retire at the end of their sporting careers (Kenny, 2015). Therefore, athletes need to develop alternative skills while simultaneously pursuing their sporting careers. However, athletes face significant challenges successfully combining these two strands (Sánchez Pato et al., 2017). Balancing the intense demands of competitive sport with educational or professional development is inherently challenging. In addition, numerous factors contribute to accentuating this challenge, including navigating daily routines, differing levels of support, or negative prejudices towards athletes (Geraniosova & Ronkainen, 2015; Li & Sum, 2017). In short, successfully combining sporting and professional ambitions is something very few athletes achieve. For instance, more than a third of German athletes describe their financial futures as not being secured (Breuer & Wicker, 2010).

In response to these challenges, numerous countries and sport federations have developed dual career support programmes (Aquilina & Henry, 2010; Morris et al., 2021; Sánchez Pato et al., 2017; Stambulova & Ryba, 2014). These programmes have principally focused on connecting athletes with education or employment opportunities or developing more general life skills. For instance, the Olympic Committees in Spain or Germany have established programmes to improve the coordination of academic studies and competitive sports (Asociación Deportes Olímpicos, 2021; Deutscher Olympischer Sportbund, 2013). However, outside of the scope of state- or federation-led programmes, there has been a growing focus on entrepreneurship's potential as a dual career pathway. University and advocacy work has called for the integration of entrepreneurship as part of dual career programmes (EU Athletes, 2015; Hakkers, 2019), and many pan-European projects have emerged on the topic (e.g. FH Joanneum University of Applied Sciences, 2017; Furim Institut, 2019; Tw1n, 2019). Yet entrepreneurship is mostly absent from European policy (European Commission, 2012) and national programmes (Morris et al., 2021; Stambulova & Ryba, 2014). Participation in sport can help develop numerous skills and networks essential to successful entrepreneurship, and athlete entrepreneurship can be an important driver of growth and innovation, but further tailored support is needed to capitalise on these opportunities (Kenny, 2015).

In the following, we aim to highlight the need, opportunities, and limitations associated with entrepreneurship education and support in the context of athlete dual careers and propose concrete avenues for integrating entrepreneurship within dual career programmes. In short, we wish to bridge the gap between these projects and current dual career athlete programmes. These reflections are based on national literature reviews, surveys, and focus groups done across eight countries as part of the Social Entrepreneurship-focused SENTA project. In total, we have interviewed over 40 national-level athletes and received nearly 300 survey responses. Therefore, though this chapter is discursive in nature, it still relies on extensive research and data collection.

Moving forward, we will first present the current status of entrepreneurship within athlete dual career programmes and policy. Afterwards, we will discuss the need and opportunities for entrepreneurship education and support within athlete dual careers and current obstacles impeding the realisation of those opportunities. Finally, we will bring these parts together and suggest future directions for entrepreneurship within dual career programmes and research. In addition, throughout, we will include the results of our research to concretely illustrate the place of entrepreneurship within the development of dual career athletes.

2 Dual Career Programmes and Entrepreneurship

The notion of a dual career for athletes involves engagement in both sports and work-related activities, such as employment or training (European Commission, 2012). However, athletes face significant challenges successfully combining these two activities. As detailed above, navigating daily routines, managing tight schedules, differing institutional support levels, or even negative prejudices towards athletes can all add significant difficulty in balancing dual careers (Geraniosova & Ronkainen, 2015; Li & Sum, 2017; Sánchez Pato et al., 2017). Indeed, numerous barriers can make it difficult to properly harmonize dual careers, such as the characteristics of the sport itself, the level of competition, access to resources, or the availability of support (López de Subijana et al., 2014). Acknowledging and responding to these challenges, an increasing focus on dual or post-athletic career development has been seen in Europe over the last decade, with a growing number of policies, programmes, and organisations working to create long-lasting career possibilities for athletes.

Most notably, in 2012, the European Commission published the *EU Guidelines on Dual Careers of Athletes,* providing the first-ever European level recognition and guidance on the topic. These guidelines were crafted to support the development of national dual career guidelines and primarily focus on employment, education, health, and financial support (European Commission, 2012). Despite these guidelines, at the national level, policies and programmes are fragmented across a wide range of actors, including state actors, sport federations, educational institutions, defence institutions, and others. In some cases, some level of dual career provision is even enshrined in law. In Poland, for example, elite athletes are guaranteed a place in physical education Universities, and Olympic medallists are ensured life-long pensions (Kuettel et al., 2020). Elsewhere, many policies and programmes are designed and led by national sport authorities such as sport confederations or Olympic committees. For instance, Germany offers multiple education-related initiatives and policies related to dual careers. Elite athletes wanting to combine work and study receive support when they go to the army, the police, the fire brigade, or customs (Hottenrott & Braumann, 2015). There have also been attempts to integrate elite sport into schools, but these attempts have faced numerous limitations and obstacles (Borggrefe & Cachay, 2012).

At the broader, European level, Aquilina and Henry (2010) worked to classify European countries based on the national approach to supporting dual career athletes in higher education. In their study, four distinct categories were mapped out: state-centric regulation, whereby the government regulates higher education institutions to support student-athletes (e.g. Spain); the state as a facilitator, where the government promotes formal, non-binding agreements to support dual career athletes (e.g. Finland and Sweden); national sporting federations as intermediaries that act on behalf of student-athletes to facilitate support (e.g. the United Kingdom); and a laisser-faire approach with no formal structures or arrangements (e.g. Slovenia). In our project, regional differences were likewise identified. While a large number of specifications and regulations related to elite athletes exist in many of the project countries (e.g. Spain, Germany, Austria), others are fragmented or have a specific focus on aspects such as a healthy lifestyle or talent scouting (e.g. Romania). Beyond the above education-focused taxonomy, many distinct organisations are involved in the provision of dual careers services. In particular, Morris et al. (2021) identified eight common types across Europe: (1) sports-friendly schools, (2) elite sport schools/colleges, (3) private club programs, (4) sport-friendly universities, (5) combined dual career systems, (6) national sports programs, (7) defence force programs, and (8) players' union programs.

What is clear from these different country and European-level analyses is that the inclusion of entrepreneurship in policy and programme design is mainly absent, leaving it to individual projects and organizations to fill this gap. Looking again to Germany, we see, for example, that the Werte Stiftung, together with German Sports Aid, has launched a start-up academy to introduce athletes to the subject of entrepreneurship. The programme supports athletes interested in founding a start-up business after their athletic career or aspiring to become an entrepreneur (Wertestiftung, 2021). Similarly, at the European level, many have called for the integration of entrepreneurship-related offers as part of dual career programmes (EU Athletes, 2015; Hakkers, 2019), and numerous pan-European education projects have emerged on the topic (FH Joanneum University of Applied Sciences, 2017; Furim Institut, 2019; Tw1n, 2019). In general, these cross-national projects work with higher education institutions and sport organisations to assess athletes' entrepreneurship needs and develop corresponding online learning tools to address these needs. For instance, the AtletyC project created a Massive Open Online Course (MOOC) to foster general entrepreneurship skills and networks for athletes (FH Joanneum University of Applied Sciences, 2017), whereas the SENTA project developed a gamification-based course related to social entrepreneurship for athletes (Furim Institut, 2019).

Taken as a whole, the current dual career landscape and the myriad of individual entrepreneurship-related projects suggest there is a significant gap in the structure and offers of dual career options. European policy and national programmes largely dismiss entrepreneurship, yet there is a growing recognition of entrepreneurship's value for dual career athletes. Ultimately, this leaves a range of individual actors to offer a disparate range of education programmes and short-term projects. As we will discuss next, there are significant opportunities and obstacles associated with better education and support around entrepreneurship in the dual career context. Entrepreneurship can be a meaningful pathway for many athletes and, for some, it is even a current, lived reality. In turn, athlete entrepreneurship can make a significant economic and societal contribution and prove to be a worthwhile investment for countries looking to boost innovation and employment. However, numerous barriers stand in the way of unlocking this potential.

3 Opportunities and Obstacles for Entrepreneurship and Dual Careers

At their heart, dual career programmes are meant to support athletes in combining their athletic careers with the development of long-term, post-athletic careers. On that basis alone, excluding entrepreneurship from dual career programmes is a rather significant oversight. Around 14% of the European adult population works on a self-employed basis (Eurostat, 2019), and the *Global Entrepreneurship Monitor* estimates that early-stage entrepreneurial activity (i.e. the percentage of the 18–64-year-old population who are either a nascent entrepreneur or are owner-manager of a new business) is at around 10% (Bosma et al., 2020). In short, entrepreneurship is a significant driver of economic activity and could represent an important opportunity for many athletes.

Many athletes expressed keen interest in entrepreneurial activities during our focus group discussions and viewed it as a potential future avenue in our work. Some even had reasonably clear ideas of what kind of entrepreneurial venture they would like to develop: 'My idea is to work in the field of consulting with a focus on personal management' (Athlete, Germany). Many others, either by planning or chance, had already become involved in some form of entrepreneurial activity. In Romania, for example, one participant spoke of starting a restaurant while, in Germany, another mentioned how she needed to register as a small business owner to process sponsorship and other revenues: 'We as athletes have to establish our own GbR to save taxes and acquire sponsors' (Athlete, Germany). Regardless of the country, there was a clear consensus that more information, education, and structures were needed to support athletes' entrepreneurial journeys. Later in this chapter, we will propose concrete ways how national authorities and sports federation can support entrepreneurship in the context of dual career programmes. However, before doing so, we must first make the case as to why that is a worthwhile investment for individual athletes and the broader community. Thus, in the following, we will highlight how entrepreneurship support can benefit both athletes and their communities.

From a societal and economic point of view, supporting athlete entrepreneurship can represent a good investment. Athlete entrepreneurship can be an important engine of growth for the sport industry (Ratten, 2018) and, overall, entrepreneurship can help promote innovation and economic growth (e.g. Bosma et al., 2018). Indeed, in Europe, youth unemployment hovers at around 17% and, in some countries, can reach almost 50% (Eurostat, 2020), highlighting the need for innovation and entrepreneurship to help tackle these challenges. Numerous studies suggest that athletes are especially well-suited to (sport) entrepreneurship and can generate positive economic impacts (Nauright & Wiggins, 2020; Ratten, 2015, 2018). Athletes interact with many people from different sectors in competitions and social events throughout their sporting life. This allows them to create wide networks that can be valuable for later entrepreneurial activities (Kenny, 2015). As Ansari et al. (2020) note, the connection between sport and a range of sectors 'such as media, data analytics, athletes and fan experiences, as well as goods and services, offers countless opportunities for entrepreneurial activities in different segments'. In addition, athletes develop numerous entrepreneurship-related skills during their careers. Though more work needs to be done to better understand athlete entrepreneurship skills, recent studies suggest that athletes develop numerous entrepreneurship skills (Matsangos et al., 2020; Steinbrink et al., 2020). In fact, our focus group participants often reflected on how the skills and contacts acquired during their careers could help support an entrepreneurial venture. Numerous interviewees highlighted how sport helped them acquire skills such as discipline, perseverance, teamwork, and communication. In addition, the opportunity to connect with influential or wealthy individuals through sport was highlighted: 'an important tool during my career was interaction with people with money' (Athlete, Romania). Overall, these skills and networks can prove to be incredibly beneficial when starting an entrepreneurial venture (Daley, 2012; Kenny, 2015). For instance, research has shown that similar job demands are associated with athletic careers and entrepreneurship, positioning athletes to be more successful with entrepreneurship as a second career choice (Steinbrink et al., 2020). Put together, these results support the contention that athletes can indeed be effective drivers of entrepreneurship. This athlete entrepreneurship, meanwhile, can act as an important driver of economic growth and support (youth) employment. Likewise, entrepreneurship can represent a viable, enticing career opportunity for athletes and allow them to capitalise on assets already acquired through their sporting careers. And, even if athletes do not specifically wish to venture into entrepreneurship, equipping athletes with a variety of entrepreneurial skills and competencies is essential for their future professional career. Skills such as flexibility, communication, and creativity are vital and it is crucial for elite athletes to be able to use these skills in their professional lives.

Yet, bridging the gap between athlete entrepreneurship's *potential* to making it a reality requires a concerted effort by national authorities and dual career service providers. At the moment, many obstacles actively impede the realisation of this potential. First and foremost, athletes generally lack awareness and education on entrepreneurship as a potential dual career opportunity. A common theme across the discussions was that athletes felt that they 'needed more information' (Athlete, Bosnia), training, and support in developing their entrepreneurial skills. And, even when athletes were involved in entrepreneurial activities, this occurred in a rather happenstance, learning-by-doing fashion: 'There is no guideline on how to establish your sailing GbR (German business), it is rather learning by doing' (Athlete, Germany). In other words, even though numerous athletes indicated some involvement in entrepreneurship, this involvement occurred due to their personal characteristics and contacts, not because it was actively supported or encouraged through dual career education or programming. Though there are increasing and interesting activities in this area—including the 'European Sport Leadership Project' (Sánchez-Pato et al., 2020) which aims to foster the athlete's leadership and employability skills—overall, we see a lack of concerted activities from dual career service providers.

4 Connecting Entrepreneurship and Dual Career Programmes

As we have detailed above, an increasing array of actors is attempting to capitalise on entrepreneurship's potential within athlete dual careers; however, European or national programmes have largely ignored this topic. In our view, this is a significant oversight, as entrepreneurship can provide many potential benefits for athletes and broader communities. There are numerous steps national authorities and dual career service providers can take to bridge this gap. First and foremost, recognition and integration of entrepreneurship in dual career policy are needed. Major European policy or national programmes rarely include entrepreneurship as a potential pathway. Explicit recognition and discussion of entrepreneurship as dual career possibilities are essential in addressing this gap. Furthermore, these policies and programmes should focus on integrating entrepreneurship education and support opportunities across the athletic lifespan.

National authorities and dual career service providers should provide a range of entrepreneurship support, and education offers suited to the different stages of an athlete's lifespan. In particular, support and education activities should occur over three different periods: when athletes are still active in sport, when they have retired from sport and are preparing to find a new occupation for the first time, and, finally, when they already have an occupation in their post-sport career (B-WISER, 2018). Among other things, that means supporting athletes through their active, athletic years and formal education and providing vocational support and support throughout retirement (Morris et al., 2021).

During active sporting careers, one of the biggest challenges for entrepreneurship education programmes is to fit into athletes' full, demanding schedules (Li & Sum, 2017). Nonetheless, it is imperative for athletes to begin laying the groundwork for their post-sporting careers at this stage. As such, tailored, flexible offers are required to match the realities and demands of athletic life (Aquilina & Henry, 2010; European Commission, 2012). Short, 'bootcamp' style courses, as well as online learning offers, can potentially help meet these requirements. Bootcamps are cornerstones of contemporary start-up ecosystems (Koning, 2016). Bootcamps directly focus on teaching practical applications for launching and managing start-ups in a short period. The primary purpose of entrepreneurship bootcamp programs is to help entrepreneurs design and bring a new venture to life. In recent years there has been a growing trend of entrepreneurship bootcamps dedicated to this type of education and training across a variety of fields, including for military veterans and people with disabilities (Hoppenfeld et al., 2013; Shaheen, 2016). In short, given their flexible, adaptable, short-term nature, entrepreneurship bootcamps can be quite suitable for athletes to explore entrepreneurship. Furthermore, there is a growing literature around sport and athlete entrepreneurship education that can be tapped into to support programme design (e.g. Ansari et al., 2020; Kenny, 2015; Ratten & Jones, 2018). Along with in-person training, national authorities should develop locally relevant distance learning materials for athletes interested in entrepreneurship. At present, many online courses are built from pan-European projects and, therefore, cannot adequately address the legal, financial, and cultural realities associated with entrepreneurship in a given country.

Support should also continue at the end of one's athletic career. Tailored guidance and mentorship are needed to promote successful entrepreneurship. Though athletes may possess significant networks from their sporting lives, connections to the broader entrepreneurship environment should be made intentionally through training, networking, or mentorship programmes. As we have highlighted above, entrepreneurship skills must be purposefully enhanced through dual career programmes, including during and after an athlete's academic career. In turn, this support and training should encourage athletes to share their experiences with their peers and allow successful entrepreneur-athletes to act as mentors for athletes in earlier entrepreneurial stages. In other words, entrepreneurship programmes should not only concern themselves with developing relevant skills but also fostering opportunities for long-term networks and mentorship. We must not abandon athletes at the conclusion of their sporting career. The transition to the world of labour and business is a moment where athletes most need support—such training and mentorship schemes can help pave the way forward.

5 Future Lines of Research

Though we have highlighted the opportunities, obstacles, and potential solutions for more integrated entrepreneurship support and education approaches in athlete dual careers, there remains a need for significant further exploration and research around this topic. Programmes need to be tailored to different types of athletes, and there remains a lack of sufficient data about the entrepreneurial skills and behaviours of athletes of different backgrounds.

Identifying the transversal competencies directly related to entrepreneurship that athletes possess and identifying skill gaps is an important starting point. An increasing number of studies have investigated this topic, including as it relates to general entrepreneurship (Steinbrink et al., 2020) and social entrepreneurship (Capella-Peris et al., 2020; Moustakas & Kalina, 2021), but there is a need for more work in this direction. The skills developed in a sporting career can be highly valuable in the entrepreneurship context (Ratten, 2015; Reyes-Hernández et al., 2021). Nonetheless, there are risks related to over-generalising specific skills. Due to the idiosyncrasy of sport and physical and sporting activities, athletes may have developed certain skills to a greater or lesser extent. Similarly, different sports lead to the development of different social networks (see Humphreys, 2011), which can influence the entrepreneurial potential of athletes. Understanding these differences is crucial to develop effectively tailored entrepreneurship education and support offers.

Likewise, it is essential to further research and understand how athletes approach their dual career planning and how entrepreneurship support can best support these different styles. Generally speaking, there are three career models in elite sports: the linear model where athletes dedicate themselves entirely to their sporting careers; the convergent model, in which the athlete focuses mainly on their sports career, but also performs an extra activity as long as it does not interfere with the sports career; and the parallel model, in which the athlete combines a sports career with another, maintaining equal levels of interest and engagement (Pallarés et al., 2011). According to these models, so-called 'strategic' athletes (convergent or parallel careers) obtain better jobs and see improved well-being later in their lives (Vilanova & Puig, 2013). However, those who practice the linear model, because they invested the majority of their time and resources in their sports careers and neglected planning for their post-athletic life, have difficulties finding a sustainable, post-sporting career occupation (Lorenzo Fernández & Bueno Moreno, 2012; Pallarés et al., 2011). Understanding these different types' characteristics and behaviours and how they perceive entrepreneurship can be a rich new avenue of inquiry. For instance, working to identify athletes who have linear careers and could have more difficulties in retirement is a valuable future research objective, and the possibilities for entrepreneurship for this group could be explored further.

6 Conclusion

Using extensive findings generated from the SENTA project, this paper has argued for the relevance of entrepreneurship within the context of athlete dual careers. In particular, we have highlighted how athletes may be uniquely well-positioned to thrive as entrepreneurs and how entrepreneurship can actively contribute to economic growth. Correspondingly, we have also proposed numerous solutions to better recognise and integrate entrepreneurship within dual career programmes, ranging from educational offers to post-career support.

For the moment, though, the glaring absence of entrepreneurship within programmes and policies is a critical gap in the current dual career landscape. Though entrepreneurship-related activities represent a significant proportion of overall occupational activity, athletes who aspire or would be well-suited to this pathway are left mainly to their own devices. Effectively, this means that the dual career programmes neglect the potential or likely pathway of upwards of 15% of their athletes (Bosma et al., 2020), or even more in some countries.

Yet this gap also presents significant opportunities. Dual career policymakers must actively recognise entrepreneurship, but they are not starting from scratch. Individual actors have developed numerous educational and support activities around athlete or sport entrepreneurship (e.g. Ansari et al., 2020; Furim Institut, 2019; Kenny, 2015; Tw1n, 2019), and these can be further combined or adapted to various national contexts. For researchers, there are also plentiful opportunities to explore how entrepreneurship programmes can best be tailored to athlete skills and approaches. Ultimately, greater efforts in this direction can help boost athlete entrepreneurship, ensure more successful post-athletic careers, and support overall economic development.

Funding This study was partially funded by the European Commission through an Erasmus+ Project Grant (603312-EPP-1-2018-1-NO-SPO-SCP). The funder did not influence the design, implementation, or interpretation of the study.

References

Ansari, P., Khoo, S., & Ismail, M. N. (2020). Designing and developing a sport entrepreneurship course: An educational design-based study. *Entrepreneurship Education, 3*(4), 411–432. https://doi.org/10.1007/s41959-020-00040-6

Aquilina, D., & Henry, I. (2010). Elite athletes and university education in Europe: A review of policy and practice in higher education in the European Union Member States. *International Journal of Sport Policy and Politics, 2*(1), 25–47. https://doi.org/10.1080/19406941003634024

Asociación Deportes Olímpicos. (2021). *Homepage*. https://ado.es

Borggrefe, C., & Cachay, K. (2012). "Dual careers": The structural coupling of elite sport and school exemplified by the German Verbundsysteme. *European Journal for Sport and Society, 9*(1–2), 57–80. https://doi.org/10.1080/16138171.2012.11687889

Bosma, N., Content, J., Sanders, M., & Stam, E. (2018). Institutions, entrepreneurship, and economic growth in Europe. *Small Business Economics, 51*(2), 483–499. https://doi.org/10.1007/s11187-018-0012-x

Bosma, N., Hill, S., Ionescu-Somers, A., Kelley, D., Levie, J., & Tarnawa, A. (2020). *Global entrepreneurship monitor*. Global Entrepreneurship Research Association.

Breuer, C., & Wicker, P. (2010, 7 February). Brüchiges Fundament: Deutschlands Spitzenathleten verdienen weniger als der Durchschnitt der deutschen Bevölkerung. Frankfurter Allgemeine Sonntagszeitung.

B-WISER. (2018). *Erasmus+ Sport project: "Be a Winner In elite Sport and Employment before and after athletic Retirement"*. http://www.vub.ac.be/topsport/b-wise

Capella-Peris, C., Gil-Gómez, J., Martí-Puig, M., & Ruíz-Bernardo, P. (2020). Development and validation of a scale to assess social entrepreneurship competency in higher education. *Journal of Social Entrepreneurship, 11*(1), 23–39. https://doi.org/10.1080/19420676.2018.1545686

Daley, J. (2012). *Why more pro athletes are scoring franchises after sports fame*. www.entrepreneur.com/article/22267

Deutscher Olympischer Sportbund. (2013). *Zehn-Punkte-Programm des DOSB zur Dualen Karriere*.

EU Athletes. (2015). *Improving dual career for players*.

European Commission. (2012). *EU guidelines on dual careers of athletes*.

Eurostat. (2019). *Self-employed persons*. https://ec.europa.eu/eurostat/web/products-eurostat-news/-/EDN-20190430-1

Eurostat. (2020). *Euro area unemployment at 7.8%*. https://ec.europa.eu/eurostat/documents/2995521/11156668/3-30072020-AP-EN.pdf/1b69a5ae-35d2-0460-f76f-12ce7f6c34be

FH Joanneum University of Applied Sciences. (2017). *AtLETyC—Athletes learning entrepreneurship*. https://www.fh-joanneum.at/en/projekt/atletyc-athletes-learning-entrepreneurship/

Furim Institut. (2019). *SENTA | athletes become social entrepreneurs*. https://www.dualcareer.net

Geraniosova, K., & Ronkainen, N. (2015). The experience of dual career through Slovak athletes' eyes. *Physical Culture and Sport, 61*, 53–64.

Hakkers, S. (2019). *How can sport clubs support a talent's dual career?* Amsterdam University of Applied Sciences.

Hoppenfeld, J., Wyckoff, T., Henson, J. A. J., Mayotte, J. N., & Kirkwood, H. P. (2013). Librarians and the entrepreneurship Bootcamp for veterans: Helping disabled veterans with business research. *Journal of Business & Finance Librarianship, 18*(4), 293–308. https://doi.org/10.1080/08963568.2013.825227

Hottenrott, K., & Braumann, K.-M. (2015). Aktuelle Situation im deutschen Spitzensport. *Sportwissenschaft, 45*(3), 111–115. https://doi.org/10.1007/s12662-015-0372-1

Humphreys, C. (2011). Who cares where I play? Linking reputation with the golfing capital and the implication for golf destinations. *Journal of Sport & Tourism, 16*(2), 105–128. https://doi.org/10.1080/14775085.2011.568086

Kenny, B. (2015). Meeting the entrepreneurial learning needs of professional athletes in career transition. *International Journal of Entrepreneurial Behavior & Research, 21*(2), 175–196. https://doi.org/10.1108/IJEBR-07-2013-0113

Koning, R. (2016). *Field experiments in networks, innovation and entrepreneurship: Evidence from a startup bootcamp* [Doctoral Dissertation]. Stanford University.

Kuettel, A., Christensen, M. K., Zysko, J., & Hansen, J. (2020). A cross-cultural comparison of dual career environments for elite athletes in Switzerland, Denmark, and Poland. *International Journal of Sport and Exercise Psychology, 18*(4), 454–471. https://doi.org/10.1080/1612197X.2018.1553889

Li, M., & Sum, R. K. W. (2017). A meta-synthesis of elite athletes' experiences in dual career development. *Asia Pacific Journal of Sport and Social Science, 19*(46), 1–19. https://doi.org/10.1080/21640599.2017.1317481

López de Subijana, C., Mascaró Ruiz, F., & Conde Pascual, E. (2014). Los servicios de asesoramiento a los Deportistas de Élite en las Universidades Españolas. *Revista Kronos, 13*(2).

Lorenzo Fernández, M., & Bueno Moreno, M. R. (2012). Recursos disponibles para la inserción sociolaboral tras la retirada deportiva de futbolistas. *Revista de Psicología del Deporte, 21*(1), 189–194.

Matsangos, N., Gargalianos, D., Coppola, S., Vastola, R., & Petromilli, A. (2020). Investigation of skills acquired by athletes during their sporting career. *Journal of Human Sport and Exercise, 15*(3). https://doi.org/10.14198/jhse.2020.153.02

Morris, R., Cartigny, E., Ryba, T. V., Wylleman, P., Henriksen, K., Torregrossa, M., Lindahl, K., & Erpič, S. C. (2021). A taxonomy of dual career development environments in European countries. *European Sport Management Quarterly, 21*(1), 134–151. https://doi.org/10.1080/16184742.2020.1725778

Moustakas, L., & Kalina, L. (2021). Sport and social entrepreneurship in Germany: exploring athlete perspectives on an emerging field. *World Journal of Entrepreneurship, Management and Sustainable Development* (ahead-of-print). https://doi.org/10.1108/WJEMSD-06-2020-0069.

Nauright, J., & Wiggins, D. K. (2020). Sports entrepreneurs and the shaping of the SportsWorld. *Sport in Society*, 1–3. https://doi.org/10.1080/17430437.2020.1777717

Pallarés, S., Azócar, F., Torregrosa, M., Selva, C., & Ramis, Y. (2011). Modelos de trayectoria deportiva en waterpolo y su implicación en la transición hacia una carrera profesional alternativa. (athletic career models in water polo and their involvement in the transition to an alternative career). *Cultura, Ciencia y Deporte, 6*(17), 93–103. https://doi.org/10.12800/ccd.v6i17.36

Ratten, V. (2015). Athletes as entrepreneurs: The role of social capital and leadership ability. *International Journal of Entrepreneurship and Small Business, 25*(4), 442. https://doi.org/10.1504/IJESB.2015.070217

Ratten, V. (2018). *Sport entrepreneurship: Developing and sustaining an entrepreneurial sports culture*. Management for Professionals. Springer. https://ebookcentral.proquest.com/lib/gbv/detail.action?docID=5267531

Ratten, V., & Jones, P. (2018). Future research directions for sport education: Toward an entrepreneurial learning approach. *Education + Training, 60*(5), 490–499. https://doi.org/10.1108/ET-02-2018-0028

Reyes-Hernández, O., Rodríguez Tristán, J. L., López-Walle, J., Prats, A. N., Verdaguer, F. X. P., Vinas, J., Reyes, S., & García-Mas, A. (2021). El proyecto ERASMUS+ ELIT-in: "Integración de los deportistas de élite al mercado laboral" (the ERASMUS+ ELIT-in project: "Integration of elite athletes into the labour market"). *Cultura, Ciencia Y Deporte, 16*(47), 59–68. https://doi.org/10.12800/ccd.v16i47.1695

Sánchez-Pato, A., Brunton, J., Leiva-Arcas, A., Isidori, E., & Decelis, A. (2020). *European sport leadership programme*. Universidad Católica de Murcia.

Sánchez Pato, A., Isıdori, E., Calderón, A., & Brunton, J. (2017). *An innovative European sports tutorship model of the dual career of student-athletes: Handbook*. Universidad Católica de Murcia.

Shaheen, G. E. (2016). "Inclusive entrepreneurship": A process for improving self-employment for people with disabilities. *Journal of Policy Practice, 15*(1–2), 58–81. https://doi.org/10.1080/15588742.2016.1109963

Stambulova, N. B., & Ryba, T. V. (2014). A critical review of career research and assistance through the cultural lens: Towards cultural praxis of athletes' careers. *International Review of Sport and Exercise Psychology, 7*(1), 1–17. https://doi.org/10.1080/1750984X.2013.851727

Steinbrink, K. M., Berger, E. S., & Kuckertz, A. (2020). Top athletes' psychological characteristics and their potential for entrepreneurship. *International Entrepreneurship and Management Journal, 16*(3), 859–878. https://doi.org/10.1007/s11365-019-00612-6

Tw1n. (2019). *ATLAS—athletes as entrepreneurs*. https://www.tw1n.eu/atlas-athletes-as-entrepreneurs/

Vilanova, A., & Puig, N. (2013). Compaginar la carrera deportiva con la carrera académica para la futura inserción laboral: ¿una cuestión de estrategia. *Revista de Psicología del Deporte, 22*(1), 61–68.

Wertestiftung. (2021). *Wir suchen das Sporthilfe Start Up des Jahres*. www.wertestiftung.org/wir-suchen-das-sporthilfe-start-up-des-jahres

How to Craft the Entrepreneurial Spirit: Entrepreneurship Education in the Dutch Creative Crafts

Marleen Hofland-Mol

Abstract The creative industries need entrepreneurship in order to survive and thrive in the global economy. The aim of this chapter is to focus on how entrepreneurship education can be utilised in the creative industries in order to promote new business activity that can value add to society. To do this, an examination of how and why individuals need to focus on cultivating an entrepreneurial spirit is stated. This helps in determining the reasons for entrepreneurship education and how this can influence growth potential. The Dutch context will be the focus of interest for this chapter and how entrepreneurship education can be embedded in teaching practices.

1 Introduction

In the last few decades, entrepreneurship has been perceived as the motor behind economic growth. Entrepreneurs are said to ensure innovation and are valued for their role as creators of jobs and can therefore be seen as one of the foundations of our common welfare and prosperity (Sarasvathy, 2001; UNCTAD & UNPD, 2010). It is for those reasons that the theme of entrepreneurship receives an abundant amount of attention among scholars and governments. Due to the pioneer role of entrepreneurship in the innovation process, the Dutch government has pointed out the Dutch creative industry as one of the nine top sectors to invest in (Advies Topteam Creatieve Industrie, 2011). With the ambition to 'become the most creative economy of Europe in 2020' (p. 1), the Dutch government recognizes the need to nourish cultural entrepreneurial desire in education programs that are part of the creative industries.

Consequently, the desire to develop entrepreneurship in the Dutch creative crafts sector is vivid (De Kok et al., 2009; Janssen & Gankema, 2012; Klamer et al., 2013; Ziemnowicx & Menefee, 2014). This desire might be related to the long history of learning a craft as an apprentice from a master in his workshop. Still, Janssen and

M. Hofland-Mol (✉)
Erasmus University, Rotterdam, Netherlands
e-mail: hofland@eshcc.eur.nl

J. Leitão, V. Ratten (eds.), *Strategic Innovation*, Contributions to Management Science, https://doi.org/10.1007/978-3-030-87112-3_7

Gankema (2012) argue that the image of the creative craftsman[1] has two sides: the image of a master (master versus entrepreneur) and the image of a teacher (master versus apprentice). In reality it is a challenge to meet the requirements needed to combine successful entrepreneurship with the master-apprentice education method (Janssen & Gankema, 2012). Hence, how do creative crafters like goldsmiths, glass blowers or furniture makers learn to start their and succeed their own workshop? This challenge is taken up on by creative craft education institutes in Netherlands teaching entrepreneurship programs to future craftsman. Due to the call to enhance these programs, it is the aim of this research to get insight on the aspects which might help to develop entrepreneurship education (EE) in creative crafts programs.

The research question which was answered in this study was how EE in Dutch creative crafts programs can be enhanced. In his study on teaching entrepreneurship, Mwasalwiba (2010) suggests that the framework he used for his analysis could be reproduced to assess specified educational courses. The study at hand followed his suggestion and took Mwasalwiba's framework as a starting point for the research. Next to that a set of sub questions were derived from his framework. These questions will be discussed further, later in this chapter. Additionally, four concepts were explored to gain a deeper understanding of first the creative crafts field in the Netherlands, second cultural versus creative crafts entrepreneurship, thirdly cultural EE and fourth and final creative crafts EE in the Netherlands. Using a case study approach five in-depth interviews with managers, teachers, and developers at four colleges on creative crafts in the Netherlands were conducted. It was the ambition of the study that the insights given by the respondents would contribute to suggestions that might help enhance EE in the Dutch creative crafts education institutes.

This chapter is organised into three sections. It starts with a theoretical section introducing the four concepts mentioned in the former paragraph. Subsequently, the concepts and the formulated research questions are discussed using the literature review and the results of the conducted interviews. Finally, the study will be completed with recommendations and some suggestions for further exploration.

2 The Context of Creative Craft Entrepreneurship Education

This literature review presents the four key concepts of this study starting with an introduction to the Dutch creative crafts field, followed by a comparative study between cultural and creative crafts entrepreneurship. Thoughts on cultural entrepreneurship are explored in the third paragraph, leading towards to the last concept of this chapter being EE in the creative crafts programs in the Netherlands.

[1] In this study the word craftsman refers to both male and female crafts persons.

2.1 Getting Acquainted with the Creative Crafts Field

Even though creative crafts have always been part of society, it does not appear to be a field of interest amongst academics as little research has been conducted. Moreover, obscure definitions and the lack of cohesive categorizations makes researching this field challenging. It was for this reason that the Dutch Social Economic Council SER (2013) developed a working definition of the concept of crafts to formulate their advice on craftsmanship and entrepreneurship in the crafts economy for the Dutch ministries of Economics, Social Affairs and Employment and Education, Culture and Science. According to this report, a profession or activity in the crafts sector should include an assembly of the following elements:

- Competent, manual and skilled creation (craftsmanship, creative character, custom made),
- Predominantly educated trough practice
- With proficiency as main value
- Practiced as an economic activity (SER, 2013, p. 12)

The concept of "crafts economy" (SER, 2013, p. 13) was introduced in 2009 by the industrial board of crafts, Hoofdbedrijfschap Ambachten (HBA), with the intention to raise awareness for the importance of crafts for the economy in the Netherlands. In their study, the HBA divided the crafts sector in nine different clusters. However, the SER (2013) suggested that spreading crafts activities among a very wide collection of clusters makes them difficult to define. Likewise, in their Creative Economy Report the UNCTAD and UNPD (2010) argue that defining and categorizing creative crafts is a complicated task. Moreover, their study recognizes the need for a common understanding as the creative craft sector plays a crucial part in the economy even though the field is frequently overlooked and cut off from public policies.

In his book, *The Craftsman*, Sennett (2008) explores the work of craftsmen past and present, identifying connections between material consciousness and ethical values. Sennett argues that craftsmanship names the basic human impulse to do a job well for its own sake, and good craftsmanship involves developing skills and focusing on the work rather than ourselves. The study from Klamer et al. (2013) helps to define the creative crafts sector further. Their analysis designates various disciplines of crafts. The foundation for these concepts rests in the distinction between skilled work and craftsmanship – where for skilled work practice and training are sufficient to reach a result, craftsmanship can only be reached through constant practice.

Additional descriptions worth touching upon in the context of this study were the notion of 'utilitarian craftspeople' and the 'creative craftspeople'. Klamer et al. (2013) puts forward that both craftspeople make use of craftsmanship. However, the production of the former category "serves a concrete purpose" and the later makes "unique objects, each with a distinctive quality and expressing the creativity of the maker" (p. 11). Similar to the study of the UNTAD and UNPD (2010), Klamer et al. (2013) also incorporate the design category in this framework resulting in the concept of 'cutting edge crafts'. This is where contemporary crafts, arts and design come together. Craftspeople belonging to this group explore new grounds, develop new practices and form a new range of artefacts. According to Klamer et al. (2013), this description could apply to 'artists' or 'designers' (p. 12). Hence, both Klamer et al. (2013) and UNCTAD and UNDP (2010) put forward that design might be a way to become economically successful as a creative crafts entrepreneur. This notation leads this study towards the following exploration of cultural entrepreneurship.

2.2 *Cultural Versus Creative Crafts Entrepreneurship: A Comparison*

The research domain on cultural entrepreneurship is a rather young field of expertise. In addition, its multidisciplinary character makes the existing literature less rich and abundant (Hagoort, 2012). Considering this context, the definition of what constitutes an entrepreneur by Zhao and Seibert (2006) forms the starting point for deliberating on cultural entrepreneurship. According to these two scholars, an entrepreneur can be defined as somebody who is the 'founder, owner, and manager of a small business and whose principal purpose is growth' (p. 263). Exploring the cultural entrepreneur, Blaug and Towse (2010) describe this person as an innovator, who works mostly on his own, creating profit from an original cultural endeavour. Still in his study Bilton (2010) inserts another dimension to this discussion as he observes a shift from 'art and artists based on the self-contained integrity of ideas, artefacts and content towards a definition of cultural production based on a collective system and networks' (p. 2). Moreover, Bilton emphasizes the role of the manager as an essential element of being a cultural entrepreneur in a context where highly skilled creatives unite to create novel pieces. In other words, where Blaug and Towse (2010) stress the significance of incremental innovation as essential part of being a cultural entrepreneur, Bilton (2010) highlights that, for instance, a prosperous furniture maker will most likely spend more time advising clienteles, ordering materials, and making a new social media campaign to keep the workshop running. This theory of juggled micromanagement contrasts significantly with the picture of the secluded artist creating a new piece.

The so-called 'arts for art's sake' principle described by Caves (2000) needs to be addressed to fully grasp the concept of cultural entrepreneurship. According to Caves, the need to create prevails over financial gain resulting in what Oakley (2014) refers to as 'voluntary poverty' (p. 153). Or as Sennett (2008) describes it rather unswervingly 'the good craftsman is a poor salesman, absorbed in doing something well, unable to explain the value of what he or she is doing' (p. 117). Moreover, in addition to the micro-management skills suggested by Bilton (2010) also certain personal skills can have a positive result on entrepreneurship. Using a framework for studying the psychology of entrepreneurship, Frese and Gielnik (2014) conclude that action characteristics like planning, social networking and personal initiative are essential for running business on the condition that acting is the utmost important component. That is, if an entrepreneur does not take any initiative, no effects can be expected of the named action characteristics either.

To sum up, a cultural entrepreneur can be described as a person using incremental innovation to develop new products, using a set of managerial skills to run a business smoothly and without financial gain as the main incentive. This brings us to the question of how this description corresponds to the creative craft entrepreneur. According to the SER (2013) in the Netherlands, entrepreneurship and arts craftsmanship frequently go hand in hand. However, in practice, the craft micro-entrepreneur finds it hard and demanding to combine craftsmanship and entrepreneurship daily. Furthermore, as merely craftsmanship is not enough the SER mentions a set of factors which are relevant to become successful in the creative crafts field, among which being creative and innovative in addition to commercial thinking are the most apparent. Moreover, the awareness of new technological trends and materials is also seen as an essential part of the entrepreneurial toolkit. Besides innovation, management skills are also emphasized by Janssen and Gankema (2012). Further suggestions to enhance the entrepreneurial attitude of the creative crafts entrepreneur are made by Klamer et al. (2013) recommending that craftspeople have to able to tell a better tale about themselves as well as about their creations in order to tutor the Dutch community on 'quality, design and creativity' (p. 8). Still, this might be a challenging suggestion as earning a sustainable income often results in arts craftspeople engaging in endeavours contradicting their personal values of handmade creations (Jacob, 2012).

Having sketched a portrait of both a cultural entrepreneur and a creative crafts entrepreneur leads us the theory on cultural entrepreneurship education.

2.3 *Cultural Entrepreneurship Education and Its Key Features*

The call for the development of EE has been there for decades. Hence, besides education institutes and scholars searching for ways to develop their EE programs, ministries of economics and policy makers are pushing these programs as entrepreneurship is recognised as being the driver of both economic and societal growth and prosperity (Henry et al., 2005; Mwasalwiba, 2010; SER, 2013). Due to this wide interest for this educational theme, criticism has been raised on whether entrepreneurship can be taught or not (Brixy et al., 2012; Henry et al., 2005; Mwasalwiba,

2010). Still, as Mwasalwiba puts forward that numerous studies confirm this theory, the study will proceed to shed light on the assumption that entrepreneurship can be taught.

Studies like the research done by Henry et al. (2005) suggest that, depending on the objectives of the program, there are a wide variety of approaches to teach entrepreneurship. Ideally the setting is not in the protective environment of the classroom, which is passive, but in the real-world where there is also room for making mistakes. By doing that, entrepreneurial skills like creative thinking and problem solving are enhanced. Rather, through logical thinking the 'science' part of entrepreneurship can be thought. However, students need to be urged to explore broader views and therefore an active experience-based approach is suggested to explore the 'art' part of entrepreneurship (p. 164). The authors further stress the need for educators to evaluate the aims of their program in order assess the program's effectiveness. Moreover, assessing the educators in these programs should also be part of the evaluation as their network and competences, a set of knowledge, skills and experience, are seen as essential factors for students to develop as an entrepreneur (Ballereau et al., 2015; Coyle, 2012). This view is shared, not only by scholars writing on cultural entrepreneurship Such as Coyle (2012) and Ballereau et al. (2015), but also by scholars in the education field like Hattie (2003) and van Alst et al. (2009).

To sum up, four elements of EE are apparent in the literature: the objectives, the teaching approach, the teachers and the evaluation. To assess the quality of EE, Mwasalwiba (2010) has designed a model based on his review of 108 research on EE. This framework contains five distinctive features for an education program on entrepreneurship. According to Mwasalwiba, a program on EE starts with establishing what the essence of entrepreneurship is. Secondly, the objectives of the education program are determined. What should be the result of the course? This can briefly be described as to learn *about*, *in* or *through* entrepreneurship and shapes the program design, the fourth feature of model on EE (Henry et al., 2005; Mwasalwiba (2010). The fifth and final step is the evaluation of the program. However, bearing in mind the aim of the study, which was to construct suggestions for developing EE in the creative crafts, it is important to reflect if the framework suggested by Mwasalwiba is a suitable starting point for these cultural entrepreneurs.

The research done by Bass et al. (2015) confirms, as suggested by Bilton (2010), that placing creative entrepreneurs in conventional entrepreneurship programs might not be an effective approach to enhance cultural entrepreneurship. Rather, the need to convert the artists' beliefs and proficiency into actual artefact prevails above seeking market opportunities. However, this could result in an 'identity-conflict' (p. 106), for the creative craftsman on how to create goods for the market instead of following his heart. In their study, Bass et al. (2015) present a framework to overcome this hindrance by bringing together the artists and entrepreneur identity to gain both creative and financial values. In addition, other studies recognize this discrepancy between a creative and a traditional entrepreneur offering suggestions for suitable pedagogical methods and educational instruments to educate cultural entrepreneurs. Van Andel and Schramme (2015), for example, have used the two opposing theories of causation, a term suggested by Sarasvathy (2001) to describe traditional entrepreneurship discovering market opportunities. And the second term is effectuation, a theory constructed by Sarasvathy (2001) where market opportunities are created to gain more profound information on how cultural entrepreneurship can be taught. A last example is the study by Concha (2015) using design thinking as an educational method to connect the inward focus of the creative entrepreneur to the needs of the market. Still, these examples are all educational methods for EE and to not provide an inclusive framework to access EE.

As this research focuses on developing suggestions for the improvement of EE programs in creative crafts courses in general instead of pedagogical methods and instruments in particular Mwasalwiba's (2010) mode on EE appeared to be a suitable base for the study. Moreover, his synthesis on scientific research on entrepreneurial development forms a guideline in formulating the questions in the interviews with managers, teachers, and developers at vocational colleges on creative crafts programs in this study.

Based on the literature study on cultural entrepreneurship, it is possible to propose incremental modifications on Mwasalwiba's (2010) model for assessing EE to make the model more applicable for assessing cultural entrepreneurship. By supporting the artistic student to explore both artistic and financial values, a stronger base would be created for the future creative entrepreneur helping him to embrace the two seemingly opposing identities of the entrepreneur and the creative craftsman. Still, to succeed suitable pedagogical methods and instruments need to be carefully selected in accordance with appropriate objectives and the targeted audiences of the education program. Moreover, Ballereau et al. (2015) maintain the importance of rebellious and experienced educators with an inside and outside network, next to the ability to coach creative students are necessary to lead successful EE programs.

The exploration of the concept of the Dutch creative crafts field showed that the view on cultural entrepreneurship contrasted with creative crafts the education and indicates their specific needs for creative craft EE. Still, there is one relevant aspect that needs to be studied to answer the research question of this study. Therefore, in the final part of this theoretical framework the structure of EE in creative crafts education programs in The Netherlands is analysed.

2.4 Entrepreneurship Education in the Dutch Creative Crafts Programs

To allow understanding the development and characteristics of EE in Dutch creative crafts programs, it is essential to have a clear perspective of the education structure in the Netherlands. The Dutch education system consists of 8 years of primary education followed by 4, 5 or 6 years of secondary education (depending on the type of education) and 2 to 6 years higher education (depending on the type and sort of education). On all levels, there are public and private institutes, the latter mostly on

Table 1 The Dutch Qualification Framework (NLQF) vs the European Qualification Framework (EQF)

EQF	NLQF	Dutch qualification	
8	8	Doctorate	
7	7	Master	
6	6	Bachelor	
5	5	Associate degree	
4	4+	VWO (university preparatory education)	
4	4	MBO 4 (senior secondary vocational education and training)	HAVO (senior general secondary education)
3	3	MBO 3 (senior secondary vocational education and training)	
2	2	MBO 2 (senior secondary vocational education and training)	VMBO 2 (preparatory secondary vocational education)
1	1	MBO 1 (senior secondary vocational education and training)	VMBO 1 (preparatory secondary vocational education)

Source: Author's own

religious or ideological grounds (Nuffic, 2014). Table 1 gives an overview of the qualification system in the Netherlands.

All creative crafts education programs are level 3, vocational training, but mainly level 4, specialist training. Apart from one associate degree course of 2 years which is more theoretical. For both level 3 and 4 programs, learning in practical forms, like a workshop, is an essential part of the program (Nuffic, 2014). The qualification and examination terms of vocational education programs are identical nationwide and developed by the Cooperation Organization for Vocational Education, Training, and the Labour Market (Over-SBB, n.d.). The SBB maintains the qualification structure as well as accredits and supports workplace companies in order for business to acquire the skilled workers they require. Additionally, the SBB advises both the Dutch Ministry of Education and Economic regarding the labour market and the vocational education field.

Eleven education institutes offer creative crafts programs in the Netherlands of which three vocational schools (vakschool) and eight are regional education centres (ROCs). With their regional function, the ROCs offer a wide range education programs at various locations depending on the regional desires and population. However, vocational schools, like CIBAP or Sint Lucas, are small, specialized education institutes offering programs in a specific field. Table 2 provides an overview of all education institutes in the Netherlands that provide creative crafts education programs.

With the exploration of the fourth and final concept, the next part provides insights on how the empirical analysis and data from the case study was used for comparative evaluations.

Table 2 Overview of institutes offering level 4 creative crafts education programs in the Netherlands

Educational institute	Creative crafts programs	Categorization
Zadkine (Vakschool Schoonhoven)	Creative craftsman (gold- and silversmithing)	ROC
Sint Lucas	Creative craftsman (ceramics, glass, leather and textile)	Vakschool
Hout en Meubilerings College (HMC)	Wood and furniture creative craftsman (wood, leather and textile)	Vakschool
Friesland College	Creative craftsman (wood, ceramics and textile)	ROC
CIBAP	Creative craftsman (wood and textile)	Vakschool
Friesland College	Creative craftsman (wood, ceramics and textile)	ROC
Koning Willem I College	Wood and furniture	ROC
ROC Deltion College	Wood and furniture	ROC
ROC Midden Nederland	Wood and furniture	ROC
ROC Twente	Wood and furniture	ROC
Summa College	Wood and furniture	ROC

Source: Author's own

3 A Case Study on Entrepreneurship Education in the Creative Craft

3.1 Mwasalwiba's Framework for Entrepreneurship Education

The research question which will be answered in this study is: How can EE in the creative crafts programs be enhanced in the Netherlands? This question is assessed through the point of view of interviewees working in the creative crafts education field. Their opinions will help develop ideas on how EE programs can be developed. In his meta-study on teaching entrepreneurship, Mwasalwiba (2010) suggests that the framework he used for his analysis could be reproduced to assess specified educational courses. This study used Mwasalwiba's framework and has derived the following sub-questions to answer the research question at hand:

1. What are the essence and objectives of entrepreneurship education courses in the creative crafts sector in the Netherlands?
2. What are the targeted audiences of entrepreneurship education courses in the creative crafts sector in the Netherlands and what does the course content consists of?
3. What are the teaching methods used in entrepreneurship education courses in the creative crafts sector in the Netherlands?
4. What are the essential skills and knowledge an educator needs to have to teach entrepreneurship?
5. How are the entrepreneurship courses evaluated and which indicators are used?

Since it was the aim of the study to propose new insights to help develop EE in the Dutch creative crafts programs, using contrasting results, or as Rowley (2002) describes it 'theoretical replication', is appropriate. Therefore, a diverse selection of creative crafts programs was invited to participate in the research, rather than a larger number of vocational education training (VET) institutes with similar programs. This led to the selection of four colleges, one of which has two locations. By choosing these colleges a diverse mixture was created of two colleges providing EE for the creative craftsman, two offering EE courses in wood and furniture and, the fifth college with programs for both programs. Table 2 provides a detailed overview of the specific creative crafts programs offered in the Netherlands.

The topics chosen for the interviews were based on the synthesis of Mwasalwiba's (2010) which is visualised in Fig. 1. Nonetheless, considering the theoretical framework developed in this study, several elements were adjusted accordingly. This results in the following topics that were researched and analysed:

1. The essence of the entrepreneurship education program
2. The objectives learn *for*, *about*, *in* and community support
3. Programme characteristics being:
   (a) The type of program
   (b) The target group involved
   (c) Course content
   (d) Outreach projects
4. Pedagogical approach being:
   (a) Teaching method
   (b) Educational model (design)
   (c) Educator
5. Evaluation method and criteria

3.2 The Interviews and Results

In the following part, the sub-questions of the study will be explored through the interviews conducted at five schools on creative crafts education in the Netherlands. In addition to the sub-questions, four explorative subjects, which have been derived from the theoretical framework, will be discussed. Prior to discussing these results, the five colleges will be shortly introduced giving an understanding of the setting each educational institute operates in.

Founded in 1895 as a school for gold-, silversmithing and watchmaking, the Vakschool Schoonhoven has the longest history of the institutes being interviewed. Since 1995, the college has been part of the ROC Zadkine based in Rotterdam. This

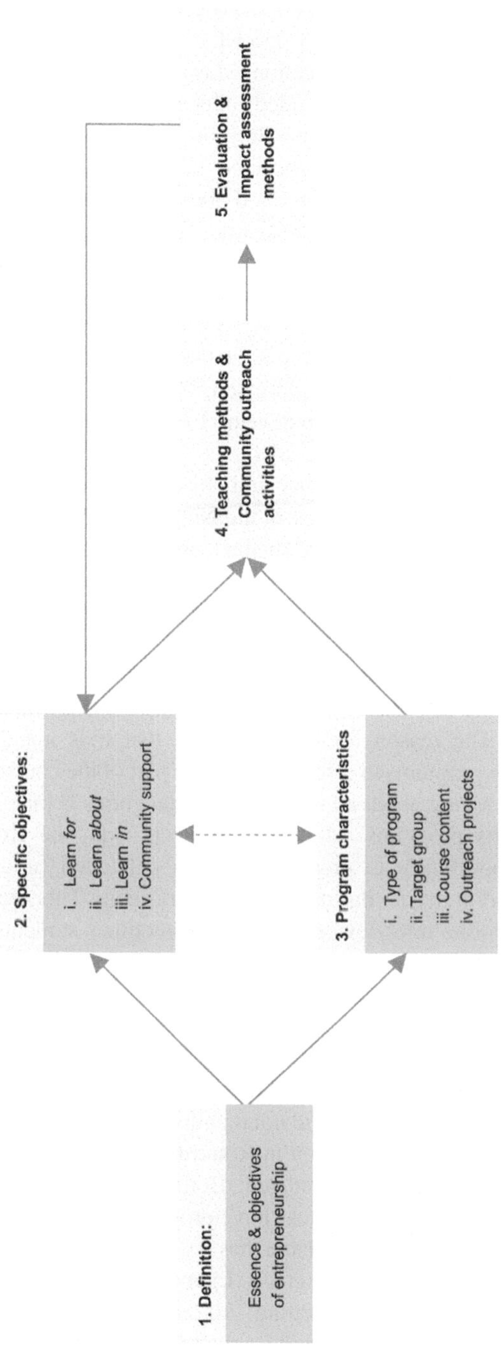

Fig. 1 Framework on entrepreneurship education. *Source:* Mwasalwiba (2010, p. 23)

college is one of the largest regional education centres in the Netherlands. (Vakschool Schoonhoven, n.d. Wikipedia). The history of the second vocational college, Sint Lucas, goes back 60 years ago when it started as a painter's college in the village Boxtel (personal communication, May 8, 2017). Around the same period the HMC college Rotterdam was founded, educating in wood and furniture programs. This third college merged with her 30 years older sister college situated in the Dutch capital Amsterdam in 1990 and became the vocational college it currently is (Historie, n.d. HMC college). The last and fourth program participating in this research belongs to the branch Construction, Infra-Architecture and Furniture Design at the ROC Koning Willem I College in s'-Hertogenbosch. Originally founded as a senior secondary technical school around 25 years ago, the college is now part of a large ROC with wide variety of branches and programs on several locations (personal communication, May 8, 2017).

Next the five sub-questions will be addressed. These questions were created using Mwasalwiba's (2010) model on how to develop EE and address the findings at hand, leading to a concrete analysis of the results.

Sub-question 1: What are the essence and objectives of entrepreneurship education courses in the creative crafts sector in the Netherlands?

Mwasalwiba (2010) identifies three distinct objectives for EE being *for, about* and *in* entrepreneurship. The first objective *for* can be described as trained to become an entrepreneur. The second *about* involves learning theories concerning entrepreneurship. And lastly the third objective *in* aspires to teach students to become entrepreneurial in their workplace. Applying this theory to the colleges being interviewed, one could say that all education programs use all three objectives for their EE program. The reason for this might be that it is mandatory in Dutch vocational education programs to offer a substantial part of the course in the working field. This way of learning about all the proposed categories is inherently integrated in the creative crafts programs. Moreover, students from the Koning Willem I College get the opportunity to create their own collection of crafted products under the guidance of a master during their apprenticeship. This seems unthinkable in other branches as one interviewee remarks, 'Sometimes students were asked to sign for the fact that they would not open their own workshop within 50 km of the shop where they did their training. Of course, we hampered that' (personal communication, May 4, 2017).

All but one college creates opportunities for their students to start their own collections for real, with registration at the chamber of commerce, or without this regulation. The HMC in Amsterdam did not mention activities like this being offered to their students. However, the location in Rotterdam also has its own 'chamber of commerce' where registration is simulated. Both Zadkine, commonly known as Vakschool Schoonhoven, and Sint Lucas have projects were students design, create and trade their own collection. The latter has its own shop in their hometown in Boxtel where students can sell their artefacts. Likewise, HMC Rotterdam plans to let students create and sell in a real-life setting. All colleges provide theoretical classes on entrepreneurship, such as finance and marketing.

In his framework Mwasalwiba (2010) suggests a fourth objective for designing a program on EE being supporting the community. Nonetheless, none of the interviewees mentioned this aim for their program. More on how the colleges integrate the remaining categories *for* and *about* entrepreneurship in their program will be explored in the paragraph on the content of the program.

While talking to the interviewees, the impression was raised that all colleges have objectives for their entrepreneurship program. However, these aims have not been put down in writing. More often the interviewees refer to qualification files from the SBB (Koning Willem I College, HMC Rotterdam and HMC Amsterdam) as the document where the objectives of their program were captured. When asked about the role the SBB plays in the development of their education program, the interviewee teacher from the HMC Rotterdam replies, ‘Nothing. We get a sheet of paper with text, and we start playing with that’ (personal communication, May 11, 2017). However, having the aims of the education program set upfront is important as it allows educators to choose the suitable pedagogical approach as well as being aware of the estimated impact (Mwasalwiba, 2010). From printed information on the education programs provided by three of the participating colleges (Vakschool Schoonhoven, Koning Willem I College and Sint Lucas), one program gave insight into the goals aimed for, derived from the vision and mission endorsed by this college, being Sint Lucas. Next to that, Sint Lucas wants entrepreneurship to be integrated in all courses offered, also in generic courses as Dutch and English, for example. This suggestion of incorporating entrepreneurship in other classes of the creative crafts program was also expressed by the Vakschool Schoonhoven.

According to the participant from the Vakschool Schoonhoven, entrepreneurship, besides creativity and technology, is one of the three pillars of the college (personal communication, May 4, 2017). The HMC College uses entrepreneurship, together with craftsmanship and creativity, as a prominent slogan on their website (HMC College, n.d. Homepage). These two examples show the importance of entrepreneurship for creative crafts colleges. When inquiring about the essence of EE, it seems to revolve more around being entrepreneurial, or ‘awareness’ (personal communication, May 11, 2017), than around being an entrepreneur. For example, another interviewee (HMC Amsterdam) mentions, ‘And you (the student) can do everything according to the book and very neat, but just try out some things’ (personal communication, May 12, 2017). The team ‘coordinator’ at Koning Willem I College describes it as ‘Having a certain attitude like: look, this is me and this what I want to be, or I dare to go for it: entrepreneurial behaviour’ (personal communication, May 18, 2017). Moreover, in their concept vision document, Sint Lucas describes the essence of entrepreneurship and entrepreneurial behaviour as ‘adding value. Value emerges when your service or product contains value for a costumer. Entrepreneurial people crab changes and take initiative. Entrepreneurs take one step further and develop changes into business models’ (Concept Visie Document, 2016, p. 3).

Sub-question 2: What are the targeted audiences of entrepreneurship education courses in the creative crafts sector in the Netherlands and what does the course content consist of?

Students following the creative crafts programs are described as hands-on and practical. Another striking characteristic mentioned by all interviewees is that creating something is important for their students. ‘They are mainly creative students who want to invent and create something’ (personal communication, May 18, 2017). Or as another interviewee puts it, ‘Nice to have that small workshop. I (the student) do not need to become rich if I can earn something of a living. But I cannot ask so much for that piece…They feel guilty’ (personal communication, May 4, 2017). From the answers given, the impression was raised that there is a general understanding of what kind of students that follow the program EE rather than more specific, segmented profile on for example social or economic background. In addition, none of the educational institutes offer programs for start-ups (Brixy et al. (2012).

In brief what strikes out the most is that all participants describe their targeted audience as creative students who want to create rather than gain profit. Becoming an entrepreneurship is not their main aim, if an aim at all, to attend a creative crafts course. Moreover, as other demographic and economic characteristics as age, social class or personal interests are lacking, it is problematic to define an overall target audience (Table 3).

In general, the content of the entrepreneurship programs mainly emphasized the finance and marketing part of starting up a business. One of the interviewees mentions, ‘It is marketing, it is administration, it is a small part organisation, and a business plan is the result of those three’ (personal communication, May 11, 2017). Moreover, writing a business plan is mandatory in all entrepreneurship programs. The way this is done differs widely among the different colleges. Some choose to write a business plan by the book (HMC Amsterdam and Rotterdam) while others seem to emphasize more the process (Vakschool Schoonhoven) and the entrepreneurial skills (Koning Willem I College, Vakschool Schoonhoven and Sint Lucas). The coordinator entrepreneurship (Sint Lucas) explains it as follows: ‘And if you (the student) want to start networking, you do not need to write down in your business plan with whom you network, attend one of our network meetings and show this way that you can do it. Because then you are doing it for real, what is more you are being entrepreneurial… You (the student) must write a business plan. Entrepreneurial behaviour is incorporated in there. That is why we have said: First entrepreneurial behaviour and after that the business (plan)’ (personal communication, May 8, 2017).

For this study, Mwasalwiba’s (2010) model for EE is used. However, the teaching subject of SME[2] management, which is suggested in his study, has not been put forward by the interviewees during the interviews. The reason for omitting SME Management might be that most creative craft entrepreneurs start on a freelance basis and therefore do not hire employees. Nonetheless, new subjects have been introduced like teaching entrepreneurial skills and design. For the design, cooperation was sought with other disciplines within the school.

[2] Small and Medium Enterprises.

Table 3 Most common subjects taught in creative crafts entrepreneurship education programs

College	Course content: subjects									
	Idea generation	Business plan	New venture creation	Risk and rationality	Marketing	Organization	managing growth	Financing	Entrepreneurial skills	Design
Zadkine (Vakschool Schoonhoven)	x	x	x	X	x		x	x	x	x
Sint Lucas	x	x	x	X	x		x	x	x	x
HMC Amsterdam	x	x		x	x	x		x		x
HMC Rotterdam	x	x	x	x	x			x	x	x
Koning Willem I College	x	x	x	x	x		x	x	x	x

Source: Author's own

There is consensus among the interviewees that entrepreneurial skills are important; still the opinion on what they consist of varies significantly. Examples of these variations are networking and research skills (Sint Lucas, Koning Willem I College), communication (Koning Willem I College) and marketing and financial skills (Vakschool Schoonhoven). Also, the term 'Twenty-first Century skills'[3] is mentioned several times when referring to entrepreneurial skills (Vakschool Schoonhoven, Sint Lucas). Using the above-mentioned modifications, Table 4 was created to give an overview of the subjects taught in entrepreneurial programs in creative crafts education.

Sub-question 3: What are the teaching methods used in entrepreneurship education courses in the creative crafts sector in the Netherlands?

In his study, Mwasalwiba (2010) makes a distinction between active (or innovative) and passive (traditional) methods used to educate in entrepreneurship programs, the first being more effective. As mentioned in the first paragraph of this chapter, all colleges can offer students business simulations in the form of an apprenticeship as a mandatory part of their vocational program. All but one college also offers a real venture setting. Sint Lucas and Koning Willem I College both participate in the Dutch Design Week in Eindhoven, enabling students to exhibit and participate in a design competition. Another activity worth mentioning is the cooperation of the Vakschool Schoonhoven with the Dutch Silver Museum in Schoonhoven which offers working benches for the goldsmith students against special rates to show customers their creative skills and to sell their own designs. Lastly, students from the HMC Rotterdam start their own furniture workshop in their final year of college. Students who are not able to start up their business immediately are given an assignment by the school.

Some methods like case studies and workshops have not been mentioned often, and videos and filming have not been mentioned at all while conducting the interviews. Still, according to my experience as a teacher on entrepreneurship in a vocational program, I presume interviewees forgot to mention these methods especially as showing videos during classes is a rather commonly used educational method also in vocational training programs.

The project approach used by Koning Willem I College is the educational design for their entire four-year program and therefore stands out from the project-based teaching approach generally used. Generally, the project-based approach is used as one pedagogical approach combined with other pedagogical approaches to form the curriculum of a program. At this point, it is therefore important to make a distinction between a pedagogical approach as a starting point for the design of an educational program or curriculum on one hand, and teaching models being used in class to teach a certain theory or skill in an appropriate manner (Coppoolse & Vroegindeweij, 2010) on the other. At the time of the interview Sint Lucas is considering a new

[3]Twenty-first century skills are an overarched concept of knowledge, skills, and dispositions that people need to possess to be able to participate in the knowledge economy (Voogt & Roblin Pareja, 2010).

Table 4 Teaching methods used in creative crafts entrepreneurship education programs

College	Teaching method											
	Real venture setting up (a)	Business simulation (a)	Games and competitions (a)	Study visits (a)	Workshops (a)	Presentations (a)	Theory based (p)	Guest speakers, role models (p)	Discussions and group work (p)	Projects (p)	case studies (p)	videos and filming (p)
Zadkine (Vakschool Schoonhoven)	x	x		x		x	x	x	x			
Sint Lucas	x	x	X	x		x	x	x	x		x	
HMC Amsterdam	x	x		x		x	x	x	x			
HMC Rotterdam		x	x	x		x	x	x	x			
Koning Willem I College	x	x	x	x		x	x	x	x	x		

Source: Author's own

educational design for their curriculum as they hold the opinion that model, they currently use, the competence-based approach,[4] is outdated ((personal communication, May 8, 2017). The basis for their entrepreneurship program lies in the design thinking method according to which the market is the starting point for creation.

The methods used in the entrepreneurship programs in creative crafts education are shown in Table 5. An active method is indicated with an 'a' and passive method with a 'p'. Generally speaking, the figure indicates that there is quite a mix between the passive and active methods used for EE at the colleges. One could argue that the passive methods are used more often. However, the amount of time in which the two methods are used in the curricula has not been measured. Therefore, this could give a lopsided perspective. Moreover, the content and methodology used in the project approach by Koning Willem I College could also be labelled as active as the students have room for learning as well as discovery (Mwasalwiba, 2010). For example, during one of these projects' students design a closet at school which they make at the workshop where they do their training. Finally, their master does the assessment of the furniture created. As Mwasalwiba (2010) already indicates in his study, activities and outreach projects are not yet often used in EE. It could be for this reason that these topics used in Mwasalwiba's model have not been brought up during the interviews with the participants of this analysis.

As the location and structure of the organisation varies among the colleges participating, the interviewees were asked with whom they participate internally and externally concerning the program on EE. The Vakschool Schoonhoven participates with the gold- and silversmith sector on all levels and with the Dutch Silver Museum mentioned above. However, participation with other sectors within Zadkine is not common; neither is cooperating with creative crafts or other vocational colleges. According to the team leader, 'This school is rather autonomous. All teaching materials are developed here...but it also has to do with our physical location' (personal communication, May 4, 2017). This is recognized at the Koning Willem I where the interviewee states, 'You (the educator) experience that sometimes it is difficult to make a solid appointment to share with each other: How do you do that? It is difficult within such inert institute. And that is a shame really, cause actually you have to benefit from each other' (personal communication, May 18, 2017). Another interviewee emphasizes the strong relationships with apprentice companies (personal communication, May 12, 2017). Nonetheless, both educators mention that a structural cooperation with other companies is not common at their college. The HMC College has its own project bureau which has contacts with companies for assignments, guest speakers and business visits. In addition, students can rent working spaces to start their own workshop at a specialized organisation (personal communication, May 11, 2017). Sint Lucas is familiar with all the forms of cooperation mentioned above and uses them in their program on entrepreneurship. Moreover, students also get the opportunity to go to the centre of entrepreneurship of

[4]As mentioned earlier in this chapter competences are described as set of knowledge, skills and experience.

the Fontys Hogeschool, a bachelor education institute, and the Technical University of Eindhoven (personal communication, May 8, 2017).

Sub-question 4: What are the essential skills and knowledge an educator needs to have to teach entrepreneurship?

The opinions on what set of skills and knowledge are needed as an educator in EE vary. Experience as an entrepreneur in the creative crafts field is seen as a benefit by all participants. Some interviewees have the impression that having the personal experience as a craftsman makes the class more practical and less theoretical (personal communication, May 11, 2017). However, the didactic and pedagogical skills are also perceived as being very important for giving an inspiring class. During the interview at the Vakschool there was said, 'You can be an entrepreneur, you can be a craftsman but that doesn't make you a good entrepreneurship teacher if you do not have the other skills' (personal communication, May 4, 2017). The interviewee from the Koning Willem I explains that if the specific knowledge is not available, then he makes sure that he finds someone to teach who does have that specific knowledge. Also, at the Vakschool Schoonhoven it is argued that they make sure that the students personal educational needs are addressed.

Regarding the skills and knowledge necessary to educate entrepreneurship, identifying the essential knowledge for an entrepreneurship educator came naturally. Interviewees mentioned examples such as knowledge of finance (Vakschool Schoonhoven, HMC Amsterdam, Koning Willem I College), marketing (Vakschool Schoonhoven) and specialized knowledge (Koning Willem I College) or knowledge trends and developments of a certain craft field (Vakschool Schoonhoven). Still, skills are more difficult to determine. Some skills that were mentioned are being innovative (Vakschool Schoonhoven), entrepreneurial (HMC Amsterdam, Sint Lucas) or according to another interviewee, 'See somebody's strengths. Look where his qualities are' (personal communication, May 11, 2017). When asked if these skills and knowledge are likewise asked from teachers of other courses than EE, the interviewees from Koning Willem I College and Vakschool Schoonhoven confirm this suggestion. However, the interviewee from the HMC Amsterdam explains, 'if you look at the product for Dutch for example it is a general exam and with entrepreneurship it is different. It is less fixed. As a teacher you must be able to handle that' (personal communication, May 12, 2017). Moreover, coordinator entrepreneurship at Sint Lucas expresses her concern on how to get other educators from Sint Lucas into an entrepreneurial mind-set. For example, creative classes which involve into entrepreneurship, need to think from the point of view of the customer, in this case the student. She explains further: 'Otherwise you (the student) keep creating a cup made of gold which everyone finds too expensive, while if you make a red cup, it is sellable. That is important. You are not making art here. You are making something that you want sell. Where you can build an existence upon' (personal communication, May 8, 2017).

Sub-question 5: How are the entrepreneurship courses evaluated and which indicators are used?

All five educational institutes evaluate their entrepreneurship program mainly by evaluation with the colleague educators involved in these programs. However, on paper no criteria are determined on how to reflect on the entrepreneurship program making it difficult for the educators to objectively evaluate the program. Most often at the end course on entrepreneurship, the team of teachers who have developed the program come together. So far it is difficult to conclude that either of the two forms of evaluation suggested by Mwasalwiba (2010) is being used at the creative crafts colleges. The first type refers to the evaluation mentioned above. This evaluation tries to appraise the general development of an EE. The second type aims to appraise the students' opinion on an entrepreneurship program by measuring predetermined indicators, which at the time of the interview is not done by any of the collaborating colleges. Still, Koning Willem I College rounds off every entrepreneurial program with a classroom conversation on how the program was experienced and the college uses these results to improve its program. Furthermore, Sint Lucas randomly evaluates classes and in the case of the creative craftsman course there is an annual anonymous survey according to a standard questionnaire. If needed, this questionnaire can also be adjusted according to specific criteria and wishes of the teachers involved. The interviewee says, 'If you ask it, they (the students) are always nice.' She therefore experiences that the anonymity of the surveys leads to more transparent answers from the participants (personal communication, May 8, 2017). Unfortunately, no information was provided to support this study.

In essence, evaluation is part of the educational process among the vast number of participating colleges. However, as hardly any written criteria are used as a base for these evaluations, the impact and results of EE cannot be objectively measured.

4 Conclusion and Discussion

Since entrepreneurship has been recognised as the catalyst for social welfare and economic growth (Sarasvathy, 2001; UNCTAD & UNPD, 2010), the interest for nurturing education on entrepreneurship is growing. Additionally, cultural sectors as the creative crafts are indicated as fields where the entrepreneurial spirit could be stronger (De Kok et al., 2009; Janssen & Gankema, 2012; Klamer et al., 2013; Ziemnowicx & Menefee, 2014). It was the aim of this study to produce suggestions for enhancing EE in the creative crafts in the Netherlands. For this purpose, a qualitative case study was conducted with team leaders, coordinators, and educators of five creative crafts programs in the Netherlands. Using Mwasalwiba's (2010) framework for assessing EE programs five sub-questions were formulated. In addition, four conjectures for suggestions were derived from the literature review to explore matters that came to light in this empirical research, but which were not pointed out by Mwasalwiba.

However, while analysing the results, there were some complicating factors that need to be resolved. Hence frequently results could not be explored since questions were not answered or given answers were ambiguous making it problematic to develop patterns. For instance, for all but one college the essence of the program on EE did not appear to have been established. Similarly, the impression was raised that objective were formed yet, they were not documented. Moreover, in most cases the evaluation of the program seemed considerably loose due to a lack of clear set criteria. And finally, the targeted audience were universally described without segmentation. With these impediments in mind, the following suggestions for enhancement might be pointed out. Hence as the data set is limited, likewise conclusions are limited.

4.1 Overall Conclusion

First, it appears that all three objectives for EE Mwasalwiba (2010) proposes being *for, about* and *in* are offered at the creative crafts colleges. Moreover, the Dutch vocational system stimulates this because an apprenticeship at a creative crafts atelier or workshop is mandatory at al vocational level four colleges. However, how the colleges go about using this to their advantage differs widely. Some schools have cooperation both internally in the school and externally with a wide variety of organisations from museums to centres of entrepreneurship at universities. By and large, the essence and objectives of the EE programs are not specifically formulated and put down in writing. Furthermore, evaluations on the program are mainly done through a reflection session among the educators, assessing the general development of the program. And for neither evaluation methods pre-determined indicators are used. The students' opinion has not been appraised by any college. Formulating objectives might give a direction on how to design a suitable program on EE. In addition, evaluation on the grounds of pre-defined criteria might give new insights and room for improvement. Finally, the view has emerged that an encompassing vision on entrepreneurship and its role throughout the organisation might result in a more cohesive educational approach.

Secondly, the qualitative research shows that according to the answers given by the interviewees the targeted audience is not described using segmentation criteria, resulting in a rather general description of the population. Nonetheless, the attending students might be described as cultural entrepreneurs. Moreover, it seems to be the view of the interviewees that the creative crafts student is mainly driven by creating something beautiful than by financial gain. In addition, theory shows that the future cultural entrepreneur has difficulties joining his or her own creative value with economic value. Specific educational models like the design model might help students to overcome this 'identity-conflict' (Bass et al., 2015). Finally, no education is offered to the young entrepreneur with some years of experience as professional craftsman (Brixy et al., 2012). This might be an additional target population to offer EE to.

Thirdly, the literature review of this study indicates that the educator plays a significant role in offering EE (Coyle, 2012; Ballereau et al., 2015; Hattie, 2003; van Alst et al., 2009). According to the interviewees specialized knowledge is essential.

Also, both didactic skills and entrepreneurial experience in the creative crafts were preferred. This resulted in a wide range of qualities an entrepreneur teacher should possess. And although this view was not supported by all participants, some would urge that all teachers should have an entrepreneurial spirit. Moreover, gaining insight on the specific skills and knowledge an entrepreneur educator should possess might be an additional recommendation for enhancing EE (Fig. 2).

Finally, Mwasalwiba's (2010) framework for EE served as a starting point for this study, giving it structure and guidance. Using existing theories and combining these with the findings from the interviews, suggestions for attuning the framework were proposed, making it more suitable for assessing creative crafts EE. Suggested alterations worth mentioning were the addition of the concept of creative personal leadership to give creative crafts people lines of approach to combine their creative value with market value. Besides, this might add to the objective learning *for* (Mwasalwiba, 2010), since the research shows that there is room for developing this aim. A second suggestion is the adjustment of the element "teaching methods and community outreach activities" as suggested by Mwasalwiba (2010) with the concept of pedagogical approach. In doing so more emphasis can be put on the role of the educator and the educational model used in combination with an appropriate teaching model.

4.2 Recommendations for Further Research

The number of concepts relevant to address in this study is too high to be explored in depth. This was by no means done out of unawareness but rather out of the wish to give the colleges who participated in this research the most beneficial insights possible. And as the information was gathered from a small samples size of only five, it is difficult to generalize any of these outcomes. Still, understandings were created, and in-depth information was assembled offering some remarkable and appreciated insights.

Nonetheless, the results have implications for other studies as there is no consensus if bridging the gap between the associate and a master's degree would benefit the entrepreneurial spirit of the creative craftsman and the creative crafts field in general. Next to that the fragmentation of the creative crafts fields, for example goldsmiths, glassblowers and furniture all create in a specific ecosystem with specific educational needs. Hence, a relevant question is what could be done to join these creative craftsmen and to give them a voice for policy makers and other stakeholders to acknowledge the economic and cultural value the craftsman creates. Moreover, what should be done on a structural basis to appraise and enhance these values and give Dutch creative crafts entrepreneurs the tools to become cutting edge.

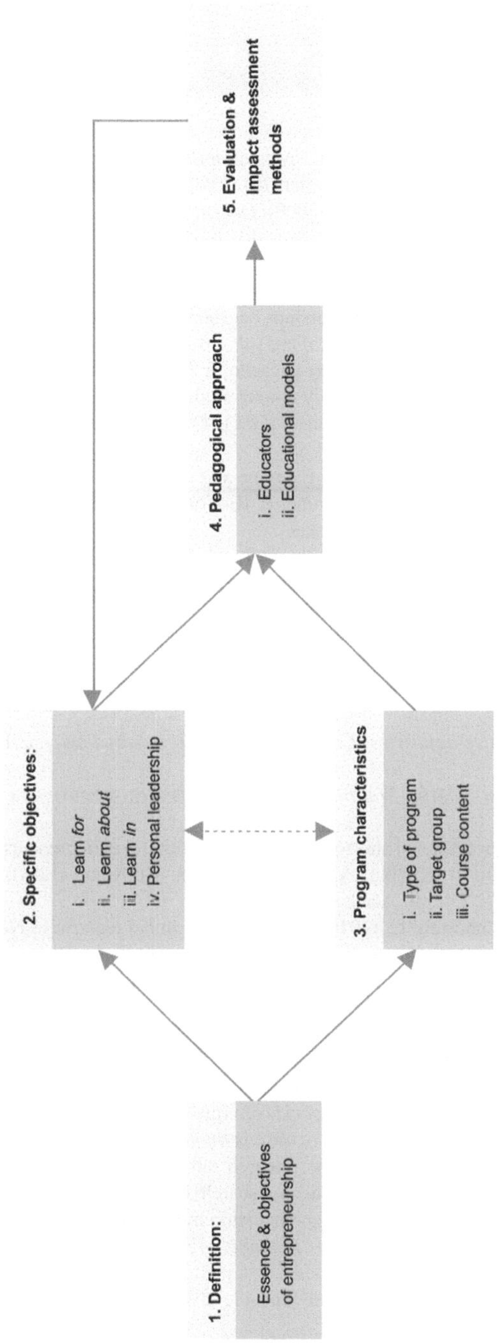

Fig. 2 Suggested framework for entrepreneurship education in the creative crafts programs. *Source*: Elaborated by the author, based on Mwasalwiba (2010)

Funding Funded by the Netherlands Organisation for Scientific Research for the Netherlands Organisation for Scientific Research in NWO project number: 023.014.018.

References

Advies Topteam Creatieve Industrie. (2011). *Creatieve industrie in topvorm.* Rijksoverheid. https://www.rijksoverheid.nl/documenten/rapporten/2011/06/17/creatieve-industrie-in-topvorm.

Alst van, J., de Jong, R., & van Keulen, H. (2009). *Docentprofessionaliteit in het Hoger onderwijs. Naar een professionele infrastructuur als voorwaarde voor studiesucces.* Instituut voor de Ontwikkeling van het Wiskunde Onderwijs.

Andel van, W., & Schramme, A. (2015). Exploring entrepreneurial actions of creative entrepreneurs and its consequences for entrepreneurship education. In O. Kuhlke, A. Schramme, & R. Kooyman (Eds.), *Creating cultural capital* (pp. 56–68). Eburon Academic Publishers.

Ballereau, V., Sinapi, C., Toutain, O., & Juno-Delgado, E. (2015) Developing a business model: the perception of entrepreneurial self-efficacy among students in cultural and creative industry. In O. Kuhlke, A. Schramme & R. Kooyman (Eds.), *Creating cultural capital* (pp. 164–177). Eburon Academic Publishers.

Bass, E., Milosevic, I., & Eesley, D. (2015) Examine and reconciling identity issues. among artist-entrepreneurs. In O. Kuhlke, A. Schramme, & R. Kooyman (Eds.), *Creating cultural capital* (pp. 99–109). Eburon Academic Publishers.

Bilton, C. (2010). *Identity, creativity and the cultural entrepreneur* [Paper presentation]. 23rd EGOS Colloquium, Vienna. http://wrap.warwick.ac.uk/60723/.

Blaug, M., & Towse, R. (2010). Cultural entrepreneurship. In R. Towse (Ed.), *A Handbook of cultural economics* (2nd ed., pp. 153–157). Edward Elgar.

Brixy, U., Sternberg, R., & Stüber, H. (2012). The selectiveness of the entrepreneurial process. *Journal of Small Business Management, 50*(1), 105–131. https://doi.org/10.1111/j.1540-627X.2011.00346.x

Caves, R. (2000). *Creative industries: Contracts between art and commerce.* Harvard University Press.

Concept Visie document. (2016). *Waarom practise, personality, creativity en Entrepreneurship.* Sint Lucas.

Concha, G. O. (2015). Professional short-term training for cultural entrepreneurs in Valdivia, Chile Innovuss Program. In O. Kuhlke, A. Schramme, & R. Kooyman (Eds.), *Creating cultural capital* (pp. 322–330). Eburon Academic Publishers.

Coppoolse, R. & Vroegindeweij, D. (2010). *75 Modellen van het onderwijs.* Noordhoff uitgevers.

Coyle, P. (2012). Entrepreneurial graduates and their contribution to the creative and cultural economies. In G. Hagoort, A. Thomassen, & R. Kooyman (Eds.), *Pioneering worldwide* (pp. 152–157). Eburon Academic Publishers.

Frese, M., & Gielnik, M. M. (2014). The psychology of entrepreneurship. *Annual Review of Organizational Psychology and Organizational Behaviour, 1*, 413–438.

Hagoort, G. (2012). On the principles of cultural entrepreneurship. In G. Hagoort, A. Thomassen & R. Kooyman (Eds.), *Pioneering minds worldwide* (pp. 4–7). Eburon Academic Publishers.

Hattie, J. (2003). *Teachers make a difference, what is the research evidence?* [Paper presentation]. Building teacher quality: What does the research tell us ACER Research Conference, Melbourne, Australia. http://research.acer.edu.au/research_conference_2003/4/.

Henry, C., Hill, F., & Leith, C. (2005). Entrepreneurship training and education: Can entrepreneurship be taught? Part II. *Education + Training, 47*(3), 158–169. https://doi.org/10.1108/00400910510592211

Historie. (n.d.). *In HMC College.* Retrieved June 11, 2017, from http://www.hmcollege.nl/hmc/historie.aspx

HMC College. (n.d.). *In homepage.* Retrieved May 21, 2017, from http://www.hmcollege.nl/

Janssen, H., & Gankema, H. (2012). *De toekomst van het creatief vakmanschap. De Opleiding als motor voor duurzame innovaties in eeuwenoude ambachten.* KPC groep.
Jacob, D. (2012). Crafting your way out of the recession? New craft entrepreneurs and the global economic downturn. *Cambridge Journal of Regions, Economy and Society, 6*, 127–140. https://doi.org/10.1093/cjres/rss022
Klamer, A., Fjeldsted, T., Goto, K., Jiang, L., Kotipalli, P., & Mignosa, A. (2013). *Crafting culture* (Final report). Stichting Economie en Cultuur.
Kok de, J. M. P., Mooibroek, M., Pleijster, F., & Wennekers, A. R. M. (2009). *Innovatief ondernemerschap in detailhandel, horeca en ambacht.* Economisch Instituut voor Midden-en kleinbedrijf (EIM).
Mwasalwiba, E. S. (2010). Entrepreneurship education: A review of its objectives, teaching methods, and impact indicators. *Education + Training, 52*(1), 20–47. https://doi.org/10.1108/00400911011017663
Nuffic. (2014). *Het onderwijssysteem van Nederland beschreven.* Nuffic.
Oakley, K. (2014). Good work? Rethinking cultural entrepreneurship. In C. Bilton & S. Cummings (Eds.), *Handbook of management and creativity* (pp. 145–159). Edward Elgar.
Over SBB. (n.d.). *In SBB.* Retrieved May 21, 2017, from https://www.s-bb.nl/over-sbb
Rowley, J. (2002). Using case studies in research. *Management Research News, 25*(1), 16–27.
Sarasvathy, S. D. (2001). Causation and effectuation: Towards a theoretical shift from economic inevitability to entrepreneurial contingency. *Academy of Management Review, 26*(2), 243–288.
Sennett, R. (2008). *The Craftsman.* Penguin Group.
Sociaal-Economische Raad. (2013). *Handmade in Holland.* Sociaal-Economische Raad (SER).
UNCTAD & UNPD. (2010). *Creative economy report: Creative economy feasible development option.* http://www.unctad.org/en/docs/ditctab20103_en.pdf.
Voogt, J., & Roblin Pareja, N. (2010). *21st Century skills. Discussienota.* Universiteit Twente.
Vakschool Schoonhoven. (n.d.) *In Wikipedia.* Retrieved June 11, from https://nl.wikipedia.org/wiki/Vakschool_Schoonhoven
Zhao, H., & Seibert, S. E. (2006). The big five personality dimensions and entrepreneurial status: A meta-analytical review. *Journal of Applied Psychology, 91*(2), 259–271. https://doi.org/10.1037/0021-9010.91.2.259
Ziemnowicx, C., & Menefee, M. (2014). *Encouraging craft, arts and micro enterprises for creative entrepreneurship and innovative business growth* [Paper presentation]. 40th ASBE Annual Conference, Memphis. http://www.aibmidwest.org/2014-proceedings.html.

Marleen Hofland-Mol, PhD Candidate, Erasmus School of History Culture and Communication at Erasmus University Rotterdam Marleen Hofland-Mol is a goldsmith, teacher Entrepreneurship at vocational institute Albeda and an external PhD candidate at Erasmus University. She holds a MA in Culture Economics and Entrepreneurship and during this program specialized in creative craft and creative craft entrepreneurship education. Her PhD-research aims to get insight into what might influence the appreciation of creative crafts in the Netherlands. The novelty of this research lies in the use of a comparative study with best practice Germany to study what attributes might influence the appreciation of creative crafts. With the rare combination of her experiences, she wishes to connect craft and theory in a creative and practical manner, and to build bridges between the wide variety of organizations the crafts field consist of. Contact Marleen Hofland-Mol is much appreciated at: https://www.linkedin.com/in/marleen-mol-195a506/

Empowering Community Out of Poverty: A Case of Kampong Bolkiah Community Development Centre, Brunei Darussalam

Khairul Hidayatullah Basir

Abstract The study explored the initiatives made by Kampong Bolkiah Community Development Centre (KBCDC) in its effort to empower the community to improve their livelihood through entrepreneurial activities in Brunei Darussalam. A qualitative approach was used and data was collected through an in-depth interview with the founder of KBCDC. The results found that by designing programs based on their needs, enhancing their entrepreneurial skills and matching them with serious and motivated buyers are the important factors. The findings are an important indicator to policy-makers and development practitioners. The future study should consider unraveling the influential factors of community participation in KBCDC to improve their livelihood.

1 Introduction

Brunei Darussalam (herein 'Brunei'), a small Islamic country, with a land area of 5765 km^2, located on the Northwest of Borneo Island, is home to 433,283 people. The oil and gas sector is the backbone of Brunei's economy, accounting for 67.7% of GDP and 95.6% of total exports. Therefore, its citizens enjoy a high level of quality of life with free education and healthcare and no income tax. Like any other country, Brunei is committed towards achieving Sustainable Development Goals (SDGs) and its national vision, *Wawasan Brunei* 2035 (Brunei Vision 2035). Under *Wawasan Brunei* 2035, Brunei aspires to be recognised for its educated, highly skilled and accomplished people, with a high quality of life and a dynamic, sustainable economy (Wawasan Brunei, n.d.). It harnesses Brunei's development strategies and policies while incorporating sustainable development perspectives.

Despite this economic advantage, poverty in Brunei remains an ongoing issue. With Brunei having no recorded poverty line, it is difficult to assess the current poverty percentage. There are multifarious government organisations established

K. H. Basir (✉)
Faculty of Agriculture, Universiti Islam Sultan Sharif Ali, Gadong, Brunei Darussalam
e-mail: hidayatullah.basir@unissa.edu.bn

J. Leitão, V. Ratten (eds.), *Strategic Innovation*, Contributions to Management Science, https://doi.org/10.1007/978-3-030-87112-3_8

with the aim to help address this issue. For instance, Monthly Welfare Assistance (BKB) is provided through the Ministry of Culture Youth and Sports (MCYS) which is designed to act as a supplement to protect the target groups from poverty and ease their hardship until they receive a sufficient source of income and become economically independent. Brunei's *zakat* (alms) system, under Ministry of Religious Affairs, provides funds for the Muslims in need. Giving zakat is a religious obligation where Muslims whose wealth sits above the minimum threshold are obligated to pay 2.5% of their collective assets. *Zakat* fund is also used to fund enrichment programs to empower eligible *zakat* recipients. In addition to government agencies, various non-governmental organisations (NGOs) also play a role in poverty alleviation, for instance, Kampong Bolkiah Community Development Centre (KBCDC).

The issue of poverty should consider manoeuvring under the basis of the paraphernalia of economic opportunities in line with the aim of Wawasan Brunei 2035, as such being in congruous with the Integrated Plan of Action on Poverty Eradication that was brought together by the Special Committee on Poverty Issues as they navigate through to achieve a reduction in dependency on welfare assistance by fortifying self-reliance with capacity building for employment and entrepreneurship (Ministry of Finance and Economy, 2020). The establishment of KBCDC is basically to give better opportunities for people and their socio-economic livelihood, and to help them get out of poverty lines, and reduce the dependency on welfare assistance. Therefore, the main objective of this chapter is to explore the initiatives made by KBCDC in its efforts to empower the community to improve their livelihood through entrepreneurial activities in Brunei Darussalam. For the rest of this chapter, the role of KBCDC will be explained in its efforts towards poverty alleviation through their community empowerment program. This is followed by exploring its motivations, initiatives, challenges and future directions. Finally, some conclusions are drawn.

2 Entrepreneurship in Community Development

The idea and practice of setting up a community development has evolved over the past decades into a familiar discipline of interest to both practitioners and academics (Kleiner et al., 2004). The decision to have Community Development by practitioners has a proclivity to arise consequently because of economic, social and physical enhancement in a community (Phillips & Pittman, 2008). There are myriads of ways to construct a community development in order to refine the living standards of rural communities to achieve a sustainable baseline for development (Hameed et al., 2016). It is also important to identify what the community is good at in terms of their skills and resources. For instance, *Program Satu Kampung Satu Produk* (literally One Village One Product) was introduced in Brunei where small and medium enterprises (SMEs) will exhibit their products in their respective villages on a particular day which includes food, handicrafts and traditional herbs. The activity also provided the entrepreneurs with the opportunity to market their products. In light of this initiative, artisan entrepreneurship should be explored.

In the literature, there has been an increased emphasis on local and handmade goods that are linked to the culture and tourism of a region (Ratten & Ferreira, 2017). According to Lounsbury and Glynn (2001), an artisan entrepreneur is a community who specialises on cultural forms of business ventures. This form of entrepreneurship is currently expanding. Most artisan entrepreneurs are in the clothing and food industries as they prefer to make their own products that are linked to their cultural heritage (Tregear, 2005). Therefore, its application in community development, in designing related programs to enhance their skills to produce and market their products, should be explored.

Many of these artisan entrepreneurs began as a hobby tied to their culture that not only incites interest but income as well. Most have turned this into a creative gamechanger by coalescing passion with marketing, resulting in a trend towards more cultural-based businesses that are clearly encouraging the tourism experience, including Brunei. However, the literature on artisan in the case of Brunei is still scarce and more coverage and studies on this should be done.

3 Methodology

Qualitative method such as in-depth interviews is employed in this study and the respondent was asked key questions and probing questions, as well as throw-away questions. The interview guide covered themes such as motivation, strategies and challenges of empowering the community through entrepreneurial activities. The interview was performed face to face in English and lasted approximately 30–45 min. The interview was recorded, transcribed and analysed to identify main ideas and themes linked to the objective of this study. As stressed by Miles and Huberman (1994), the transcribed data were coded and scaled down to meaningful themes. This was further highlighted by Gioia et al. (2013) where the analysis developed on transcripts from interviews and data obtained were categorised into themes. Thematic analysis is also used in this study to analyse and organise the data. Due to the occasional use of Brunei-Malay terms, a list of translated Brunei-Malay terms is provided in the Appendix.

4 The Kampong Bolkiah Community Development Centre

The Kampong Bolkiah Community Development Centre (herein 'KBCDC') is located in Kampong Bolkiah, Kampong Ayer, Bandar Seri Begawan, Brunei Darussalam. Translated, "Kampong Ayer" directly means "Water Village" and this centuries-old floating village consists of ten interconnected floating neighborhoods, housing close to 30,000 inhabitants through wooden bridges and walkways

(Jingwei, 2019). This scenic "Venice of the East" is the world's largest floating village and it is located along the banks of the Brunei River.

KBCDC was founded in August 2020 by the Big BWN Project under the initiative of Yayasan Sultan Haji Hassanal Bolkiah's (YSHHB) Ristaan Abadi. Big BWN Project emphasises on building platforms and projects for young entrepreneurs to build their brands whilst providing mass exposure for both up-and-starting businesses and established ones as well as providing a channel to connect with their customers. Under the YSHHB Foundation's Project, this KBCDC will act as a platform to hold community and entrepreneurship projects for Kampong Bolkiah A & Kampong Bolkiah B of Kampong Ayer. The main objective of KBCDC is to give better opportunities for people and their socio-economic livelihood, and to help them get out of poverty lines, and not relying on government benefits. Over the next few years, they will be working with a lot of local and regional partners; conducting a lot of different activities, events, workshops, and more—all to create opportunities and to empower the local Kampong community, and to preserve culture and heritage. Since its opening, KBCDC has held various events and activities as summarised in Table 1.

5 Findings and Discussions

This section provides the findings from the interview with the founder of KBCDC. From the interviews, the following themes were extracted.

1. Overwhelming response

   As most of the participants of KBCDC are women, Bolkiah Women's Club was consequently established. The participants in the club produced their handmade traditional and modern weaving and handicrafts as well as food and drinks. To get in touch with them, a WhatsApp hotline was created.

   > I created Bolkiah Women's Club where I've got more than 30 women joined on our WhatsApp group. Recently in April 2021, I successfully registered 22 women on business from Kampong Bolkiah

2. Building relationships within the community

   Community engagement is a strong value and fundamental practice. It is very important to build relationships with the local community as it will result in a profound impact on their base line especially in understanding their situations.

   > For me I have a very good relationship with the people here and I don't hate it and I enjoy working with the people here. Surprisingly they always make me feel like I belong. Very oddly, but when some of them saw me here, they would invite me to have a chat and light snacks with them. I have built such a great relationship to the point when they bumped into me they would greet me and even waved at me from their house when they saw me which is nice. Of course that was the first base for me because I mean I thought about it like I am an outsider you know and I don't want to come in and intrude. So the best way I think that's why I kind of succeeded compared with the others because I really involved

Table 1 KBCDC activities

Date	Events
9 June 2021	*Kuih* order for Muara Maritime Services
8 May 2021	'Sponsor a *Baju Raya*' drive—over 400 pcs (targeted 200 pieces) for under-privileged and low-income families at Kg. Bolkiah
28 April 2021	Distributed some donation items from @theimpianproject for underprivileged special needs families at Kg Bolkiah
Early April 2021	Joint leadership workshop with @sealentpb19 (led by Universiti Brunei Darussalam Discovery Year Community Outreach Programme, UBD DY COP, student)
9 April 2021	Marketing workshop with @agribiz.bn (led by UBD DY COP students)
2 April 2021	Basic Self-Defense workshop with @thepanthersguild
March 21	Hosted Zero Waste Activities with @zerowastebwn during school holiday
21 March 2021	*Gulingtangan* and traditional music workshop with @seri_laila_irama.bn and @kesturi.hijau (part of UBD DY COP students)
Early March 2021	Twenty successfully registered women owned small businesses (coincided with International Women's Day)
5 March 2021	*Ambuyat* session with Bolkiah Women's Club
19 February 2021	Hosted six sessions of @girls4girlsbrunei's Bolkiah circle
7 February 2021	Delivered second Bolkiah Donation Drive (collected during 3–5 February) (led by UBD DY COP students)
6 December 2020	Market on the River—Cultural Demo & Activities, *kuih* making, community vendors (in conjunction with Brunei December estival)
30 November 2020	Closing ceremony for Entrepreneurship Training Program; 15 local small businesses
	Hosted @bruneiansread's Travelling with Books for kids
29 November 2020	Bolkiah Mini Festival
22 November 2020	Let's Rewind—a forum on history and heritage of Brunei Darussalam
15 November 2020	Arts & Crafts Workshop—activities by Universiti Brunei Darussalam (UBD)'s Design & Creative Industries students
14 November 2020	Official launching of @balkish.official—(part of UBD students internship projects)
13 November 2020	Burgembira Night with @meatman.bn (part of UBD students internship projects)
10 November 2020	Engaged with Ta-Pow! for KBCDC's locally made food
8 November 2020	Hosted for Progresif's Buzzcut for Charity with @snips.ent and @barberku.bn
7 November 2020	*Kamayan* (a communal-style Filipino feast) feast with @arquilato_kusina
4 November 2020	Community Donation Drive—led by UBD DY student
1 November 2020	Breast Cancer Awareness with @hpcbrunei
	Delivered First Bolkiah Donation Drive (collected during 26–30 October)

(continued)

Table 1 (continued)

Date	Events
23 October 2020	Basic First Aid course with @pulseline.nursing
11 October 2020	Youth Business Talk co-organised with @ybt.brunei for 50 youths
9 October 2020	Fun fitness Zumba—in support of breast cancer awareness month
3 October 2020	Greek Food on Brunei River
20 September 2020	*Santai* Sunday—*Penyaram* making, bag weaving, local products and food
17 September 2020	Zero Waste Activity with 30 kids of Kg. Bolkiah during school term holiday—led by UBD DY students
5 September 2020	Seafood Saturday
30 August 2020	Hosted a *Mukun* party
22 August 2020	KBCDC held Open Day
10 August 2020	Organised an afternoon tea session; formed Kelab Wanita Bolkiah (Bolkiah Women's Club)
22 May 2020	Two-day "Sponsor a *Baju Raya*" drive
10 February 2020	Signed MOU with YSHHB to conduct community and entrepreneurship projects in Kg Bolkiah A & Kg Bolkiah B

Source: Author's own compilation from @bigbwnproject Instagram Account

> in community as much as I could and I think they appreciated that. I have been doing community development for so long I know how to like connect with everyone.

3. Designing programs based on the community needs

   Engaging community members in problem-solving solutions to issues that affect them is very important. In KBCDC, a survey with the residents is normally held monthly in order to suggest the type of programs and trainings to be offered by KBCDC in the respective month.

> I do survey with them and I try my best to have monthly hi-tea gathering. I usually give a survey form and ask them to fill in for them to help us. For example, tailoring workshop that we conducted today is based on their request. There will be a different workshop in the next 2 weeks. It could be entrepreneurship or weaving workshop. It depends on what they request.

Therefore, it is very important to involve community members in all activities—from identifying the relevant issues and making decisions about how to address them to evaluating and sharing the results with the community. Thus, the Entrepreneurship Training Programme reinforces and strengthens entrepreneurial competencies that involve diagnostics.

4. Outsourcing training

   There are different engaging programs on vocational training, workshops and activities on community capacity building in order to develop their skills and talents by implementing high value content with collaborations and partnerships from other organisations and stakeholders.

> After they suggest, I will reach out to people because I'm obviously not experienced in a lot of things like I can't teach sewing. Previously, I had invited some from insurance companies to talk about financial management and investment. A few weeks back we had first aid and fire safety courses.

Execution on this notion is conceivable as some companies are integrating corporate social responsibility programs (CSR programs) into their business and aligning themselves with pressing social movements.

> I engaged—because a lot of companies are doing CSR so I check to them so you know do you want to do—I provided with venue just come in and do it.

Trainers are not restricted to companies. Attachment students who have the skills and background are also welcome to give the training.

> I have a lot of plans to do and currently I am waiting for new interns to apply. I encourage more university students to join us and create the impact especially in giving the training or conducting workshops.

5. The use of social media and e-commerce platform 'Ta-Pow!'

   BigBWNProject Instagram has attracted potential customers and these customers will reach KBCDC through Instagram. To date, it has 11,500 followers. This is very important as the unpredictability of income has always been a challenge for entrepreneurs.

   > People contacted me through our Instagram. They (including companies) follow our activities on Instagram and found out about Bolkiah Women's Club. There was a time, a company place an order of 550 pieces of door gift. The ladies get to earn and I'm very happy to support. It was during Hari Raya that they've made BND1000 (AUD1000).

The role of social media is not overlooked. To reach mass market in Brunei, for food entrepreneurs, they are included into the e-commerce platform Ta-pow! to boost their sales and get more potential customers and motivated buyers.

> Most of them in food businesses I've put them on *Ta-pow*!. Some of them supply catering food to local companies. There is a local company which always uses our catering services. Some companies will order our local *kuih* (local snacks) as their corporate gift or door gift.

6. Organising activities to promote local culture

   Most of the activities at KBCDC are held every Sunday. For example, *Santai* Sunday event gives the public the opportunity to learn how to weave and make traditional snacks like *Penyaram*. Not only will it benefit the public where the skills will be passed down to the next generation, this will also help to showcase and market their products to the public.
7. The businesses are registered

   It is a requirement for businesses in Brunei to be registered. It is an achievement for KBCDC that most of the businesses are legally registered which entails that they are committed to run and sustain their businesses. As KBCDC provides different ranges of programs, for instance financial management; this will enable and assist them should they face issues or challenges throughout their business operation or decide on expanding.

8. Future planning

   There are a lot of opportunities that can be utilised from KCBDC – for instance, domestic tourism where the locals or foreigners in Brunei could experience Kampong Ayer life, from the cuisines to the traditional games. Especially during this pandemic where outbound traveling is restricted, this opportunity should be grabbed.

   > As they are good in cooking, I would like to do weekend Kampong Ayer experience. For example, enjoying traditional local cuisine like *ambuyat* and then you could play Kampong game like *congkak*. I have seen other districts have done similar things. I mean not—to be honest I don't see anybody do it properly except like sunset walk which I feel too mainstream. We did Kampong market last time and I think this is a good idea.

9. KBCDC Branding

   > I would also like to have a nice KBCDC branding and supply the products in Brunei's market. As a start, we could consider supplying the local foods to the local education institutions, for example their cafeteria. As we have Ta-Pow!, our delivery guys could deliver the food over on consignment basis.

10. The involvement of the other community

    KBCDC has its own limitations in terms of its capacity. Thus, it is very important for the public and other organisations to get involved through their CSR programs to support such initiatives.

    > I'm hoping for community to come and join us because at the end of the day like we want to encourage people to be involved, to try to contribute to them back, because in the fact that we are part of Kampong Ayer and it is part of Brunei's identity and sadly we start to lose that. We encourage people to come back to Kampong Ayer and do things and interact with community here, learn different skills from community itself and see how we can work together.

6 Challenges

From the interview, there are a few challenges identified as follows:

Firstly, in terms of mindset. The biggest challenge was to change the mindset of the locals from the community and to gain their confidence to do activities with KBCDC and join programs offered by KBCDC as many are still very reserved.

> There are some who are very hardworking and committed to joining all our programs and trainings, and some are only on an occasional basis. There has always been a problem of preferring and relying on government assistance.
>
> Sometimes there are situations where once you help you will open that door so people keep on asking so many things. They can actually put in the effort to get these things and do yourself.

Secondly, accessibility by water taxi (*Perahu Tambang*). Water taxi is a kind of speed boat made of wood to commute people from point A to point B, along the river in Brunei. Due to the discouraging number of people using water taxi, the availability of water taxi is rare and the price can be very expensive.

> I did a few events where people outside of Kampong Ayer came. I have to liaise with the water taxi driver and they tend to overcharge which I don't like.

People still can drive to KBCDC. However, it means that the visitor will miss the whole experience of riding the water taxi and enjoying the magnificent scenery along Brunei River to KBCDC.

7 Conclusion and Recommendations

This study has shown that NGOs do play a role in poverty alleviation through the provision of community empowerment program at community development centre in order to empower the village residents to improve their livelihood. Proposed programs should be designed based on community needs which enable them to enhance their entrepreneurial skills. Another important factor is to assist and match them with serious and motivated buyers in order for them to be able to sell their products. In today's digital age, the strong influence of social media should not be underestimated. It could be seen that potential buyers and companies that wish to help the village residents by contributing in the empowerment program found them through the social media. Therefore, all activities should continue to be posted on social media to reach the mass market and grab more opportunities. Despite the increasing number of the community, the number of men joining KBCDC is still lacking. More survey with the men should be done in order to devise strategies to attract them to participate and be more involved with KBCDC.

The village residents are the important artisan entrepreneurs of Brunei as they continue to produce local products such as hand-made traditional and modern weaving and handicraft as well as local or national foods. Their entrepreneurial activities and interests have been linked and tied to their culture in which they choose to use as a source of income. Thus, these initiatives and efforts should continue and eventually will contribute to the tourism industry should KBCDC wish to expand their portfolio to inbound or domestic tourism. The collaboration and support from other agencies are important to help assist and improve the programs and overcome challenges KBCDC is currently facing.

At this stage, the progress of the community empowerment programs at KBCDC shows to benefit the poor. Policy-makers and development thinkers must realise the fact that establishing the empowerment program at community level by NGOs play a pivotal role in realising the fruit of development equitably and effectively so that the village residents can be independent and less reliant on welfare assistance. The village residents, especially the men, should utilise the centre in further enhancing their skills and training for entrepreneurship, technical and vocational education and culture. Local terms are used in the name of activities.

As this study focuses on the founder of KBCDC, future study should engage the participants of KBCDC to find out the influential factors of their participation in KBCDC and what the issues and challenges are being faced while they are in the program. The findings are an important indicator to policy-makers and development practitioners.

Acknowledgement and disclaimer This is a non-funded research. The author would like to thank Noorhafizah Rashid, the founder of Big BWN Project for her willingness to be interviewed for the purpose of this research. The author would also like to thank his research assistant Mohamad Bazly Fakhri bin Bakri for transcribing the interview and collection of data. The views expressed in this publication are those of the author and do not necessarily represent the official stance of Universiti Islam Sultan Sharif Ali (UNISSA).

Appendix

List of Brunei-Malay Terms

Ambuyat	The sticky national dish of Brunei, made with sago palm tree starch that gets cooked into a substance similar to glue
Baju Raya	A traditional Malay costume for both men and women worn during the Eid festival
Congkak	A traditional mancala game of Malay
Gulingtangan	A traditional Bruneian musical instrument
Kuih	Snack
Mukun	A cultural performance
Penyaram	A traditional cake
Perahu Tambang	Water taxi
Santai	Relax
Ta-Pow	Take-away

References

Gioia, D. A., Corley, K. G., & Hamilton, A. L. (2013). Seeking qualitative rigor in inductive research: Notes on the Gioia methodology. *Organizational Research Methods, 16*(1), 15–31. https://doi.org/10.1177/1094428112452151

Hameed, G., Saboor, A., Khan, A. U., Ali, I., & Wazir, M. K. (2016). Impact of community development in poverty reduction: Reflections of Azad Jammu and Kashmir community development program. *Social Indicators Research, 130*(3), 1073–1086. https://doi.org/10.1007/s11205-016-1235-3

Jingwei, S. (2019) *Kampong Ayer: The world's largest water village in Brunei.* Retrieved July 10, 2021, from https://news.cgtn.com/news/3d3d414f7855544e34457a6333566d54/index.html

Kleiner, B., Raue, K., Silverstein, G., Bell, R., & Wells, J. (2004). *Evaluation of the Appalachian regional commission's community capacity building projects*, Appalachian Regional Commission.

Lounsbury, M., & Glynn, M. A. (2001). Cultural entrepreneurship stories, legitimacy and the acquisition of resources. *Strategic Management Journal, 22*, 545–564.

Miles, M. B., & Huberman, A. M. (1994). *An expanded sourcebook: Qualitative data analysis*. Sage Publication.

Ministry of Finance and Economy. (2020). *Voluntary national review (VNR) report at the 2020 high-level political forum for sustainable development.* Brunei Darussalam. Retrieved July 6, 2021, from https://sustainabledevelopment.un.org/content/documents/26410VNR_2020_Brunei_Report.pdf

Phillips, R., & Pittman, R. H. (2008). *An introduction to community development.* Taylor & Francis.

Ratten, V., & Ferreira, J. (2017). Future research direction for cultural entrepreneurship and regional innovation. *International Journal of Entrepreneurship and Innovation, 21*(3), 163–169.

Tregear, A. (2005). Lifestyle growth or community involvement? The balance of goals of artisan food producers. *Entrepreneurship and Regional Development, 17*(1), 1–15.

Wawasan Brunei. (n.d.) *Wawasan Brunei 2035.* Retrieved July 6, 2021, from http://wawasanbrunei.gov.bn/SitePages/Our%20Vision%20For%202035.aspx

Khairul Hidayatullah Basir is an Assistant Lecturer in Agribusiness, Faculty of Agriculture, Universiti Islam Sultan Sharif Ali (UNISSA), Brunei Darussalam.

How Does the Effect of Absorptive Capacity on Innovation Capacity Change According to Countries' Technology Manufacturing Value-Added Levels?

Nuri Görkem Yönkul and Hülya Ünlü

Abstract The aim of this study is to analyze the effects of countries' absorptive capacity on their innovation capacity according to their tendency to produce medium and high technology. In this context, the number of patent applications is used to represent innovation capacity. Ethics and corruption, foreign direct investment, tertiary education enrollment rate, technological literacy, university-industry research collaboration, and scientific and technical publications are used to represent social and technological absorption capacity. The variables used in the data set are taken from the Competitive Industrial Index, Global Innovation Index, and Global Competition Index. The study uses a special type of simultaneous equation models which is error correction two-stage least squares model for a panel data for years 2013–2017 and 60 countries. According to the analysis' result, absorptive capacity has a significant impact on innovation capacity for both country groups. In addition, while in countries with a high value added on medium- and high-technology production technological readiness has an impact on innovation capacity, ethics and corruption are more effective in the group of countries with a low rate of value added on medium- and high-technology manufacturing.

This chapter is based on the MSc dissertation entitled "The Effect of Absorptive Capacity in Innovation Capacity", by Nuri Görkem Yönkul, under supervisoion of Dr. Hülya ÜNLÜ in the Department of Economics at Cankiri Karatekin University/Turkey in 2021.

N. G. Yönkul
Cankiri Karatekin University, Çankırı, Turkey

H. Ünlü (✉)
Department of Economics, Cankiri Karatekin University, Çankırı, Turkey
e-mail: hunlu@karatekin.edu.tr

J. Leitão, V. Ratten (eds.), *Strategic Innovation*, Contributions to Management Science, https://doi.org/10.1007/978-3-030-87112-3_9

1 Introduction

Although the concept of technology is generally thought to have been formed recently, it has been used since the very existence of humanity. Our ancestors have made their lives easier by using different technologies at different times and have conveyed them to future generations. Due to the reason that technology is old as much as the history of mankind, it has had an economic impact, and it has been experienced with the first industrial revolution. Muscle power, which was used intensively before the industrial revolution, was replaced by steam machines, and production booms were experienced in production with the intensive use of technology. In particular, 200 years ago, the per capita GDP figures of the countries were on average, almost wealth was evenly distributed (Verspagen, 2004). The change of production methods with the first industrial revolution has led to an increase in this difference rather than the preservation of indifference between countries. With the emergence of this difference, economists have started to make different suggestions on growth models in the long run. Solow (1956) accepted technology as an external factor in his growth model and tried to explain this difference along with using workforce and capital as only inputs in the production function. With the external acceptance of technology, growth is explained by the ratio of capital per labor, which, at a certain point, concludes that the growth of countries will stop. In this model, Solow concluded that countries would reach the same point even in different periods, and as a result, convergence would occur worldwide.

Some countries are technological leaders and others are lagging behind. This technological gap constitutes a "big promise" for economic growth for the lagging behind (Gerschenkron, 1962). One of the biggest examples of Gerschenkron is the industrialization between Germany and England about 120 years ago. When England was industrialized at that time, technology was often labor-intensive and small-scale. While Germany was showing up on the scene, technology changed and became more capital-intensive and large-scale. Therefore, Germany needed several institutions and capabilities to overcome the challenges of industrialization, most importantly in the financial sector. What Gerschenkron wants to emphasize is the existence of institutions and capacities that countries need to achieve in order to exploit the advantage of technological backwardness (Arrow & Intriligator, 2000).

Like Gerschenkron, Abramovitz pointed out the differences in economic growth. Abramovitz (1986) put forward the terms "forging ahead," "catching up," and "falling behind" and tried to define the differences between countries with these terms. While constructing this hypothesis, Abramovitz observed the USA and other western countries that succeeded in introducing backlog and unexploited technology into the production process after World War II. While the USA used this unexploited technology including production methods and industrial and organizational methods at the time, other western countries did not. As a result, the USA came forward and became the "leader," while other western countries remained as "followers." In this hypothesis, Abramovitz emphasizes that followers have a chance to "catch up" the leading country and that this difference will determine the growth rates of followers.

As a result, Abramovitz said that there is a difference in the short term but that convergence will take place in the long term (Abramovitz, 1986).

Thereafter Schumpeter laid the foundations of the concept of innovation, using this concept has been popular among the scholars in order to explain economics performance both at the country level (Castellacci, 2011; Hasan & Tucci, 2010; Fagerberg & Srholec, 2008; Özbek and Atik, 2013; Ulku, 2004) and at the firm level (Escribano et al., 2009; Kostopoulos et al., 2011; Nieto & Quevedo, 2005). Despite the fact that positive effects of innovation activities on development and growth rates are already shown in many studies in the literature (Fagerberg et al., 2007; Fagerberg & Srholec, 2008; Ulku, 2004), social capability, technological capability, and absorptive capacity, which those are determinant concepts of innovation capacity, are still study subjects. In the light of current literature, social capability (Abramovitz, 1986; Gerschenkron, 1962), technological capability (Archibugi & Coco, 2004; Kim, 1980; Lall, 1992), and absorptive capacity (Cohen & Levinthal, 1989, 1990; Todorova & Durisin, 2007; Zahra & George, 2002) are studied in order to monitor the effects of those concepts on both innovation activities and economic growth and development.

Due to the reason that technology (or knowledge) has started to perform crucial function in economic indicators all nearby the world, the concept of absorptive capacity has become one of the most crucial terms in the last three decades (Cohen & Levinthal, 1989, 1990, Todorova & Durisin, 2007, Zahra & George, 2002). The term of absorptive capacity has been conceptualized by Cohen and Levinthal's (1989, 1990) works. Absorptive capacity is described as "a firm's ability to recognize new external knowledge, assimilate it, and link it to a commercial outcome" (Cohen & Levinthal, 1990, p. 128). On the other hand, Camisón and Forés (2010) defined absorptive capacity as a dynamic capacity that lets firms produce a new value and benefit and preserve the comparative advantage along with using external knowledge. In both definitions of absorptive capacity, firms' prior knowledge base plays a critical role. Consequently, many studies in the literature examine the influence of absorptive capacity on innovation capacity on a firm and industrial scale. Studies have measured how increasing the absorption capacity will affect the innovation and business performance of firms (Flor et al., 2018; Kostopoulos et al., 2011; Liao et al., 2007; Nieto & Quevedo, 2005; Xie et al., 2018). On the other side, there are a few studies that investigate the effect of the absorptive capacity on innovation capacity for cross-country analysis (Castellacci & Natera, 2013).

Due to the fact that many scholars had studied convergence among economies, the absorptive capacity concept gained importance in order to explain the catching-up process. As Verspagen (2004) mentioned before, the technological gap among countries has been increasing, and in order to close that gap, followers need to better understand absorptive capacity concepts and increase their knowledge base. Thus, we employ absorptive capacity components to examine their effect on the convergence process. Absorptive capacity is divided into two sets of indicators which are technological capability and social capability. Innovation capacity is represented by the number of patent applications. By examining the effects of different capabilities on innovation capacity for selected countries, it is aimed to make comparisons between these countries and contribute to the literature.

Abramovitz (1986) mentioned the "big promise" concept and "forging ahead," "catching up," and "falling behind" terms to illustrate technology difference between technology leaders and lagging behind countries. According to convergence theory, some countries are technological leaders and others are lagging behind. Therefore, countries' technology levels, ability to use knowledge to produce more complex goods, or capacity to gain benefit by using knowledge vary from one country to another. Consequently, the impact of the concepts such as social capability or technological capability could show different outcomes for technological leaders and others. Gani (2009) used the technological achievement index (TAI) prepared by United Nations Development Programme to categorize the country groups in order to get more accurate outcomes about countries' technology base to interpret, and countries are divided into three groups: technological leaders, potential leaders, and dynamic adopters. Thus, we use medium- and high-technology manufacturing value-added share in total manufacturing value added, which is prepared by competitive industrial performance in order to create country groups and to monitor the effects of capabilities on innovation capacity.

This study has the data on 60 countries for the period 2013–2017 to attain two objectives. First, the effects of the absorptive capacity on innovation capacity are examined for selected countries. Secondly, the study also monitors the effect of a country being whether have a high rate of intensity on medium- and high-technology production, on absorptive capacity.

In section two, studies that the technological and social capabilities are examined and the results of these studies are given. In section three, the data set, empirical strategy, and method that will be used in the study are explained. In section four, findings of the empirical analysis are given. Finally, in section five, the outcome of the study and interpretation is written.

2 Capabilities That Affect Innovation Capacity

Since the first industrial revolution, knowledge was gained a vital role to identify countries' economic performance. Like Kim (1980) and Lall (1992), scholars have been studying on the notion of technological capabilities for efficient usage of knowledge in terms of production. Kim (1980) suggested that by using technological capabilities, countries, especially lagged behind the technological leader, increase their growth rate and boost their developments. Firms in the late industrialization countries need existing technology in developed countries to acquire and diffuse them within the company. In order to adapt and diffuse the existing technology, these firms should develop their technological capabilities (Berger & Diez, 2006).

Economists generally think that R&D produces a single product: new knowledge. In their study, Cohen and Levinthal (1989) state that R&D does not only produce new knowledge but also provides an ability for firms to identify, assimilate, and exploit information from the environment and define it as the capacity to learn or "absorbing." As can be understood from the definition, Cohen and Levinthal's "absorptive capacity" and "technological capability" defined by Linsu Kim are similar (Fagerberg & Srholec, 2008). Absorptive capacity not only contributes firms with the understanding to imitate new product or process innovations but also gives those with the capability to take advantage of intermediate knowledge, such as simple key findings that lay the base for future applied R&D. In this context, the absorptive capacity is a different kind of learning from learning by doing. "Learning by doing" is an automated process in which it is more effective and experienced by doing what it does. In contrast, absorptive capacity provides a firm to acquire outward knowledge that allows it to do a little differently with it (Cohen & Levinthal, 1989). With the experience they have gained from previous R&D studies, firms develop the ability to understand future findings (Cohen & Levinthal, 1990; Griffith et al., 2003). Therefore, the absorptive capacity of a firm depends on the knowledge stock, which indicates that it will be higher among companies that have previously invested in information-producing activities such as R&D (Harris & Le, 2019). Moreover, absorptive capacity is a crucial indicator of whether companies use R&D or they do not, because firms with higher absorptive capacity will use knowledge from outside and inside, benefit from them, and thus receive a higher return on investment in R&D (Kostopoulos et al., 2011). Mancusi (2008) emphasizes that the difference in technology between a follower and the leader affects the absorptive capacity's efficiency. A country with a great amount of technological gap between the technological pioneer and the ability to absorb and benefit from external information is low but larger for the country has the potential to improve its ability (Mancusi, 2008).

The effect of innovation on the growth and competitiveness of countries makes it important to investigate the factors affecting innovation capacity. In the light of the definitions in the literature, these factors can be grouped as technological and social capabilities. Developed countries are relatively superior in both capabilities and innovation capacity compared to developing countries. The capabilities of developing countries affect their ability to absorb, imitate, and benefit from the knowledge that comes from developed countries through knowledge spillover channels. Therefore, it is critical to know what role these capabilities play in the development stage for policymakers in the policymaking process to make more effective policies to increase the level of innovation capacity.

2.1 Social Capabilities

When Abramovitz (1986) put forward the "catching-up" hypothesis, one of the necessary and most important conditions was that the follower country had the necessary "social capability." At that time, Abramovitz tried to find the necessary variables for social ability but could not reach certain indicators because the necessary data sets were not completed. In one of his studies, he states the duration of education as a rough indicator and also emphasizes that political, economic, industrial, and financial institutions of a country are suitable for measuring social capability (Abramovitz, 1986). Social capability is based on more than firm organizations and training. Openness to competition affects the social capabilities in other economic factors such as the establishment and activities of new firms, purchasing, selling of new goods and services, honesty, the sense of trust of society, and the degree of development of national and international capital markets (Abramovitz, 1986).

The difference in production levels between countries creates a strong convergence potential for those who come later (under the condition that they have enough social ability to absorb more advanced technology). Factors such as corporate capital and human capital components, parts of social ability, technological opportunity, and organization and education that respond to the needs of benefit from this opportunity are developing slowly. The speed of realization of the catching-up potential is attached to a number of other aspects that control information dissemination, resource mobility, and investment rate (Abramovitz, 1986).

Table 1 shows studies related to social capability indicators. When the literature is examined, several studies suggest social capability indicators, which are education (Castellacci & Natera, 2013; Fleisher et al., 2010; Ulku, 2004; Varsakelis, 2006), government institutions and corruption (Abramovitz, 1986; Gerschenkron, 1962; Lall, 1992; Mauro, 1995; Varsakelis, 2006), and openness (Coe & Helpman, 1995; Lesser, 2008; Ulku, 2004).

In the following part, the most commonly used social capabilities affecting innovation capacity are given.

2.1.1 Education

Abramovitz (1986) defined social capability as a necessary tool for countries, especially for lagging behind, to catch up the technological leaders. This capability creates an opportunity for those countries by interacting with the technological gap. Even though he mentioned some measurements to observe social capability effect such as education or government and industrial institutions, he could not give exact measurements. However, in the following years, scholars have been using education measurements as one of the social capabilities (Ali et al., 2018; Bassanini & Ernst, 2002; Fleisher et al., 2010; Lee et al., 2016; Ulku, 2004; Varsakelis, 2006).

Ulku (2004) in her study on 20 OECD member countries and 10 non-OECD member countries between 1981 and 1997, although this education variable expects the high t value and positive coefficient in all countries, this education variable was significant and positive only in low-income OECD member countries. Ali et al. (2018) examined the effects of human capital and social capabilities on economic growth in their study using data from 132 countries between 1996 and 2011. It includes the variable schooling year defined as human capital and its return. In the study, it was emphasized that some social ability dimensions interacted with human capital positively affecting economic growth. Fleisher et al. (2010) analyzed the

Table 1 Social capability indicators

	Social capabilities					
Author name (year)	Sample size	Sample years	Dependent variable	Social capabilities as an independent variable	Other independent variables	Method
Castellacci and Natera (2013)	87 countries	1980–2007	Number of patent applications	– Tertiary enrollment ratio – Secondary enrollment ratio – Corruption perception index	– Openness – Electricity consumption – Number of fixed and mobile phone subscribers – R&D expenditure – Number of articles	Panel data analysis
Ali et al. (2018)	132 countries	1996–2011	GDP per capita	– Years of schooling (under human capital index) (+) – Quality of legal institutions and property rights (+)	– Stock of physical capital – Employed labor force – Economic opportunities	Panel data analysis
Fleisher et al. (2010)	China	1988–2003	TFP growth	– Employees with secondary or higher education (+)	– İnfrastructure capital – Physical-capital vintage effects – FDI – Marketization – Regional technology spillovers	Common correlated effects pooled estimator (CCEP)
Varsakelis (2006)	29 countries	1995–2000	Number of patent applications	– Corruption perception index (+) – Political right index (−) – Civil liberties index (−) – Press freedom (−) – Number of students in higher education (−)	– The scores in mathematics – The scores in natural sciences – R&D expenditure	Panel data analysis
Coe and Helpman (1995)	22 countries	1970–1990	TFP growth	– Foreign R&D capital stock (+)	– Domestic R&D capital stock – Fraction of import to GDP	OLS analysis Pooled cointegrated analysis

(continued)

Table 1 (continued)

	Social capabilities					
Author name (year)	Sample size	Sample years	Dependent variable	Social capabilities as an independent variable	Other independent variables	Method
Hulya Ulku (2004)	30 countries	1981–1997	TFP	– Degree of trade liberalization (+)	– Patent applications – Secondary school enrollment – Expropriation risk	Generalized method of moments (GMM)

Source: Author's own

relationship between human capital and economic growth in their China-based studies covering various years. In the study, they emphasized that trained workers have a direct impact on productivity, and employees who have more than primary education have more marginal production than those who do not. In addition, scholars said that human capital (measured by employees with secondary or higher education) had a positive and significant influence on TFP growth (Fleisher et al., 2010).

Varsakelis (2006) carried out a study investigating education system and government' institutions' efficiency on innovation covering 29 countries for the 1995–2005 time period. As Abramovitz described the general structure of social capabilities such as education and institutions, Varsakelis (2006) found out the effectiveness of government institutions and quality of education system impact, positively innovation performance. Moreover, the author underlined policy link to those indicators also important for sustainable growth. Lee et al. (2016) used 40 countries for the 1999–2013 period for analyzing the main drivers of technological innovation. According to the study's results, higher education is statistically significant on innovation productivity, and education implements human capital and knowledge for innovation. The results that Lee et al. (2016) reached are in line with what Varsakelis (2006) found out.

Abramovitz (1986) stressed that social capabilities not only contain education and government institutions but also consist of other factors affecting the economy itself. Along similar lines with Abramovitz (1986), Sterlacchini (2008) argued that even if recent economic growth rates in EU countries are significantly positively affected by education acquisition, which is represented by adults with tertiary education, this effect does not provide a certain equal growth rate among those countries. Therefore, systematic linkages between the main player in the system, presence of socioeconomic supportive approach to the one new to market, and broader and systematic well-functioning policy framework are crucial (Sterlacchini, 2008).

2.1.2 Government Institutions and Corruption

In the theoretical studies in the literature (Abramovitz, 1986; Gerschenkron, 1962; Lall, 1992), it was emphasized that institutions are an important factor in terms of enabling high growth rates and sustainable development by using technology difference. Especially in the social capabilities defined by Abramovitz (1986), it is one of the tools that regulate social life and provide awareness of people against information and economic order. However, there was no emphasis on which indicators could be put use to measure the impacts of institutions on innovation and growth at that time.

Educational institutions, which are the first institutions that come to mind when it comes to social ability in literature, have been shown in studies that have an impact on innovation (e.g., Ali et al., 2018; Varsakelis, 2006). However, when it comes to the institutions that provide political and social order, there are not many studies in the literature. In his study examining the perception of corruption, bureaucratic activity, and growth, Mauro (1995) emphasized that poor countries tend to have corruption, have unfavorable bureaucracy, and be politically unwilling. It has been shown that the ineffectiveness of institutions for the long term and the existence of corrupt institutions in the past may be one of the reasons for low economic growth. He also said that governments have made an unbalanced and insufficient investment in education due to the positive correlation between corruption and growth. Varsakelis (2006) pointed out the effect of education and political institutions on novelties in his study covering 29 countries between 1995 and 2000. In this study, the index of human rights, freedom of the press, political rights, and the perception of corruption was created to define political institutions. Under the light of the study's results, it was emphasized that the variables used to define government institutions have a remarkable and positive impact on patenting, and as a result, they were significant on innovation and growth. Therefore, it is said that a more productive innovation system will be achieved with the development of government institutions (Ünlü & Karacaer Ulusoy, 2021; Varsakelis, 2006).

2.1.3 Openness

In the process of catching the leader, the technological difference and social capability determine the long-term potential of the follower country in production. Determining the potential capture rate of the country still depends on many factors. One of these factors is the state of international trade. A falling behind country by using trade channels with the leader receives technological knowledge from the technological leader, which means rapid growth and an increase in production for the backward country (Abramovitz, 1986).

> The importance of a national innovation system in mediating the import of technology from international sources underlines the interaction between national institutions and international trade and technology flows. Although some scientists oppose this characterization, There is no doubt that national innovation systems of most industrial economies are more open to international influences compared to the 1950s and 1960s (Mowery & Oxley, 1995, p. 87).

With the globalizing world, the borders of the countries have disappeared, and there has been an increase in international goods and services trade, foreign direct investment, sharing, and diffusion of knowledge. For this reason, the production level of a country is attached to not only on its R&D activities but also on the R&D activities executed by the trading partners (Coe & Helpman, 1995). For this reason, the production levels of the countries are determined not only with their knowledge and innovation activities but also with the trade channels they create. Coe and Helpman (1995) examined the effects of both local and foreign R&D on TFP among 22 countries between 1970 and 1990. Researchers pointed out a country's TFP is affected not only by the local R&D capital stock but also by foreign R&D capital stocks. As the country's tolerance to interstate trade increases, the influence of foreign R&D activities on TFP in that country becomes stronger. In his study on the Finnish telephone equipment industry, Lesser (2008) emphasized that Finnish trade and investment policies have a crucial and significant effect on the formation of the necessary framework for innovation, especially in Finland in 20 years. Regional trade liberalizations have enabled Finnish firms to purchase equipment and parts including technological knowledge from outside. In addition, globalization in Finland and globalization in the global telephone market have created a competitive environment in the Finnish telephone equipment industry and led firms to innovate more (Lesser, 2008). Ulku (2004) used the openness variable that shows the degree of trade liberalizations of countries in her study conducted among OECD and non-OECD member countries and found effective and powerful linkage on most observations. This trade liberalization means that it is an important factor in determining GDP levels per capita in countries. In the same study, she emphasized that trade liberalization is a significant and positive relationship with the GDP per labor, except in developed G-7 countries and non-OECD countries.

2.2 Technological Capabilities

Abramovitz (1986) and Gerschenkron (1962) analyzed the prewar and postwar periods of the USA and the western countries in terms of the capabilities of the lagged behind countries to close the gap between the followers. However, there are many examples of catching up not only on the western side but also in Asia. One of them is how South Korea, made by Linsu Kim, coming from one of the poorest countries to became one of the wealthy countries around the world in 30 years. Kim defines "technological capability" as the effective use of technological knowledge to assimilate, use, adapt, and modify existing technologies (Kim, 1980). It also permits the creation of new knowledge and the development of new products and methods (Fagerberg & Srholec, 2008). In his study of the South Korean electronics industry, Kim emphasizes that technological development consists of three basic steps: implementation, assimilation, and improvement. In all three stages, players in the sector need technological and production knowledge and provide it from different sources (e.g., international technology transfer in the implementation phase and local R&D studies in the development phase). However, South Korea's technological capability during the catching up to the leader, as well as the government's trade, technology, and science policies with incentives, is one of the keys to success (Kim, 1980).

The technological capabilities are defined by Kim (1980) as effectively using technological knowledge to assimilate, use, adapt, and change existing technologies. Therefore, countries need infrastructure to acquire technological knowledge and use it effectively, to catch high growth rates, and to close the technology gap with the leader. Firms in the late industrialization countries need existing technology in developed countries to acquire and diffuse them within the company. In order to adapt and diffuse the existing technology, these firms should develop their technological capabilities (Berger & Diez, 2006).

Lall (1992) has made significant contributions to the literature in terms of technological capability with his work both at firm level and at country level. The interplay of "capabilities" (physical investment, human capital, and technological effort), "incentives" (to ensure the smooth functioning of capabilities and to eliminate market failures), and "institutions" (industrial, educational, and technological institutions) determine national technology capability. The improvement of technological capabilities is realized by the interaction of these three actors in a complex structure. In addition, government policies play an effective role in all three stages (Lall, 1992). Archibugi and Coco (2004) tried to measure the "technological capacity" with the ArCo technology index they created and determine the indicators of this capacity. The ArCo technology index consists of three dimensions: technology creation (patents and scientific articles), technological infrastructure (internet penetration, telephone penetration, and electricity consumption), and human skills development (graduate and engineering enrollment, average education time, literacy rate).

It is an inevitable fact that technological change causes economic differences between countries. Certainly, no economist can therefore deny the role of knowledge in economic growth. For this reason, Arrow (1971) defined the acquisition of knowledge, in his "learning by doing" model, as learning and said that it is necessary to experience to learn. Learning takes place only during problem-solving and occurs only during activity. Solving the same problem over and over again will be subject to decreasing returns in learning, and to achieve increased performance, stimulating situations need to evolve and change (Arrow, 1971).

In Table 2, some empirical analyses related to technological capability indicators are shown.

2.2.1 R&D Expenditure

After the conceptualization of technological capability by Kim (1980) and Lall (1992), the notion of technological capability has gained importance to use knowledge effectively in the production process. In order to understand which inputs define this notion, many measurements that are using to represent technological capability have been proposed, and one of these most common measurements is R&D expenditure (Coombs and Bierly, 2006; Kostopoulos et al., 2011; Lall, 1992; Schoenecker & Swanson, 2002; Ulku, 2004; Zachariadis, 2003).

Cohen and Levinthal (1990) emphasized that R&D activities not only create new knowledge but also give firms the skill to absorb the knowledge that is available outside, assimilate it, and use it. For this reason, knowledge production activities such as R&D create a capability in firms (or countries) to recognize external knowledge and gain economic benefits by using it. While Schoenecker and Swanson (2002) treated R&D expenditures as an input assessment of technological capabilities, on the other hand, Coombs and Bierly (2006) emphasized that R&D expenditure is on the good generally used measurement of technological capabilities.

In the light of current literature, R&D expenditures are used in several studies to investigate the effect of technological capability on innovation capacity.

Table 2 Technological capability indicators

	Technological capabilities					
Author name (year)	Sample size	Sample years	Dependent variable	Technological capabilities as an independent variable	Other independent variables	Method
Kostopoulos et al. (2011)	461 firms	2000–2002	–	– Firms' total R&D expenditure (+) – Number of employees with a bachelor degrees (+) – Performed R&D activities (dummy) (+) – Personnel training (dummy) (+)	– Network knowledge inflows (four-point scale) – Firms' annual new or improved products/services sales – Return of sales – Return of assets	Path analysis
Simon Teitel (1994)	68 countries	1976–1985	Number of patents granted	– R&D expenditures (+) – Number of scientists and engineers available in a country (+)	– Income per capita – Population	OLS regression analysis
Tüylüoğlu and Saraç (2012)	44 countries	1998–2007	Number of patent applications	– R&D expenditure to GDP (+) – Product/services import to GDP (+) – FDI (–)	– GDP per capita – Royalty and license payments	Dynamic ordinary squares
Furman et al. (2002)	17 countries	1973–1995	Number of patents granted	– Number of scientists and engineers (+) – Openness to trade (+) – R&D expenditures (+)	– Stringency of antitrust policy – Higher education investment – Private R&D funding – Specialization – University R&D performance – Strength of venture capital – GDP per capita	Panel data analysis
Furman and Hayes (2004)	29 countries	1978–1999	Number of patents granted	– Personnel employed in R&D (+) – R&D expenditure (+) – Openness to trade (+)	– Strength of protection for intellectual property – Share of GDP spent on secondary and tertiary education – Percentage of R&D founded by private sector	Panel data analysis

(continued)

Table 2 (continued)

	Technological capabilities					
Author name (year)	Sample size	Sample years	Dependent variable	Technological capabilities as an independent variable	Other independent variables	Method
					– Percentage of R&D performed by university – GDP per capita	
Doyle and O'Connor (2013)	23 countries	1993–2005	Number of patents granted	– Personnel employed in R&D (insignificant) – R&D expenditure (+) –Freedom to trade (+)	– Secondary and tertiary education investment – Percentage of R&D funded by private industry – Specialization – Percentage of R&D performed by universities – Legal structure and security of property rights	Panel data analysis
Escribano et al. (2009)	2265 firms	2000–2002	New or improved product sales Innovation (dummy)	– R&D expenditure (+) – R&D fully staffed department (dummy) (+) – Training for R&D personnel (dummy) (+) – Ratio of R&D employees to total employees (+)	– Knowledge inflow sources (four-point scale) – Innovation process (PCA method) – Sector appropriability – Strategic protection	OLS regression analysis

Mayor et al. (2012)	30 countries	2010–2011	–	– Number of active fixed telephone lines – Number of mobile cellular subscribers – Number of estimated Internet users	– Number of scientists and engineers – R&D spending – ICT-related laws – University-industry collaboration in R&D – Firm-level technology absorption – FDI and technology transfer – Capacity for innovation – IP protection – Government procurement of advanced technology goods – Quality of scientific research investment institutions	Cluster analysis

Source: Author's own

Kostopoulos et al. (2011) used R&D expenditures as an indicator of absorptive capacity in the study covering 461 production and service firms between 2000 and 2002. The study emphasizes that the flow of knowledge from outside improves innovation performance through absorptive capacity. This points to the following: If firms understand the worth of outward knowledge, internalize them, and benefit them, they gain novelty benefits from this new outward knowledge. The study also shows that absorptive capacity helps firms improve innovation performance, as well as providing financial benefits with long-term innovation. In other words, absorptive capacity directly improves financial performance by indirectly improving innovation performance. Especially when firms' absorptive capacity and countries' absorptive capacities are linked, policies that increase firms' absorption capacity will help the country to be more open to benefit from the international flow of knowledge. Ulku (2004) stated that a powerfully effective linkage between innovation and growth is in both OECD member countries and non-OECD countries, but OECD member countries with large markets have improved their R&D capabilities by investing in R&D.

In addition to these, Garcia et al. (2012) attached importance to the direct linkage between R&D investments and learning from exporting. By using R&D intensity, scholars pointed out that any firm investing in R&D more than the average R&D investment level of that firm's sector is more likely to gain benefit in terms of productivity after making sales abroad. Moreover, showing this tendency to benefit more from investing in R&D matches up with the importance of absorptive capacity, which is conceptualized by Cohen and Levinthal (1990). Even if a firm gets advanced knowledge through knowledge spillover channels, that firm still needs technological capabilities to understand, use, and benefit from that knowledge (Garcia et al., 2012). Unlike Garcia et al. (2012) demonstrating the impact of R&D expenditures on getting benefits from knowledge spillovers, Anand and Kogut (1997) found out unfavorable results. According to the study's results, there is not a clear indication that higher R&D expenditure sectors in the USA are getting new FDI when compared to the other nations (Anand & Kogut, 1997). Wakelin (2001) analyzed the linkage between R&D investments and growth in productivity in her study covering 170 firms in the United Kingdom. The result shows that R&D expenditure has effective influence on productivity growth in the sample group. However, the return of a firms' R&D investments is affected by the sector that they are in. If a firm is a sector with innovation users, that firm will have a greater amount of return in terms of R&D expenditure. Besides, as Anand and Kogut (1997) pointed out there is not a linkage between R&D expenditure and knowledge spillovers, Wakelin (2001) could not notice enough sign to reinforce the linkage between R&D expenditure and benefiting from knowledge spillovers.

2.2.2 Number of Scientists and Engineers in R&D

The ratio of the number of scientists and engineers employed in R&D departments to the total population for the measurement of technological capabilities is another common measurement. Although the quality of scientists and engineers in R&D

departments varies according to countries and their economic contribution varies according to R&D activity types, the indicator is used in measurement when communal technology capacity measurement is concerned (Lall, 1992).

Rothwell and Dodgson (1991) stated that as a result of the survey conducted with 170 firms, the lack of appropriate qualified scientists and engineers can prevent small firms from their ability to absorb the technological know-how and further developing, even if they manage to obtain them from external sources. Amsden and Mourshed (1997) found out that the number of scientists and engineers per million population is highly positive correlated with both patents and publications, which are possible indicators for innovation capacity. Shefer and Frenkel (2005) suggested that the ratio of employees hired in R&D operations with the rate of R&D expenditure is in the negative and significant relationship with the size of the firm in the group of the firm in the high-tech sector.

In their study, Escribano et al. (2009) monitored the impact of the absorptive capacity and the effect of absorptive capacity on innovation performance with the number of scientists and engineers employed in R&D activities. As a result, it was uncovered that the number of R&D operations by employed scientists and engineers are crucially effective on innovation productivity. Besides, the researchers emphasized that firms with higher absorptive capacity are better equipped to detect the existence of outward knowledge spillovers and to use them effectively. However, Paolillo and Brown (1978) mentioned that an abundant amount of scientists and engineers could be seen as an obstacle to innovation. This issue might arise the question that the quality of scientists and engineers employed in R&D is crucial rather than quantity of it when it comes to innovation performance. Furthermore, innovation productivity is not just influenced by the number of scientists and engineers but also the working environment of employees, and the structure of R&D organization impacts the innovation performance (Paolillo & Brown, 1978).

2.2.3 Technological Infrastructure

Technologically lagging behind countries are inadequate in producing advanced technology. These countries have the chance to produce advanced technology in the future and close the technology gap with the technological leader by assimilating existing ones before producing new technologies. The technological infrastructure must be developed in order to obtain the knowledge that is outside and to produce new technology using it. Therefore, public investments in technology infrastructure play a vital role in successful economic development (Freeman, 2004). Nowadays, some knowledge is in human capital as a "tacit." On the other hand, "codified" knowledge is embedded in equipment, machinery, and infrastructure. Archibugi and Coco (2004), on the technology index they created, saw the Internet, telephone, and electricity indicators that respond to the industrial revolutions of the twentieth century as technological infrastructure. Although not directly linked to industrial capabilities, the production of knowledge depends on their existence and diffusion (Archibugi & Coco, 2004).

Mayor et al. (2012), in the study involving 30 African countries, investigated how technological infrastructure causes different levels of innovation in countries. The researchers, who define the technological infrastructure as an "available base," used the variables fixed telephone line, mobile telephone subscriptions, and Internet users. As a result of the clusters created in the study, developed and high-infrastructure countries are at the forefront of innovation performance and economic development. On the other hand, low absorptive capacity has emerged in countries with a weak infrastructure. Castellacci and Natera (2013) analyzed the factors affecting the national innovation system in their studies covering 87 countries in 1980–2007. As the technological infrastructure indicator, a kilowatt of electricity consumed, the number of fixed and mobile phone subscribers are used in the ArCo technology index. As a result of the study, it has shown that innovation capacity and absorptive capacity have a long-term structural relationship, and technological product has a bilateral dynamic link with infrastructures. At the same time, infrastructures develop and increase scientific and innovative outputs in one way.

2.2.4 Foreign Direct Investment

In the light of current literature, foreign direct investment may be seen as one of the crucial factors affecting technological capability. Foreign direct investment (FDI) not only helps the host country in terms of finance, employment, or production but also creates a knowledge spillover channel that could arise the technological capability of the host country. Thus, in the last two decades, investigation on the impacts of FDI on innovation capacity has been dramatically increased. When literature is inspected, it is clearly noticed that FDI is a channel for knowledge spillover and boost tool for technological capacity (Costa & de Queiroz, 2002; Di Vita, 2013; Fu, 2008; Jin et al., 2019; Kogut & Chang, 1991; Salim et al., 2017; Shi, 2001).

Di Vita (2013) monitors how the protection of intellectual property rights (IPR) affects innovation. Scholar argued that by creating strong protection of IPR, two possible technology transfer channels can be observed, and those are FDI and imitation of technology, which occurs from the northern hemisphere to the southern hemisphere. By using FDI variable in his study, the scholar pointed out that FDI is the key carrier to transfer technology from technology leader countries to lagging behind countries. In addition to this, the protection of IPR could promote the transfer of technology.

As Di Vita (2013) implied FDI is a key channel to transfer technology, Fu (2008) referred that FDI is a driven force for the development of innovation capacity, especially for the host state. Moreover, the effects of FDI on the host country highly depend on the host state's absorptive capacity and technological capabilities. For instance, in the coastal region of China, which provides well-educated R&D staff and trained employees, a well-functioning set of institutions such as top universities and R&D institutions, and a well-organized industrial area that focuses more on asset-seeking, FDI has a more effective influence on innovation capacity. Notwithstanding, in the inland provinces of China, which have not that many capabilities listed above, it is hard to see the impact of foreign direct investment on both innovation capacity and economic growth (Fu, 2008).

Even if technology transfers through FDI give chance to domestic firms to upgrade their technology base and create a more competitive market in the host country, it still has a harmful threat for domestic firms, especially lagging behind firms. In the host country, technology leading firms might be under competitive pressure due to the reason of FDI. Accordingly, those firms try to invest more in innovation activities that have uncertainty themselves and might put those firms in a riskier situation (Jin et al., 2019).

3 Data and Method

3.1 Data Set and Variables

As we mentioned before, the aim of the study is proposing a relationship between absorptive capacity and innovation capacity. For this reason, we used special data from the Global Innovation Index (GII), global competitiveness index (GCI), and competitive industrial performance (CIP). The main reason for this is that although variables explaining both innovation capacity and absorptive capacity are available in developed countries, these data are not available in a single source in developing countries (Dechezleprétre et al., 2013; Di Vita, 2013). In addition to the data diversity problem, there are also problems related to country constraints and time zones. The variables used in the study and the sources to be obtained are presented in Table 1.

The dependent variable is the patent application per million, which is the indication of the innovation capacity of a state (Castellacci, 2011; Fagerberg et al., 2007; Fagerberg & Srholec, 2008; Hasan & Tucci, 2010; Ulku, 2004). The theoretical models explaining the effects of social capabilities appear in the literature with three possible channels for a stronger innovation capacity: (a) education, (b) government institutions and corruption, and (c) openness. In consideration of this fact, we add ethics and corruption and tertiary education enrollment to represent social capability. Due to the lack of data for chosen countries, we are not able to test the effect of openness.

Similarly, with social capabilities, the channels of technological capabilities are given in the literature for a strong innovation capacity: (a) foreign direct investment, (b) technological readiness, and (c) scientific and technical publications. The effect of international transfers of technology is given by using foreign direct investment (Di Vita, 2013).

Another explanatory variable we use is university-industry collaboration in research, which often creates an alternative input for innovation (Mayor et al., 2012; Philbin, 2008). Guimón (2013) argued that collaboration between industry and research institutions such as universities is a crucial factor for training and education improvement; for the creation, adoption, and acquirement of knowledge, which are the process of knowledge absorption; and also for enhancement of entrepreneurship. Furthermore, Marotta et al. (2007) suggested that enhancing the interaction of industry and research institutions such as universities is the key element of increasing the innovation environment. Moreover, scholars also mentioned that innovation activities are affected not only by these interactions between research institutions and industries but also by technology infrastructure, linkages between the public-private sector, and also government's science, technology, and innovation policies. This variable is also a link between basic research and applied research and represents both social and technological capabilities.

Table 3 presents the variable list that are employed in the study. The sources, shortenings, and descriptions are also given. We have a patent application variable that will be used as the dependent variable (Castellacci, 2011; Fagerberg et al., 2007; Fagerberg & Srholec, 2008; Hasan & Tucci, 2010; Ulku, 2004). In the analysis, we took the logarithmic form of patent application. In order to explain what affects innovation capacity, we obtain social and technological capabilities. We employ ethics and corruption (Ali et al., 2018; Castellacci & Natera, 2013; Varsakelis, 2006) and tertiary education enrollment (Castellacci & Natera, 2013; Doyle & O'Connor, 2013; Fleisher et al., 2010; Ulku, 2004) as social capabilities. To observe the impacts of technological capabilities on innovation capacity, we use technological readiness (Alfaki & Ahmed, 2013; Archibugi et al., 2009; Moldabekova et al., 2021; Razavi et al., 2011), scientific and technical publications (Amsden & Mourshed, 1997; Archibugi et al., 2009; Fagerberg et al., 2007), and foreign direct investment (Costa & de Queiroz, 2002; Jin et al., 2019; Salim et al., 2017). When universities are the main origin of knowledge creation and industries are the place where to put a theoretical framework into practice, we also add university-industry research collaboration variable, which represents both social and technological capabilities (Mayor et al., 2012; Tseng et al., 2020).

The impact of the social and technological capabilities on innovation capacity may differentiate according to the technological status of a country. This may cause a heterogeneity issue, and it is preferred to use two different samples in the study. In order to observe this, the sample was divided according to medium- and high-technology value-added status of countries.

The medium- and high-technology (MHT) manufacturing value-added share in total manufacturing value added is obtained from United Nations' (UN) competitive industrial performance (CIP) report. The first 30 countries are the one whom industry sector is more focused on high-tech manufacturing, and the second 30 countries are the one who has less concentration. Table 4 shows a high share of medium- and high-tech manufacturing value-added countries and less share of medium- and high-tech manufacturing value-added countries, respectively.

Our data contains 30 countries that has more intensity to produce medium- and high-technology value added (see Table 4) and 30 countries that has the least intention to produce medium- and high-technology value added (cf. Table 5), a total of 60 countries covering 5 (2013–2017) years. Table 6 presents the descriptive statistic of two country groups, both for countries with high intensity and the least

Table 3 Description and source of variables

	Variable name	Description	Shortening	Source of the data
Dependent variable	Patent applications	Log of patent applications per million people	LPCT	Global competitiveness index
Independent variables	Ethics and corruption	It is main index including "diversion of public funds," "public trust in politicians," and "irregular payments and bribes." [Value: From 1 (worst) to 7 (best)]	EAC	Global competitiveness index
	Foreign direct investment	Net inflows of investments to acquire a lasting management interest in an enterprise operating in an economy other than that of the investors (% of GDP).	FDII	Global Innovation Index
	Tertiary education enrollment	Gross tertiary education enrollment rate	TEEI	Global competitiveness index
	Technological readiness	Technological readiness [value: from 1 (worst) to 7 (best)]	THP	Global competitiveness index
	University-industry collaboration in research	In your country, to what extent do business and universities collaborate on research and development (R&D)? (Score, 100 = max strength, 0 = weakest)	UIRC	Global Innovation Index
Endogenous variable	Scientific and technical publications	The number of scientific and engineering articles published in the following fields: physics, biology, chemistry, mathematics, clinical medicine, biomedical, research, engineering and technology, and earth and space science (score, 100 = max strength, 0 = weakest)	STP	Global Innovation Index
Instrumental variables	Availability of scientists and engineers	In your country, to what extent are scientists and engineers available? (1 = not available at all; 7 = widely available)	ASE	Global competitiveness index
	Quality of scientific research institutions	In your country, how do you assess the quality of scientific research institutions? (1 = extremely poor, among the worst in the world; 7 = extremely good, among the best in the world)	QSRI	Global competitiveness index

Source: Author's own

Table 4 Countries having more share of medium- and high-technology manufacturing value added in terms of total manufacturing value added

Austria	Belgium	China
Czech Republic	Denmark	Finland
France	Germany	Hungary
India	Ireland	Israel
Italy	Japan	Korea, Republic
Malaysia	Mexico	Netherlands
Norway	Philippines	Qatar
Romania	Singapore	Slovenia
Spain	Sweden	Switzerland
Thailand	United Kingdom	USA

Table 5 Countries having less share of medium- and high-technology manufacturing value added in terms of total manufacturing value added

Argentina	Australia	Bahrain
Brazil	Bulgaria	Canada
Croatia	Cyprus	Estonia
Greece	Indonesia	Jordan
Kuwait	Latvia	Lithuania
Malta	Morocco	Nigeria
Pakistan	Poland	Portugal
Russian Federation	Saudi Arabia	Serbia
South Africa	Tunisia	Turkey
Ukraine	United Arab Emirates	Vietnam

intensity to produce MHT, and correlation table for variables, respectively. Our data set constitutes strongly balanced panel data.

The correlation of all variables with each other for two country groups may be seen in Tables 7 and 8, countries having the high intensity to produce MHT and countries having less intensity to produce MHT, respectively. Unlike Xie et al. (2019) finding out the low correlation between innovation indicator and corruption, our corruption variable is considerably highly correlated with patent applications (lpct) in countries having high intensity to produce MHT with respect to other country group.

As well as lpct is highly correlated with ethics and corruption (eac), lpct is also highly correlated with technological readiness (thp) and quality of scientific research institutions (qsri). Another conspicuous outcome is that qsri is positively and highly correlated with technological readiness and university-industry research collaboration (uirc) variables for both two country groups. As Razavi et al. (2011) pointed out that FDI has the least correlation with quality of scientific and research institutions, we reached similar results for both country groups as well (Tables 7 and 8).

Table 6 Summary statistic of variables

Countries having high intensity to produce medium- and high-technology value added					
	Count	Mean	SD	Min	Max
LPCT	150	3.822845	1.919681	−1.297549	5.815278
EAC	150	4.525577	1.22885	2.356359	6.428324
FDII	150	34.914	21.15469	0	100
TEEI	150	62.45033	21.4979	11.6063	103.1111
THP	150	5.319762	0.9130853	2.732743	6.413285
UIRC	150	62.678	12.58745	34.7	82.8
STP	150	46.67573	26.6977	0.76	100
ASE	150	4.739394	0.5581106	3.602801	6.297107
QSRI	150	5.203112	0.767995	3.396321	6.550109
NxT	30 × 5				
Countries having less intensity to produce medium- and high-technology value added					
	Count	mean	SD	Min	Max
LPCT	150	1.108081	2.060823	−4.911119	4.500455
EAC	150	3.69333	0.9838411	2.024296	6.30795
FDII	150	34.502	11.83498	13.4	84
TEEI	150	51.91221	25.33192	8.32041	116.6216
THP	150	4.492129	0.8487044	2.734656	5.912302
UIRC	150	45.45333	10.43805	25.3	68.3
STP	150	31.76933	24.66067	0	99.4
ASE	150	4.25953	0.5590228	3.254099	5.44392
QSRI	150	4.074779	0.7200271	2.522501	5.815563
NxT	30 × 5				

Table 7 Correlation table for countries having a high intensity to produce MHT

Variable	(1)	(2)	(3)	(4)	(5)	(6)	(7)	(8)	(9)
(1) LPCT	1.000								
(2) EAC	0.635*	1.000							
(3) FDİİ	0.066*	0.168*	1.000						
(4) TEEİ	0.717*	0.231*	0.123*	1.000					
(5) THP	0.876*	0.699*	0.144*	0.675*	1.000				
(6) UİRC	0.666*	0.832*	0.119*	0.273*	0.680*	1.000			
(7) STP	0.719*	0.412*	−0.013	0.646*	0.667*	0.377*	1.000		
(8) ASE	0.514*	0.678*	0.034	0.187*	0.489*	0.740*	0.123*	1.000	
(9) QSRİ	0.813*	0.776*	0.104*	0.385*	0.812*	0.886*	0.548*	0.657*	1.000

*Significance level 5%

3.2 Empirical Strategy

The empirical analysis to be carried out in this study examines the social and technological capabilities affecting innovation capacity at the country level between

Table 8 Correlation table for countries having less intensity to produce MHT

Variable	(1)	(2)	(3)	(4)	(5)	(6)	(7)	(8)	(9)
(1) LPCT	1.000								
(2) EAC	0.440*	1.000							
(3) FDIİ	0.177*	0.074*	1.000						
(4) TEEİ	0.658*	0.012	0.088*	1.000					
(5) THP	0.826*	0.618*	0.247*	0.433*	1.000				
(6) UİRC	0.472*	0.564*	0.025	0.088*	0.514*	1.000			
(7) STP	0.587*	0.139*	0.225*	0.504*	0.446*	0.211*	1.000		
(8) ASE	0.213*	0.593*	−0.038	0.217*	0.269*	0.327*	0.222*	1.000	
(9) QSRİ	0.666*	0.536*	0.123*	0.389*	0.676*	0.844*	0.494*	0.366*	1.000

*Significance level 5%

2013 and 2017. The study discusses the effects of these factors separately for whether a country is focusing more on medium- and high-technology production value added or less. Since the data to be used includes both the time series extent and the cross-section extent, panel data methods are applied in the analyses.

3.2.1 Econometric Model

Besides using panel data methods in this study, it is also believed that a specific type of simultaneous equation models, which is two-stage least squares method (2SLS), should be used. Wooldridge (2010) imply that in any equation, endogeneity might come from any kind of source. It can help to think the error term has an omitted variable. The 2SLS method is derived from the reduced form of simultaneous equation model. In this type of model, rather than using an endogenous variable, instrumental variable is used.

Whereas it is known that innovation production has been affected by the production of academia (Archibugi & Coco, 2004; Castellacci, 2011; Castellacci & Natera, 2013; Fagerberg et al., 2007; Fagerberg & Srholec, 2008), according to Beaudry and Allaoui (2012), there is a possible endogeneity problem when innovation production tried to be explained by the number of scientific publications. Beaudry and Allaoui (2012) pointed out that they tried to find variables to explain the difference in the number of publications. However, they stated that they could not find the variable to explain the difference due to the lack of data. Unlike them, the availability of scientists and engineers and the quality of scientific research institutions are used in this study in order to explain how the production of the academy has changed.

Our econometric model based on panel data could be presented as follows:

$$\boldsymbol{lpct}_{i,t} = \boldsymbol{\alpha} + \boldsymbol{\beta}'[\boldsymbol{X}]_{i,t} + \boldsymbol{stp}_{i,t} + \boldsymbol{e}_{i,t} \quad (1)$$

Firstly, we start to run Pooled Least Squares (POLS) method for our regression. Due to the reason that POLS method assumes there are not country-specific effects, we also bring Fixed Effects (FE) and Random Effects (RE) to the estimations in order to use. In order to decide which model between FE and RE we should use in our estimations, we use the Hausman specification test (Wooldridge, 2010). Hausman specification test hypothesis is as follows:

$$\mathrm{H_0}: \text{No correlation exists between regressors and unobserved country} \\ -\text{specific effects.}$$

$$\mathrm{H_1}: \text{Correlation exists between regressors and unobserved country} \\ -\text{specific effects.}$$

Before solving the possible endogeneity problem, we need to consider heteroscedasticity, serial correlation, and cross-sectional dependence problems. Torres-Reyna (2007) suggests that serial correlation tests should be applied to a macro panel with a long time period. It is not a problem to solve for like our macro panel data with a short term. The same applies to the cross-sectional dependence as well. Testing cross-section dependence needs a long time period. In our data set ($N > T$), we have data for 5 years and 60 countries which are divided into two groups including 30 countries in it. However, we need to monitor heteroscedasticity in our model.

While examining the endogeneity problem, in order to solve heteroscedasticity, we use a robust Hausman test based on bootstrap. Kaiser (2014) implies that the traditional Hausman test needs one estimator to be fully effective under the null hypothesis. This is frequently broken in microeconomics data. The conventional Hausman test cannot be used in any existence of serial correlation or heteroscedasticity. Godfrey and Tremayne (2005) suggest that using the robust Hausman test gives reliable outcomes compared to the conventional Hausman test under the presence of heteroscedasticity. As we mentioned above, we are aware of possible endogeneity problem.

In order to solve the endogeneity problem, using the method of instrumental variables gives a common solution to the problem of endogeneity. Wooldridge (2010) states that under its assumptions, two-stage least squares (2SLS) estimator is the most coherent estimator for instrumental variables. To use our instrumental variables, we need to employ the two-stage least squares (2SLS) method for RE, FE, and Baltagi's Error Component (EC) estimators (Baltagi & Liu, 2009).

As we mentioned above, the goal of the study consists in determining whether a country with more intensity to produce MHT and better technological infrastructure generates more patent in terms of innovation activity. On the score of our dependent variables is patent application counts, we take the logarithmic form of patent applications.

$$\boldsymbol{lpct}_{i,t} = \boldsymbol{\alpha} + \boldsymbol{\beta}'[\boldsymbol{X}]_{i,t} + \boldsymbol{stp}_{i,t} + \boldsymbol{\mu}_{i,t} \tag{2}$$

$$stp_{i,t} = \Upsilon + \theta'[Z]_{i,t} + \mu_{i,t} \tag{3}$$

$$i = 1, 2, \ldots .N t = 1, 2, \ldots .T$$

In Eq. (2), patent applications are admitted as a dependent variable. X refers to our explanatory variables including ethics and corruption, foreign direct investment, tertiary education enrollment, technological readiness, and university-industry research collaboration. In the model, α refers to the coefficient expressing the alter in the dependent variable other than explanatory variables, $\mu_{i,\ t}$ is an independently distributed error term, and the subindices unit i and t represent the cross-section size and the time dimension. The number of cross-section observations is expressed in N and the time dimension in T.

Consequently, we employ two instrumental variables (those are the availability of scientists and engineers (ase) and quality of scientific research institutions (qsri)) to explain our endogenous variable, which is scientific and technical publications in Eq. (3).

4 Findings

As we mentioned before, according to countries' intensity to produce MHT value added, we divided our sample size into two groups, which are a country who has more intensity to produce and who has less intensity to produce MHT value added. Therefore, we applied our regression analysis both for two groups. Tables 9 and 10 represent estimation results of country groups for innovation capacity. In the tables, there are six columns, which represent different estimator results. From 1 to 6, column (1) gives Pooled Least Squares, column (2) presents Fixed Effects, column (3) provides Random Effects, and columns (4), (5), and (6) illustrate Fixed Effects Two-Stage Least Squares (FE2SLS), Random Effects Two-Stage Least Squares (RE2SLS), and Error Components Two-Stage Least Squares (EC2SLS), respectively.

Table 9 shows the estimation result of countries having more intensity to produce MHT for innovation capacity which is represented by the logarithmic form of patent application numbers. We started to run Pooled Least Squares estimator, which is in column (1). In order to observe country-specific effects, we brought FE as well as RE to our analysis. Firstly, in order to decide which model between POLS and RE is more appropriate, we employ the Breusch-Pagan LM test for RE. The result of LM test for POLS and RE rejected the null hypothesis, which says that Random Effects is a more convenient model. Secondly, we used the Hausman specification test in order to test which model between FE and RE is suitable for our regression. As stated in the Hausman specification test result, which is 0.0005 (p-value), the null hypothesis is rejected, and FE model is more appropriate.

We performed Wald test, which controls the existence of heteroscedasticity. The null hypothesis of Wald test is constant variance. The p-value of Wald test is 0.0000,

Table 9 Estimation results of countries having high intensity to produce MHT

	(1) POLS	(2) FE	(3) RE	(4) FE2SLS	(5) RE2SLS	(6) EC2SLS
Ethics and corruption	0.0548 (0.606)	−0.0695 (0.449)	−0.0116 (0.894)	−0.0766 (0.474)	−0.0550 (0.715)	−0.0643 (0.631)
Foreign direct investment	−0.00513 (0.102)	0.00177 (0.181)	0.00138 (0.310)	0.00193 (0.289)	0.00256* (0.088)	0.00283** (0.011)
Tertiary education enrollment	0.0235*** (0.000)	0.00937* (0.052)	0.0155*** (0.000)	0.00951* (0.052)	0.0113** (0.018)	0.0104** (0.037)
Technological readiness	0.868*** (0.000)	0.411*** (0.000)	0.591*** (0.000)	0.417*** (0.000)	0.532*** (0.001)	0.520*** (0.003)
University-industry research collaboration	0.0345*** (0.000)	0.00495 (0.525)	0.0220*** (0.001)	0.00670 (0.669)	0.0257*** (0.001)	0.0264*** (0.000)
Scientific and technical publications	0.0124*** (0.001)	0.00879 (0.115)	0.0190*** (0.000)	0.0124 (0.667)	0.0368*** (0.002)	0.0406*** (0.000)
Constant	−5.074*** (0.000)	0.582 (0.536)	−2.549*** (0.000)	0.289 (0.906)	−2.922*** (0.003)	−2.989*** (0.001)
Observations	150	150	150	150	145	145
N_g		30	30	30	30	30
R^2	0.844	0.788	0.825	0.783	0.773	0.760
Hausman test (*p*-value)			0.000		0.854	0.985
LM test (chi^2)			239.04			
Wald test (*p*-value)		0.000				
Sargan-Hansen chi^2 (*p*-value)						12.172 (0.1437)

p-values in parentheses
$^{*}p < 0.1$, $^{**}p < 0.05$, $^{***}p < 0.01$

Table 10 Estimation results of countries having less intensity to produce MHT

	(1) POLS	(2) FE	(3) RE	(4) FE2SLS	(5) RE2SLS	(6) EC2SLS
Ethics and corruption	0.00675 (0.950)	0.249 (0.073)	0.331^{**} (0.011)	0.181 (0.271)	0.304^{**} (0.029)	0.359^{**} (0.016)
Foreign direct investment	−0.00477 (0.464)	0.00531^{**} (0.028)	0.00257 (0.328)	0.00448 (0.108)	0.00111 (0.709)	0.00363^{*} (0.099)
Tertiary education enrollment	0.0271^{***} (0.000)	0.0130^{***} (0.004)	0.0215^{***} (0.000)	0.00901 (0.124)	0.0226^{***} (0.000)	0.0212^{***} (0.000)
Technological readiness	1.350^{***} (0.000)	0.130 (0.283)	0.346^{***} (0.006)	0.232 (0.138)	0.481^{***} (0.003)	0.245^{*} (0.071)
University-industry research collaboration	0.0246^{***} (0.006)	0.00281 (0.684)	0.0174^{**} (0.013)	−0.0101 (0.406)	0.0127 (0.135)	0.0234^{**} (0.031)
Scientific and technical publications	0.0126^{***} (0.001)	−0.00397 (0.468)	0.0104^{**} (0.030)	−0.0361 (0.131)	−0.0102 (0.530)	0.0318^{**} (0.005)
Constant	-7.739^{***} (0.000)	-1.258^{*} (0.097)	-3.992^{***} (0.000)	0.380 (0.794)	-3.642^{***} (0.000)	-4.615^{***} (0.000)
Observations	150	150	150	150	150	150
N_g		30	30	30	30	30
R^2	0.822	0.635	0.777	0.052	0.671	0.710
Hausman test (*p*-value)			0.0017		0.870	0.737
LM test chi^2			195.13			
Wald test (*p*-value)		0.000				
Sargan-Hansen chi^2 (*p*-value)						12.568 (0.1276)

p-values in parentheses $^{*}p< 0.1$, $^{**}p< 0.05$, $^{***}p< 0.01$

which rejects the null hypothesis, and it means the presence of heteroscedasticity. We have data with heteroscedasticity and possible endogeneity. Consequently, we use a two-stage panel model. The robust Hausman test statistics is 0.9643, which does not reject the null hypothesis of the Hausman test, and it refers that RE2SLS estimator is more suitable than FE2SLS. Besides, we tested FE2SLS and EC2SLS estimators, and the test statistics (p-value 0.9957) do not reject the null hypothesis, which means that EC2SLS is suggested for our data set. When we bring together the parameter estimations obtained by the Two-Stage Least Squares Method, one of the panel data estimation methods for the Error Component Model used in the study, the following results are obtained for countries having the high intensity to produce MHT.

Due to the reason that we also should check our instrumental variables are valid or overidentifying, we employ Sargan-Hansen's test of overidentifying restrictions. Sargan-Hansen test controls the correct use of instrumental variables under the null hypothesis that excluded instruments are valid instruments, and rejection of it causes suspicion on the validity of the instruments (Schaffer & Stillman, 2010). Therefore, we performed the Sargan-Hansen test in order to see the validity of our instrumental variables. According to test results, the null hypothesis is not rejected with a 0.1437 p-value, and it means that our instrumental variables are valid in this model.

According to EC2SLS estimator, the estimated coefficients of foreign direct investment, tertiary education enrollment, technological readiness, university-industry collaboration, and scientific and technical publications are positive and all statistically significant at a 90% significance level. However, ethics and corruption variable is insignificant for our model.

Nowadays, in information societies, technological readiness is getting crucial. It is wildly crucial to find out how to use knowledge, how to adapt existing knowledge to production lines, or how to increase competitiveness by using that knowledge. The gaining ability to understand the technology that already existed could help people to use information and communication technology (ICT) more efficiently and also could be the main framework for future innovation activities. As Razavi et al. (2011) demonstrated that technological readiness has effective impact on novelty, we found similar results. The scope of estimated technological readiness coefficient in the equation is 0.520 which refers that a one-point increase in technological readiness increases patent application number per million by 0.520%. When compared to other variables in the equation, the effect of technological readiness is way more effective than others.

As technological readiness has a significant effect on innovation capacity, other absorptive capacity variables have a positive effect as well. University-industry research collaboration and foreign direct investment have a similar effect on innovation capacity. Any 1% increase for both university-industry collaboration and foreign direct investment enlarges innovation capacity by 0.0264% and 0.0029%, respectively. If in any country tertiary education enrollment increases 1%, innovation capacity will be increased by 0.011%. As we mentioned above, we use instrumental variables in order to avoid possible endogeneity problem. We employ scientific and technical publications, which is explained by two instrumental variables: availability of scientists and engineers and quality of scientific research institutions. Scientific and technical publications have effective and statistically significant influence on innovation capacity. Any one-point increase in scientific and technical publications, innovation capacity will be enhanced by 0.0406%.

Table 10 represents estimation results of the impact of absorptive capacity upon innovation capacity for countries having less intention to produce MHT value added. Firstly, we run POLS estimator, and it gives that tertiary education enrollment, technological readiness, university-industry research collaboration, and scientific and technical publication have positive and statistically significant effects on innovation capacity, while ethics and corruption and foreign direct investment are insignificant. Secondly, we run FE and RE estimators to observe the country-specific effects. We use LM test in order to decide which estimator between POLS and RE is more suitable for our model. According to LM test results, which is 0.0000 (p-value), the null hypothesis is rejected, and RE model is more appropriate. After deciding between POLS and RE, we run the Hausman specification test to determine between FE and RE. In proportion to the Hausman test result (0.001, p-value), we accepted the alternative hypothesis, which means that FE estimator is more proper than RE estimator.

Before running 2SLS estimators, we run the Wald test to monitor the existence of heteroscedasticity. According to the Wald test result, which is 0.000 p-value, it rejects the null hypothesis that is constant variance and concluded that our data is heteroscedastic. Furthermore, we employ the instrumental variables in order to prevent potential endogeneity problem. We use the availability of scientists and engineers and the quality of scientific research institutions as an instrumental variable for scientific and technical publications. While examining the effect of absorptive capacity on innovation capacity by using 2SLS method, we employ three estimators: Fixed Effects, Random Effects, and Error Components. As we mentioned earlier, we have data with heteroscedasticity. Thus, we use the robust Hausman test based on bootstrap. In order to find out which estimators we should use, we run the robust Hausman test for FE2SLS and EC2SLS, and the Hausman test result with 0.6338 p-value does not reject the null hypothesis. According to the Hausman result, we accept EC2SLS as an estimator for our model. As stated in EC2SLS estimator, our model of countries with less intention to produce MHT value added is as follows:

As we mentioned above, we run Sargan-Hansen's test of overidentifying restrictions to control whether our instrumental variables are fit in the model or not. The null hypothesis of Sargan-Hansen's test is not rejected with a 0.1276 p-value, and it says our instrumental variables are valid in our model.

At a 90% significance level, ethics and corruption, foreign direct investment, tertiary education enrollment, technological readiness, university-industry research collaboration, and scientific and technical publications are significant. We have R^2 with 71%, and it means that our explanatory variables in the model are significant to explain the chancing in patent applications and also can explain the change in patent applications by about 71%.

Acemoglu (2004) pointed out that institutions are one of the crucial factors to shape economic performance. Moreover, institutions are the main element to understand the cross-country difference both for welfare and development. Therefore, countries must be sure that they have a well-functioning institution structure. Besides, creating an ethical culture both for public and private sectors, being a more transparent as well as well-functioning judicial system, and having public awareness might help countries about developing. In our model, we have ethics and corruption variable which represents institutions. The coefficient of ethics and corruption variable is 0.359 which means that with a one-point increase in ethics and corruption, the innovation capacity of any country in our sample group will increase by 0.359%. According to our estimation results, it is seen that ethics and corruption has more power to affect innovation capacity than other variables for countries having less intention to produce MHT value added.

We mentioned above the importance of technological preparation in the information age we are in. Even if the impact of technological readiness is not as great as in countries having high intention to produce MHT, technological readiness still has a critical dimension on innovation capacity. For countries having less intention to produce MHT value added, the coefficient of the technological readiness is 0.245, meaning that a one-point increase in technological readiness results in a 0.245% increase in innovation capacity for those countries.

Our other explanatory variables have positive and statistical significance on innovation capacity as well. For instance, a 1% increase in tertiary education enrollment will affect patent applications per million people by 0.0212%. University-industry research collaboration and scientific and technical publications have similar magnitude power on innovation capacity. A one-score raising in both uirc and stp creates a 0.0234% and 0.0318% increase in innovation capacity, respectively. Furthermore, foreign direct investment has a positive coefficient on innovation capacity. Any 1% increase in foreign direct investment arises patent applications per million by 0.00363%.

5 Conclusion

It is a fact that from the very beginning of humans, the importance of technology has become more influential to daily life. Until the first industrial revolution, the effect of technology was not that much on economies. After the revolution, methods of production, essential resources, production inputs, lifestyles, and most importantly distribution of income over the world have changed and keep still changing. Among the poorest and richest countries, the gap of wealth is increasing, and it is precisely where technology being distinctive. While a country having either enough infrastructure to create technology or to get it externally keeps growing by using that technology, a country having neither enough infrastructure to create nor to get it externally makes no progress. Therefore, the notion of absorptive capacity has gained interest in order to explain the growing technology and wealth gap.

Absorptive capacity might be described as the general capability to acquire existing knowledge, define, adapt, and use it in order to benefit both economically and socially (for more information, see Cohen & Levinthal, 1989, 1990; Kim, 1980; Mowery & Oxley, 1995; Todorova & Durisin, 2007; Zahra & George, 2002). Thus, absorptive capacity might help countries, especially those technologically underdeveloped countries.

In light of the current literature, our study mainly has two objectives. In the first place, we would like to investigate the impact of absorptive capacity on innovation capacity from a cross-country perspective. On the other hand, we would like to observe the effect of whether being a country having more intention to export medium and high technology or being a country having least intention to export medium and high technology on absorptive capacity and innovation capacity relationship.

To accomplish these goals, we have panel data containing 60 countries for 2013–2017. Data are obtained from three different sources: GII, GCI, and UN's CIP. We used patent application counts representing innovation capacity as a dependent variable and have ethics and corruption, foreign direct investment, tertiary education enrollment, technological readiness, university-industry research collaboration, and scientific and technical publications as explanatory variables. We employed two instrumental variables to avoid possible endogeneity. Moreover, we analyzed the data by using Two-Stage Least Squares, which is one of the panel data methods.

As we spoke of before, for strong and consistent economies, it is inevitable to have a well-functioning set of institutions and ethical culture for both production and management sides. A country that accomplished to create such a strong infrastructure probably will be more successful at such as creating novelties, opening new markets, making new contacts, or speeding up development compared to a country that does not have such infrastructure. Accordingly, we employ ethics and corruption in order to observe its effect on innovation capacity. In our model, ethics and corruption is significant for countries having less intention to produce MHT value added, while it is insignificant for those having more intention to produce MHT value added. This result shows the similarity with Chadee and Roxas's (2013) study which underlined that a higher corruption rate decreases the innovation performance. This outcome might be the reason those countries having high intention already succeed at building such infrastructure. According to our estimation results, for those having less intention to produce MHT value added, ethics and corruption takes the biggest slice of the pie to affect innovation capacity. They primarily need to focus on this issue in order to raise their innovation capacities.

As well as institutional framework, education, especially higher education, is crucial about development and being wealthy. The reason why tertiary education plays more important than other education levels might be that students are taught for particular goals or specialized fields. Even if the quality of tertiary education might be another study subject, it still keeps an important role in increasing the knowledge base and awareness. The study is carried out by Castellacci and Natera (2013) demonstrating that even if tertiary education does not have a direct effect on innovation capacity, it provides sustainable economic growth. On the other hand, our results are like what we expect which is tertiary education has a direct effect on innovation capacity. If the enrollment rate in tertiary education increase, it will have waited that patent application count increase for two country groups.

Due to the reason that innovation has uncertainty itself, creating novelty needs an enormous amount of investment. As well as internal resources, external resources are another key factor for a sustainable innovation environment. Foreign direct investment might serve as a solution for that need. FDI not only is an investment resource for the host country but also is one of the most important knowledge spillover channels. Jin et al. (2019) mentioned that foreign competition affects firms with a strong technological capability negatively much more than firms with less technological capabilities. We put FDI our model due to reason that we would like to see how FDI affects innovation capacity according to countries' MHT value-added production levels. We assumed that countries having more intention to produce MHT value added already have a higher knowledge base when compared to those having less intention. Therefore, we expected that the effect of FDI in countries having less intention to produce MHT value added is much more than countries having more intention. Our model suggests a similar outcome to what we expected. The reason behind this outcome might be those countries having more intention to produce MHT value added have more existing knowledge than countries having less intention. In the literature, spillovers go through FDI from developed countries to developing countries. According to coefficients of FDI for two country groups, we may assume that countries having more intention to produce MHT value added is more developed than countries having less intention in terms of technology.

Even if each country has different kinds of resources, culture, expertise, or capital, they are all in the same era, technology. At such a time when knowledge is so precious, getting, understanding, and practicing that knowledge seem to be an important issue for countries. Therefore, we use technological readiness in order to observe it. For both country groups, technological readiness plays a crucial role in order to increase their innovation capacities. As Razavi et al. (2011) and Moldabekova et al. (2021) pointed out that there is a positive relationship between technological readiness and innovation capacity, our results suggest that countries having high intention to produce MHT value added need to develop technological readiness in the first place in order to get more returns in innovation capacity.

According to the definition of innovation, two conditions are required for something to be innovated; it should be something new and economically beneficial. Moreover, knowledge emerges in institutions such as universities, whose purpose is education and research, while in industry, the developed thoughts, ideas, or theories are put into practice. As a result of the cooperation of these two institutions, it is seen that innovation is achieved in two necessary conditions. Thus, university-industry collaborations can be a tool to increase innovation capacity. Guan and Zhao (2013) showed the positive effect of university on innovation performance. While university-industry research collaboration has a positive impact on innovation, Ponds et al. (2009) indicated that even if university plays a critical role to transfer the knowledge, the distances between receiver and transmitter are determinant of the effect. On the other hand, our findings demonstrate that with strong university-industry research collaboration, countries will have more innovation capacities than those without.

As we mentioned above, innovation has two main requirements: novelty and economic benefit. Even if research institutions such as universities are nonprofit institutions, they are still effective in economics in terms of producing novelties, and they are one of the creating novelty sources by publishing a scientific paper. As well as publishing papers not only creates novelty, but also it increases the knowledge base that helps absorption and adaption. In the current literature, on the one hand, Amsden and Mourshed (1997) have already shown the positive relationship between scientific publications and innovation. On the other hand, Archibugi et al. (2009) have demonstrated the crucial role of scientific and technical articles in knowledge generation. Thus, we employed scientific and technical publications in order to examine its effect on innovation capacity. Estimation result pointed out that publication has a positive impact on innovation capacity for both country groups. Any increase in scientific and technical publication will result in an increase in patent application numbers.

As a conclusion, in a globalized world, boundaries no longer exist, knowledge spillovers are rapidly increased, and the proportion of knowledge in the production process is enlarged. Therefore, in such a world, technologically underdeveloped countries are needed to make a set of improvements for closing the gap and catching the technological leaders. As much as technologically underdeveloped countries' effort, technological leaders should keep their activities in order to hold the lead. Analysis results clearly reveal that absorptive capacity, which is one of the most crucial elements of the boosting innovation, cannot be considered independent from development in innovation activities. While countries having high intention to produce MHT value added, which are seen as technological leaders, have already increased fundamental economic requirements, such as democracy, transparency, easy access to finance, IPR protections, and education systems, to increase their innovation capacity and economic development, countries having less intention to produce MHT value added, which are seen as technologically developing countries, should focus on essential economy needs, such as sustainable investment to R&D, modern education system, democracy culture, freedom of speech, or strong trading partners.

References

Abramovitz, M. (1986). Catching up, forging ahead, and falling behind. *The Journal of Economic History, 46*(2), 385–406.

Acemoglu, D. (2004). *Understanding institutions* (pp. 23–25). Lionel Robbins Lectures, London School of Economics.

Alfaki, I. M. A., & Ahmed, A. (2013). Technological readiness in the United Arab Emirates towards global competitiveness. *World Journal of Entrepreneurship, Management and Sustainable Development, 9*(1), 4–13.

Ali, M., Egbetokun, A., & Memon, M. H. (2018). Human capital, social capabilities and economic growth. *Economies, 6*(1), 2.
Amsden, A. H., & Mourshed, M. (1997). Scientific publications, patents and technological capabilities in late-industrializing countries. *Technology Analysis & Strategic Management, 9*(3), 343–360.
Anand, J., & Kogut, B. (1997). Technological capabilities of countries, firm rivalry and foreign direct investment. *Journal of International Business Studies, 28*(3), 445–465.
Archibugi, D., & Coco, A. (2004). A new indicator of technological capabilities for developed and developing countries (ArCo). *World Development, 32*(4), 629–654.
Archibugi, D., Denni, M., & Filippetti, A. (2009). The technological capabilities of nations: The state of the art of synthetic indicators. *Technological Forecasting and Social Change, 76*(7), 917–931.
Arrow, K. J. (1971). The economic implications of learning by doing. In *Readings in the theory of growth* (pp. 131–149). Palgrave Macmillan.
Arrow, K., & Intriligator, M. (2000). *Handbook of mathematical economics* (Vol. 1). Elsevier.
Baltagi, B. H., & Liu, L. (2009). A note on the application of EC2SLS and EC3SLS estimators in panel data models. *Statistics & Probability Letters, 79*(20), 2189–2192.
Bassanini, A., & Ernst, E. (2002). *Labour market institutions, product market regulation, and innovation: Cross-country evidence.*
Beaudry, C., & Allaoui, S. (2012). Impact of public and private research funding on scientific production: The case of nanotechnology. *Research Policy, 41*(9), 1589–1606.
Berger, M., & Diez, J. R. (2006). Technological capabilities and innovation in Southeast Asia: Results from innovation surveys in Singapore, Penang and Bangkok. *Science Technology and Society, 11*(1), 109–148.
Camisón, C., & Forés, B. (2010). Knowledge absorptive capacity: New insights for its conceptualization and measurement. *Journal of Business Research, 63*(7), 707–715.
Castellacci, F. (2011). Closing the technology gap? *Review of Development Economics, 15*(1), 180–197.
Castellacci, F., & Natera, J. M. (2013). The dynamics of national innovation systems: A panel cointegration analysis of the coevolution between innovative capability and absorptive capacity. *Research Policy, 42*(3), 579–594.
Chadee, D., & Roxas, B. (2013). Institutional environment, innovation capacity and firm performance in Russia. *Critical Perspectives on International Business, 9*(1–2), 19–39.
Coe, D. T., & Helpman, E. (1995). International r & d spillovers. *European Economic Review, 39*(5), 859–887.
Cohen, W. M., & Levinthal, D. A. (1989). Innovation and learning: The two faces of R & D. *The Economic Journal, 99*(397), 569–596.
Cohen, W. M., & Levinthal, D. A. (1990). Absorptive capacity: A new perspective on learning and innovation. *Administrative Science Quarterly, 35*(1), 128–152.
Coombs, J. E., & Bierly, P. E., III. (2006). Measuring technological capability and performance. *R&D Management, 36*(4), 421–438. https://doi.org/10.1111/j.1467-9310.2006.00444.x
Costa, I., & de Queiroz, S. R. R. (2002). Foreign direct investment and technological capabilities in Brazilian industry. *Research Policy, 31*(8–9), 1431–1443.
Dechezleprêtre, A., Glachant, M., & Ménière, Y. (2013). What drives the international transfer of climate change mitigation technologies? Empirical evidence from patent data. *Environmental and Resource Economics, 54*, 161–178. https://doi.org/10.1007/s10640-012-9592-0
Di Vita, G. (2013). The TRIPs agreement and technological innovation. *Journal of Policy Modeling, 35*(6), 964–977.
Doyle, E., & O'Connor, F. (2013). Innovation capacities in advanced economies: Relative performance of small open economies. *Research in International Business and Finance, 27*(1), 106–123.
Escribano, A., Fosfuri, A., & Tribó, J. A. (2009). Managing external knowledge flows: The moderating role of absorptive capacity. *Research Policy, 38*(1), 96–105.

Fagerberg, J., & Srholec, M. (2008). National innovation systems, capabilities and economic development. *Research Policy, 37*(9), 1417–1435.
Fagerberg, J., Srholec, M., & Knell, M. (2007). The competitiveness of nations: Why some countries prosper while others fall behind. *World Development, 35*(10), 1595–1620.
Fleisher, B., Li, H., & Zhao, M. Q. (2010). Human capital, economic growth, and regional inequality in China. *Journal of Development Economics, 92*(2), 215–231.
Flor, M. L., Cooper, S. Y., & Oltra, M. J. (2018). External knowledge search, absorptive capacity and radical innovation in high-technology firms. *European Management Journal, 36*(2), 183–194.
Freeman, C. (2004). Technological infrastructure and international competitiveness. *Industrial and Corporate Change, 13*(3), 541–569.
Fu, X. (2008). Foreign direct investment, absorptive capacity and regional innovation capabilities: Evidence from China. *Oxford Development Studies, 36*(1), 89–110.
Furman, J. L., & Hayes, R. (2004). Catching up or standing still?: National innovative productivity among 'follower' countries, 1978–1999. *Research Policy, 33*(9), 1329–1354.
Furman, J. L., Porter, M. E., & Stern, S. (2002). The determinants of national innovative capacity. *Research Policy, 31*(6), 899–933.
Gani, A. (2009). Technological achievement, high technology exports and growth. *Journal of Comparative International Management, 12*(2), 31–47.
García, F., Avella, L., & Fernández, E. (2012). Learning from exporting: The moderating effect of technological capabilities. *International Business Review, 21*(6), 1099–1111.
Gerschenkron, A. (1962). *Economic backwardness in historical perspective: A book of essays* (No. 330.947 G381). Belknap Press of Harvard University Press.
Godfrey, L. G., & Tremayne, A. R. (2005). The wild bootstrap and heteroskedasticity-robust tests for serial correlation in dynamic regression models. *Computational Statistics & Data Analysis, 49*(2), 377–395.
Griffith, R., Redding, S., & Van Reenen, J. (2003). R&D and absorptive capacity: Theory and empirical evidence. *Scandinavian Journal of Economics, 105*(1), 99–118.
Guan, J., & Zhao, Q. (2013). The impact of university–industry collaboration networks on innovation in nano biopharmaceuticals. *Technological Forecasting and Social Change, 80*(7), 1271–1286.
Guimón, J. (2013). Promoting university-industry collaboration in developing countries. *World Bank, 3*, 12–48.
Hasan, I., & Tucci, C. L. (2010). The innovation–economic growth nexus: Global evidence. *Research Policy, 39*(10), 1264–1276.
Harris, R., & Le, T. (2019). Absorptive capacity in New Zealand firms: Measurement and importance. *Science and Public Policy, 46*(2), 290–309.
Jin, B., García, F., & Salomon, R. (2019). Inward foreign direct investment and local firm innovation: The moderating role of technological capabilities. *Journal of International Business Studies, 50*(5), 847–855.
Kaiser, B. (2014). *RHAUSMAN: Stata module to perform a (cluster-) robust Hausman test*. University of Bern.
Kim, L. (1980). Stages of development of industrial technology in a developing country: A model. *Research Policy, 9*(3), 254–277.
Kogut, B., & Chang, S. J. (1991). Technological capabilities and Japanese foreign direct investment in the United States. *The Review of Economics and Statistics, 73*(3), 401–413.
Kostopoulos, K., Papalexandris, A., Papachroni, M., & Ioannou, G. (2011). Absorptive capacity, innovation, and financial performance. *Journal of Business Research, 64*(12), 1335–1343.
Lall, S. (1992). Technological capabilities and industrialization. *World Development, 20*(2), 165–186.
Lee, S., Nam, Y., Lee, S., & Son, H. (2016). Determinants of ICT innovations: A cross-country empirical study. *Technological Forecasting and Social Change, 110*, 71–77.

Lesser, C. (2008). Market openness, trade liberalisation and innovation capacity in the finish telecom equipment industry. *OECD Journal: General Papers, 2008*(4), 65–107.

Liao, S. H., Fei, W. C., & Chen, C. C. (2007). Knowledge sharing, absorptive capacity, and innovation capability: An empirical study of Taiwan's knowledge-intensive industries. *Journal of Information Science, 33*(3), 340–359.

Mancusi, M. L. (2008). International spillovers and absorptive capacity: A cross-country cross-sector analysis based on patents and citations. *Journal of International Economics, 76*(2), 155–165.

Marotta, D., Mark, M., Blom, A., & Thorn, K. (2007). *Human capital and university-industry linkages' role in fostering firm innovation: An empirical study of Chile and Colombia*. The World Bank.

Mauro, P. (1995). Corruption and growth. *The Quarterly Journal of Economics, 110*(3), 681–712.

Mayor, M. G. O., de la Hera, M. L. B., & Ruiz, E. D. D. (2012). Empirical study of national technological innovation capability in Africa. *South African Journal of Economic and Management Sciences, 15*(4), 440–463.

Moldabekova, A., Philipp, R., Satybaldin, A. A., & Prause, G. (2021). Technological readiness and innovation as drivers for logistics 4.0. *The Journal of Asian Finance, Economics and Business, 8*(1), 145–156. https://doi.org/10.13106/JAFEB.2021.VOL8.NO1.145

Mowery, D. C., & Oxley, J. E. (1995). Inward technology transfer and competitiveness: The role of national innovation systems. *Cambridge Journal of Economics, 19*(1), 67–93.

Nieto, M., & Quevedo, P. (2005). Absorptive capacity, technological opportunity, knowledge spillovers, and innovative effort. *Technovation, 25*(10), 1141–1157.

Özbek, H., & Atik, H. (2013). Inovasyon Göstergeleri Bakimindan Türkiye'nin Avrupa Birliği Ülkeleri Arasindaki Yeri: Istatistiksel Bir Analiz. *Erciyes Üniversitesi İktisadi ve İdari Bilimler Fakültesi Dergisi, 0*(42), 193–210. Retrieved from https://dergipark.org.tr/en/pub/erciyesiibd/issue/5899/77997

Paolillo, J. G., & Brown, W. B. (1978). How organizational factors affect R&D innovation. *Research Management, 21*(2), 12–15.

Philbin, S. (2008). Process model for university-industry research collaboration. *European Journal of Innovation Management, 11*(4), 488–521.

Ponds, R., Oort, F. V., & Frenken, K. (2009). Innovation, spillover Sand university–industry collaboration: An extended knowledge production function approach. *Journal of Economic Geography, 10*(2), 231–255.

Razavi, S., Mostafa, G., Rohollah, A. B., & Kashani, M. (2011). Relationship between technological readiness and innovation: A secondary analysis of countries global competitiveness. *European Journal of Scientific Research, 59*(3), 318–328.

Rothwell, R., & Dodgson, M. (1991). External linkages and innovation in small and medium-sized enterprises. *R&D Management, 21*(2), 125–138.

Salim, A., Razavi, M. R., & Afshari-Mofrad, M. (2017). Foreign direct investment and technology spillover in Iran: The role of technological capabilities of subsidiaries. *Technological Forecasting and Social Change, 122*, 207–214.

Schaffer, M. E., & Stillman, S. (2010). xtoverid: Stata module to calculate tests of overidentifying restrictions after xtreg, xtivreg, xtivreg2 and xthtaylor.

Schoenecker, T., & Swanson, L. (2002). Indicators of firm technological capability: Validity and performance implications. *IEEE Transactions on Engineering Management, 49*(1), 36–44.

Shefer, D., & Frenkel, A. (2005). R&D, firm size and innovation: An empirical analysis. *Technovation, 25*(1), 25–32.

Shi, Y. (2001). Technological capabilities and international production strategy of firms: The case of foreign direct investment in China. *Journal of World Business, 36*(2), 184–204.

Solow, R. M. (1956). A contribution to the theory of economic growth. *The Quarterly Journal of Economics, 70*(1), 65–94.

Sterlacchini, A. (2008). R&D, higher education and regional growth: Uneven linkages among European regions. *Research Policy, 37*(6–7), 1096–1107.
Teitel, S. (1994). Patents, R&D expenditures, country size, and per-capita income: An international comparison. *Scientometrics, 29*, 137–159.
Todorova, G., & Durisin, B. (2007). Absorptive capacity: Valuing a reconceptualization. *Academy of Management Review, 32*(3), 774–786.
Torres-Reyna, O. (2007). *Panel data analysis fixed and random effects using Stata* (v. 4.2). Data & Statistical Services, Princeton University (pp. 1–40).
Tseng, F. C., Huang, M. H., & Chen, D. Z. (2020). Factors of university–industry collaboration affecting university innovation performance. *The Journal of Technology Transfer, 45*(2), 560–577.
Tüylüoğlu, Ş., & Saraç, Ş. (2012). Gelişmiş ve gelişmekte olan ülkelerde inovasyonun belirleyicileri: Ampirik bir analiz. *Eskişehir Osmangazi Üniversitesi İktisadi ve İdari Bilimler Dergisi, 7*(1), 39–74.
Ulku, H. (2004). *Rand D, innovation, and economic growth: An empirical analysis* (No. 4–185). International Monetary Fund.
Ünlü, H., & Karacaer Ulusoy, M. (2021). Innovation and corruption in Turkey: "Grease the Wheels" or "Sand the Wheels". In A. Rafay (Ed.), *Handbook of research on theory and practice of financial crimes* (pp. 80–103). IGI Global. https://doi.org/10.4018/978-1-7998-5567-5.ch006
Varsakelis, N. C. (2006). Education, political institutions and innovative activity: A cross-country empirical investigation. *Research Policy, 35*, 1083–1090.
Verspagen, B. (2004). Innovation and economic growth. In J. Fagerberg, D. Mowery, & R. Nelson (Ed.), *The handbook of innovation* (pp. 487–513). Oxford University Press.
Wakelin, K. (2001). Productivity growth and R&D expenditure in UK manufacturing firms. *Research Policy, 30*(7), 1079–1090.
Wooldridge, J. M. (2010). *Econometric analysis of cross section and panel data*. MIT press.
Xie, X., Qi, G., & Zhu, K. X. (2019). Corruption and new product innovation: Examining firms' ethical dilemmas in transition economies. *Journal of Business Ethics, 160*(1), 107–125.
Xie, X., Zou, H., & Qi, G. (2018). Knowledge absorptive capacity and innovation performance in high-tech companies: A multi-mediating analysis. *Journal of Business Research, 88*, 289–297.
Zachariadis, M. (2003). R&D, innovation, and technological progress: A test of the Schumpeterian framework without scale effects. *Canadian Journal of Economics/ Revuecanadiennedʼéconomique, 36*(3), 566–586.
Zahra, S. A., & George, G. (2002). Absorptive capacity: A review, reconceptualization, and extension. *Academy of Management Review, 27*(2), 185–203.

Nuri Görkem Yönkul is working as a foreign trade specialist in the food industry and has completed his master's degree in innovation at Çankırı Karatekin University, Turkey.

Hülya Ünlü holds a Ph.D. in Banking and Finance from the Yildirim Beyazit University in Ankara, Turkey. Currently, she is an Assistant Professor of Economics at Cankiri Karatekin University, Turkey. She has an MSc in Financial Economics and Econometrics from the University of Essex in the UK. Her research interests are Economics of Innovation and Technology, Financial Econometrics, and Applied Microeconometrics.

Reinforcing the Labor Market Resilience: Exploring the Relationship Between Minimum Wage, Official Economy, and Informal Economy Using Granger Causality and Scenario Simulations

Adriana AnaMaria Davidescu

Abstract This chapter focuses on labor market resilience following changing environmental conditions occurring in the marketplace. The country context of Romania is utilized in order to understand the effect of the informal economy on labor markets and economic conditions. This enables more detail to be acquired on how resilience through entrepreneurship can occur via labor market intervention, thereby bridging the labor market literature with the resilience and entrepreneurship schools of thought. The chapter offers a perspective of minimum wage developments in Romania, which is a country characterized by a large proportion of informal entrepreneurs.

1 Introduction

Resilient labor markets are "labour markets that weather economic downturns with limited social costs or, more formally, limited losses in worker welfare" (OECD, 2012: 57). The resilience of labor market depends fundamentally on macroeconomic and labor market policy settings. In times of crises, macroeconomic policies are effective in limiting employment declines and preventing cyclical increases in unemployment from becoming structural (Hijzen et al., 2018). The shadow economy acts a "safety valve" for the formal economy in crisis creating employment and income opportunities, causing an increase in supply (Davidescu & Schneider, 2017).

Many articles have been written about the minimum wage in the literature, with its advantages and disadvantages. There are pros and cons, both based on solid arguments. From the state's point of view, things are good. From a private point of view, the news is bad. The employer has to pay more and therefore more to the state,

A. A. Davidescu (✉)
Department of Statistics and Economics/Department of Education, Training and Labour Market, Bucharest Academy of Economic Studies/National Scientific Research Institute for Labour and Social Protection, Bucharest, Romania
e-mail: adriana.alexandru@csie.ase.ro

J. Leitão, V. Ratten (eds.), *Strategic Innovation*, Contributions to Management Science, https://doi.org/10.1007/978-3-030-87112-3_10

which directly affects its profitability or its losses. It should be noted that the number of employees with a minimum wage in the public sector is twice as small as in the private sector.

On the one hand, the increase of the minimum wage would increase the budget revenues, but on the other hand, the private sector suffers from the increase of the minimum wage. This induces additional costs, and in order to maintain a balance the CAS should be reduced to absorb the impact on labor costs. So, as a consequence, there is an increase in consumption, which comes at the same time as the growth of the underground economy.

Also, some companies may refuse to pay these increased minimum wages and move employees into the unofficial economy. However, the increase in costs is marginal and the reverse phenomenon can occur, of pressure from the employee to be registered in the formal economy, given the increase in the minimum wage. On the other hand, at low-income levels, the vast majority of any additional income goes into current food consumption. Thus, the VAT revenues related to this consumption will also increase, taking into account the 50% share of the underground economy in the food trade.

Wage increases can lead to inflation or exchange rates, amid low productivity, because the difference between these increases and labor productivity results in either inflation or exchange rate depreciation. Although a potentially useful tool for redistribution, raising the minimum wage does nothing but raise the net income of unskilled workers at the expense of other factors of production and can slip into involuntary unemployment.

In such a context, it is of major importance to investigate how these increases in the minimum wage could affect the Romanian shadow activity through three forecasting scenarios having as starting point the results provided by two previous publications: Davidescu and Schneider (2019) and Popescu et al. (2018).

Davidescu and Schneider (2019) clearly point out that the minimum wage at least for the Romanian economy is a "sustaining factor of the shadow economy" but only in the long term, a potential relationship not being supported in the short run.

In this equation, another important piece of the puzzle is the official economy, both economies being substitutes, the unofficial economy playing the role of social buffer at least for certain periods of time and certain categories of individuals (young or low-skilled workers).

Therefore, it will make sense to simulate how different increases of the minimum wage based on two scenarios (7% respectively 15%) would affect the size of the Romanian shadow economy.

The series of the Romanian shadow economy has been used from Popescu et al. (2018) estimated using the MIMIC model and revealing a declining trend until the end of 2017, with a slight reverse trend during the period of economic crisis followed by a slow decrease until the end of 2017.

Therefore, the results on both scenarios highlighted that a future increase in the minimum wage, under the hypothesis of a quarterly economic growth of 4%, will lead to a new increase in informal economic activity, causing a loss of jobs primarily for low-skilled employees who will search for work in the unofficial sector.

Furthermore, future increases in the minimum wage need to be regarded with caution, especially if these increases seem not to take into account the labor market developments. Thus, these increases should not be encouraged before assessing the potential effect that such a measure might have on the economy for all actors involved.

This chapter is organized into five sections. The introductory section is dedicated to briefly presenting the minimum wage developments in Romania. The third section presents data and working methodology, while the following shows the empirical results. The last section includes the results of the main scenarios together with main conclusions and recommendations.

2 Shedding Light on the Romanian Minimum Wage in the European Context

The informal economy in Romania is a topic that has been approached in recent years by both Romanian and foreign specialists.

The impact of minimum wages on both formal and informal sectors is reflected in the literature through dual sectoral models. These models highlight that the minimum wage level above the equilibrium level leads to a limitation in labor demand, resulting in an increase in the number of the unemployed that will favor the informal sector (Hohberg & Lay, 2015, Krstić & Schneider, 2015).

Neumark et al. (2000) as well as Gindling and Terrell (2005, 2007) highlight the mixed impact of the minimum wage on the workforce. Thus, for employees with salaries close to the minimum, the positive effect of salary growth is presented: on the one hand, the positive effect as a result of salary increase, and on the other hand, the negative effect that will lead to an increase in unemployment, which will gradually become an alternative to the informal sector.

In most countries experiencing a high percentage of low wage, a high level of informality, and with a rather well-established legislation in this direction, it is difficult to delineate the effect of wage growth in the formal sector comparing with that from the informal sector.

At the level of low social security countries, instead of unemployment, people choose to work as a priority in the informal sector (Carneiro and Henley 2001; Maloney and Mendez 2004; Muravyev and Oshchepkov 2013).

At the EU level, the impact of raising the minimum wage is the same: for older Member States it is negative determining the reduction in the proportion of non-contract workers; for the new Member States the impact is positive (resulting in contract growth; Hazans (2011; Packard et al. 2012).

The minimum wage expressed as the ratio of average earnings is seen as putting more pressure on employment, due to the mismatch between the differential of productivity and that of wages in the sectors with medium and higher qualifications, relative to the sectors with low qualifications, and the way to adjust this is to increase employment in the informal sector or increase evasion by declaring to a greater extent the salaries at a minimum level.

On the one hand, the increase of minimum wage could decrease formal employment, as the capacity of the informal sector to attract labor surplus is higher. On the other hand, this minimum wage increase could lead to an increase in the employment of a large proportion of people who were previously active in the informal sector as a result of greater incentives to look for a formal job (Bhorat et al., 2014; Magruder, 2013).

Regarding the impact of the minimum wage on informal labor market sector, Filion (2009) argued that on the one hand informal workers will be encouraged to work in the formal sector of the economy, and on the other hand, the increase in salary costs may determine employers not to declare all employees or to pay official salaries for part-time jobs, even if workers are employed full-time, which determines illegal salary payments.

Therefore, raising the minimum wage can both generate a decrease in evasion by reducing the gap between the actual salary paid and the one registered in accounting and an increase in evasion, if previous salaries greater than the minimum wage will be declared at this level.

In this context, the main purpose of this chapter is to analyze the potential impact of different increases in the minimum wage on the incidence of shadow activity using forecasting scenarios under the vector error correction (VECM) models, Granger causality analyses for quarterly data covering the 2000–2019 period.

Within the chapter, the shadow economy is defined as "all market-based legal production of goods and services that are deliberately concealed from public authorities for the following reasons: to avoid payment of income, value added or other taxes; to avoid payment of social security contributions; to avoid certain legal labour market standards, such as minimum wages, maximum working hours, safety standards; to avoid complying with certain administrative procedures, such as completing statistical questionnaires or other administrative forms" (Schneider et al., 2010, pp. 3–4).

Romanian employees have the third lowest minimum gross salary in the European Union, according to data from January 1, 2021, published by Eurostat. On January 1, 2021, the minimum gross salary per economy in Romania was 2230 lei, and from mid-January 2021, the government decided to slightly increase the minimum gross salary to 2300 lei per month.

The minimum gross salary in Romania, of about 458 euros, was the third lowest in the EU. The minimum wages in Bulgaria (332 euros) and Hungary (442 euros) were lower. On the other hand, the highest levels of the minimum wage in the EU were in Luxembourg (€ 2202), Ireland (€ 1724), and the Netherlands (€ 1685). In Spain, an important destination for the Romanian labor force, the minimum wage in the economy was 1108 euros per month. In France, the minimum gross salary was 1555 euros, and in Germany, 1614 euros. In six countries in the 27 EU Member States, there is no national minimum wage system in the economy: Italy, Finland, Denmark, Sweden, Austria, and Cyprus.

Across the 21 Member States concerned, the highest minimum wage in the EU was 6.6 times higher than the lowest. By eliminating price differences, minimum wages ranged from 623 PPS per month in Bulgaria to 1668 PPS in Luxembourg, meaning that the highest minimum wage was 2.7 times higher than the lowest.

Minimum wages may also be measured in relative terms, as a proportion of the median earnings. In Romania, however, the median earnings are not high either, this being the main reason why there is a higher proportion of the minimum wage than the median income compared to rich EU countries. Thus, in Romania the minimum wage is 61% of the median income, and in Luxembourg and the Netherlands, their minimum wage is 57% of their median income, in Ireland the proportion is 53%, and in Germany, 52%.

The minimum wage in Romania could increase in the future, but this time due to a possible decision of the European Commission. The latest statistics show that almost 1.6 million citizens are remunerated with the minimum legal income for the work performed, 2.300 lei gross. Since 2000, the minimum wage has increased constantly yearly or several times per year. After the denomination from 2005 and upon joining the European Union, the minimum wage registered increases. The first year without an increase in the minimum income was the year of 2010 against the background of the economic crisis that affected the whole world. The year 2012 comes with new increases and also the next 3 years have been marked by new biannual increases. The minimum wage also increased in 2016, reaching RON 1250, while in 2017, Romanians enjoyed a slightly more consistent growth, with minimum wages reaching RON 1450.

A new increase took place in 2018, and from January 1, the minimum wage reached 1900 lei. The consistent increase is justified by the fact that the contributions have been transferred from employer to employee. In 2019, Romanians will once again receive more money on their salary, reaching 2080 lei. The penultimate salary increase took place in 2020, when the salary increased to 2230 lei, and in 2021, it brings a new salary increase, a little modest, to 2300 RON.

If in nominal terms, the minimum wage increased by 33 times since 2000, in real terms, the increase was nearly eight times. In terms of average gross earnings, the minimum wage ratio increased from 26.3% at the beginning of 2000 to almost 46.4% at the beginning of 2019.

Therefore, Romanians still earn very little; the pay gap is quite large, given that the richest states can afford to offer minimum wages about seven times higher than those at the bottom of the rankings.

In Romania, minimum wage increases were in no way related to the concepts of productivity and labor market performance, but creating a supplementary pressure on the wage distribution accelerating the transition of low-skilled and youth workers into unemployment or the informal sector.

3 The Minimum Wage Feeds the Romanian Shadow Activity? An Empirical Approach Based on Granger Causality and Simulation Scenarios

3.1 Data and Methodology

In order to capture the potential impact of several minimum wage alternative increases on the magnitude of the Romanian shadow activity, two main research papers have been used as starting points within our empirical demarche: Davidescu and Schneider (2019) and Popescu et al. (2018). The whole analysis relies on quarterly data covering the period 2000Q1–2017Q3.

Therefore, we can use the conceptual framework of Davidescu and Schneider (2019), in which the long-term impact of minimum wage on the incidence of the Romanian shadow activity has been proved using three different VAR/VECM models for different specifications of minimum wage and shadow economy: real SE activity per capita, real SE activity or real monthly minimum wage, minimum wage as a ratio of average gross earnings (%), as well as minimum wage as a ratio of GDP per capita. The analysis used quarterly data for the period 2000–2015.

Keeping the same reasoning, the whole estimation process has been repeated expanding the period to 2000Q1–2017Q3, using this time the estimated series of the informal economy of Popescu et al. (2018) built on an innovative methodology - an improved MIMIC (multiple causes multiple indicators) specification in which the causal variables have been grounded in an evidence-based approach using a micro–macro approach, incorporating the points of view of Romanian entrepreneurs, gained from a national representative survey.

Furthermore, the chapter explores the dynamics of the independencies between real shadow economy per capita and real minimum wage in the presence of the official economy proxied by real GDP per capita and including several control variables: share of employed persons having a second job, several dummy variables (Labour Code amendment, decline of public sector salaries, VAT increases or decreases). The main sources of data used in the analysis have been the Tempo database and Eurostat quarterly databases LFS and CPI.

The main methods used in the investigation are the analysis of non-stationarity based on unit root tests, VAR models, Johansen (1991) cointegration test, vector error correction models, Granger causality analysis, impulse response function, and forecasting scenarios based on different economic hypotheses. Pesaran and Shin's (1998) generalized impulse response functions have been used to measure the effect and the time lag of a shock in the minimum wage on the Romanian informal sector. A detailed description of the technical methodology has been already provided in Davidescu and Schneider (2019) and Lütkepohl (2007).

Therefore, we used the series of Romanian shadow economy for the period 2000Q1–2017Q3 in order to test and to evaluate a relationship with the minimum wage and then we investigated how well the model performs until the end of 2019.

Furthermore, based on three different forecasting scenarios, the analysis aims to evaluate the change in the level of shadow activity, based on the hypothesis of a future increase in the minimum wage, considering in an economic context an average quarterly economic growth of 4%. The forecasting will be realized for the first quarter of 2020Q1 when the minimum wage increased at 2230 lei and for those with higher education was set at 2350 lei.

Therefore, the impact of an increase in the minimum wage in the level of shadow activity will be analyzed using three scenarios:

- Baseline scenario in which the minimum wage, the share of employed persons having a second job, and the GDP per capita have a growth rate generated by the model.
- Scenario 1 in which the minimum wage will increase by 7% in 2020Q1 (to the level of 2230 lei according to the latest statements) and assuming an economic growth over the same quarter of the previous year of 4% and keeping the same level of share for employed persons having a second job as in the same quarter of the previous year.
- Scenario 2 in which the minimum wage will increase by 15% in 2020Q1 (to 2400 lei) and assuming an economic growth over the same quarter of the previous year of 4% and keeping the same level of share for employed persons having a second job as in the same quarter of the previous year.

3.2 *Empirical Results*

The empirical results of the improved version of MIMIC model grounded on evidence-based approach used for the estimation of the Romanian shadow economy as % of official GDP revealed that "the main causes for the Romanian SE were self-employment, unemployment, part-time employment, and the lack of trust in public institutions, while the effects of this phenomenon can be reflected by the fluctuations in currency and labour force" (Popescu et al., 2018, p. 1).

Unemployment acts as a "safety valve for the official sector" especially in recession periods, in which the shadow economy could represent an alternative for many individuals willing to supplement their earnings (Dell'Anno, 2003; Dell'Anno and Solomon, 2008; Dell'Anno et al., 2007). Self-employment rate can be seen as a potential factor in explaining the equation of the Romanian shadow economy, since the proportion of those individuals is relatively high, and additionally, they have more possibilities to evade. Part-time employment was found to be significant in all specifications, stipulating that at least a proportion of those employees is working in both sectors, going also in the unofficial economy in order to supplement their revenues.

A core variable in this shadow economy equation is the lack of trust in public institutions, associated also with corruption, who push both entrepreneurs and individuals in the unofficial sector in order to avoid taxes and bureaucracy.

Incorporating all these causes and calibrating the model, the empirical findings revealed a phenomenon with a significant incidence characterized by a cyclical pattern, with successions such as decrease–increase and decrease–increase even if of different magnitudes during the period 2000–2017. Therefore, even if until the end of 2008, the general trend was a decreasing one, characterized by a significant decrease of 5 percentage points from 2000, during the economic crisis, there is a reverse trend, the magnitude of the SE reaching the value of 32.3% in 2010.

Then, for another 6 years, the trend followed a decreasing direction, reaching the value of 27.7% in 2016, while from the beginning of 2017, due to the modifications brought to the Labour Code and Fiscal Code, political instability, and the increasing lack of trust in public officials under the perspective of a future "Tax Revolution" (implying the transfer of contributions from employer to the employee), the phenomenon registered an increase of more than 1 ppt. in the second quarter of 2017, reaching 28.6% of official GDP.

Analyzing the evolution between real minimum wage and real shadow activity per capita during the period 2000–2017, a co-movement relationship can be highlighted, the correlation coefficient value of 0.94 revealing a direct and strong linear relationship between both variables.

In line with the methodological considerations, the series used in the analysis have been tested for non-stationarity using unit root tests, the empirical results supporting the hypothesis that all-time series are I (1), being non-stationary and requiring a first difference in order to achieve stationarity. Having this first condition accomplished, it makes sense to further investigate a potential long-run relationship under a VAR framework in level, based on which the optimal lag length was found to be 1 based on AIC and SBC values, on stability condition and the validation of the main residuals' hypotheses.

For exploring a potential long-run relationship, Johansen (1991) cointegration approach has been applied highlighting a unique equilibrium relationship between variables, allowing for the estimation of a vector error correction model. The long-run model can be specified as follows:

$$ECT_{t-1} = 1.00 \cdot \log\,(\text{realSEcaptia})_t - 0.14 \log\,(\text{real MW})_t - 0.61 \log\,(\text{real GDP}_{\text{capita}})_t - 0.06\,(\text{employed persons having a second job})_t - 0.006\,\text{trend} + 4.97 \quad (1)$$

The term error correction, ECT_{t-1}, quantifies that last period deviation from long-run equilibrium (the error) influences the short-run dynamics of the shadow economy. Therefore, the coefficient of ECT is called the speed of adjustment, measuring the speed at which the shadow economy returns to equilibrium after a change in the minimum wage.

The empirical results of both long-run and short-run model within the VECM model are presented in Table 1.

The most important empirical finding was the one related to the existence of a long-run relationship between real shadow economic activity per capita, real minimum wage, real GDP per capita, and the share of those employed persons having a second job. All long-run coefficients are positive and highly significant proving the validity of such a relationship. There is enough empirical evidence to support the

Table 1 The empirical results of VECM model

Cointegrating equation	CointEq1
LOG(real SE_D11(−1))	1.000000
LOG(real minimum wage(−1))	−0.143615**
	(0.05592)
	[−2.56827]
LOG(REAL_GDP_CAPITA_D11(−1))	−0.619617**
	(0.12151)
	[−5.09925]
SECOND_JOB_D11(−1)	−0.060423**
	(0.01272)
	[−4.75119]
@TREND(00Q1)	−0.006470**
	(0.00201)
	[−3.22510]
C	4.977904**
Error correction:	D(LOG(REAL_SE_D11))
CointEq1	−0.362797***
	(0.13906)
	[−2.60892]
D(LOG(real SE_D11(−1)))	−0.121733
	(0.17691)
	[−0.68812]
D(LOG(real minimum wage (−1)))	−0.037357
	(0.04572)
	[−0.81715]
D(LOG(REAL_GDP_CAPITA_D11(−1)))	0.724526***
	(0.24249)
	[2.98786]
D(SECOND_JOB_D11(−1))	−0.013300
	(0.00701)
	[−1.89697]
C	0.008234
	(0.00454)
	[1.81277]
D3	−0.002807
	(0.00965)
	[−0.29092]
D1	−0.005898
	(0.00825)
	[−0.71504]
R-squared	0.299734
Adj. *R*-squared	0.205468
Sum sq. resids	0.030794

(continued)

Table 1 (continued)

Cointegrating equation	CointEq1
S.E. equation	0.024335
F-statistic	3.179646
Log likelihood	142.1070
Akaike AIC	−4.470234
Schwarz SC	−4.190988

Source: Author's own
*** means statistically significant at 1%
** means statistically significant at 5%
* means statistically significant at 10%

positive long-run relationship between minimum wage and the size of the shadow activity per capita; a raise of 1% in the minimum wage will increase the incidence of such a phenomenon with 0.14% in the long run, ceteris paribus. The empirical results strongly supported the hypothesis of complementarity between both economies both in the long run and in the short run, proving the positive sign of the real GDP per capita.

Therefore, when the official economy increases by 1%, the shadow activity is expected to increase by 0.62%, ceteris paribus, proving that both economies are complements and at least partially people are coming in the unofficial economy to supplement their revenues (Davidescu, 2014).

Also, the shadow activity is positively related to the second job; therefore, people who have a second job are more inclined to work at least partially after or even during working hours in informal economic activities. The impact is a direct one, with a resulting increase of almost 0.06% in the incidence of the shadow activity.

There is enough empirical evidence to support the existence of a long-run causality, proved by the negative and statistically significant coefficient of ECT, stating that the shadow activity restored the deviation from the long-term equilibrium by 36% each quarter.

The short-run model does not exhibit a statistical significant validity, since almost all the short-run coefficients suffer from the lack of statistical significance, the only exception being the coefficient of official economy which has also been shown to have a significant and direct impact in the short term.

Therefore, both in the long run and in the short run, both economies are rather complements, so when one grows, the other also grows, proving that people go in the unofficial sector to supplement their revenues.

The model has proven its statistical validity in terms of Fisher test, and the degree of determination was 29.9%, stipulating that all the considered factors explained almost 30% of the whole variation in the shadow activity, the difference being attributed to other factors not included in the model. The main hypotheses on residuals have been tested using Jarque–Bera test, serial correlation LM test, and White test, highlighting that the model residuals can be considered white noise. The dummy variables addressing different legislative changes as well as the former

Table 2 Granger Causality test results[a]

Null hypothesis/lag level	F-stat	$t_{ECT_{t-1}}$	Results
Real minimum wage does not Granger cause real SE per capita	0.66	−2.60[a]	Long-run causality

[a]Means significant at the 0.05 level (2-tailed)

economic crisis do not present any impact on the size of the informal sector in Romania.

Under the VECM framework, the Granger causality analysis has been tested both in the long run and short run, proving the existence of a unidirectional causality in the long run running from the minimum wage to shadow activity in the presence of official economy and the employment rate of second job, since the value of t-test and the sign of the ECT coefficient conform to the technical considerations. Therefore, the negative sign of ECT and the statistical significance of this coefficient proved that there is a unidirectional long-run causality. The short-run causality has been verified by the statistical significance of short-run coefficients of the minimum wage, the official economy, or employment rate of those having a second job, proving that the only short-run causality identified was the one running from the official economy to the unofficial economy, due to the statistical significance of the short-run coefficient of real GDP per capita.

Therefore, the direction is the one coming from the official economy to the unofficial economy, confirming what professor Schneider et al. (2010) stated that making the official economy more attractive could be the key solution of monitoring the shadow economy.

It is worth mentioning that the shadow economic activity does not exhibit any dynamic pattern, not being influenced by its past. Also, the minimum wage and the rate of employment of those having a second job do not manifest any statistical impact in the short run, invalidating a potential Granger causality in the short run (Table 2).

In order to capture the short-run effect of a shock in the minimum wage on the level of shadow activity, the generalized impulse response functions of Pesaran and Shin (1998) have been applied, revealing that a raise of 1% in the minimum wage would increase the real shadow activity per capita with approximately 0.86%, the initial shock reaching its saturation potential on the horizon of the fourth quarter; thereafter, the trend flattens.

As a final remark, it is important to point out the direct relationship between both economies in the short run and in the long run and also to highlight the significant impact of the minimum wage on the magnitude of such a type of economic activity but only in the long term (Fig. 1).

Based on the information provided by the impulse response function, we have built three alternative scenarios to capture the change in the level of shadow activity, based on the hypothesis of a future increase in the minimum wage. In order to do that, we have used stochastic simulations, taking into account the same sort of errors

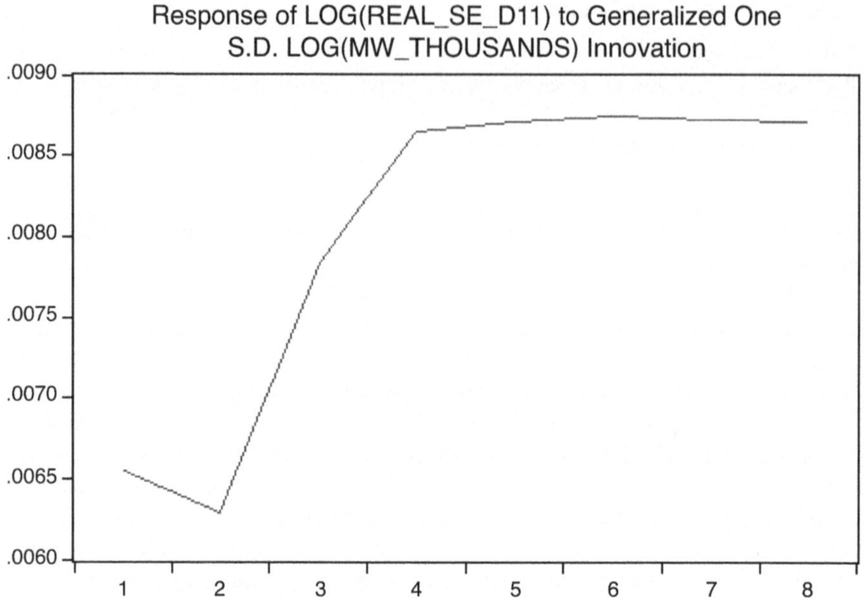

Fig. 1 Generalized impulse responses of shadow activity per capita to one S.D. shock in the minimum wage

occurring in the future as seen over historical data and the fact that the coefficients of our model are estimated not fixed as known values.

The empirical results of baseline scenario revealed that an increase in the minimum wage together with an average quarterly economic growth of 4% over the same quarter of the previous year showed a slow rise in the level of shadow activity per capita (Fig. 2).

Scenario 1 stipulates that the minimum wage will increase by 7% in 2020Q1 (according to the latest statements, attaining the value of 2230 lei from January 2020) and assuming an economic growth over the same quarter of the previous year of 4% and keeping the same level of share for employed persons having a second job as in the same quarter of the previous year. The empirical results revealed an even greater increase of the shadow activity per capita as a consequence of minimum wage increase (Fig. 3).

The empirical results of Scenario 2 which stipulates now an increase of the minimum wage of 15% in 2020Q1 (to the value of 2400 lei), assuming an economic growth over the same quarter of the previous year of 4% and keeping the same level of share for employed persons having a second job as in the same quarter of the previous year, revealed an even greater increase in the shadow activity per capita as a result of a higher increase in the minimum wage (Fig. 4).

Analyzing the results from both scenarios comparatively, it can be highlighted that a future increase in the minimum wage, under the hypothesis of a quarterly

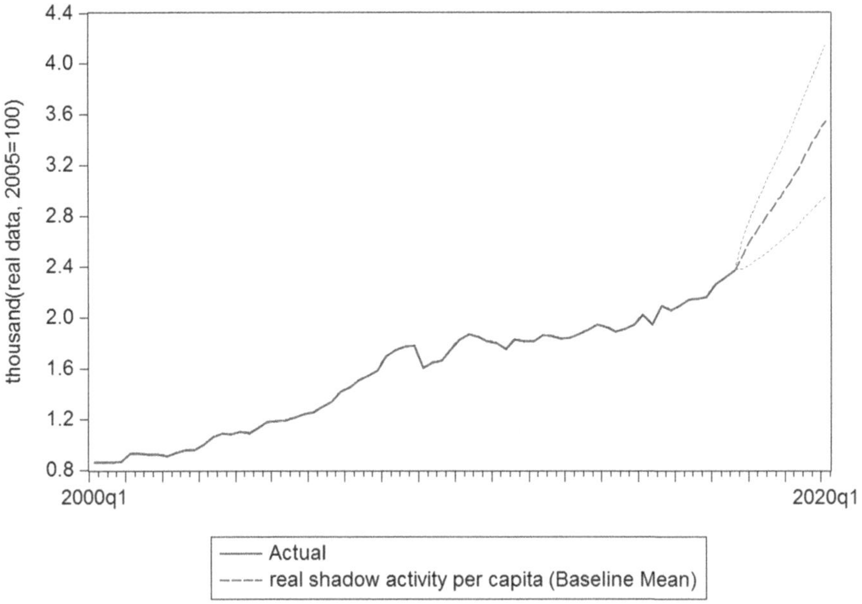

Fig. 2 The empirical results of baseline scenario

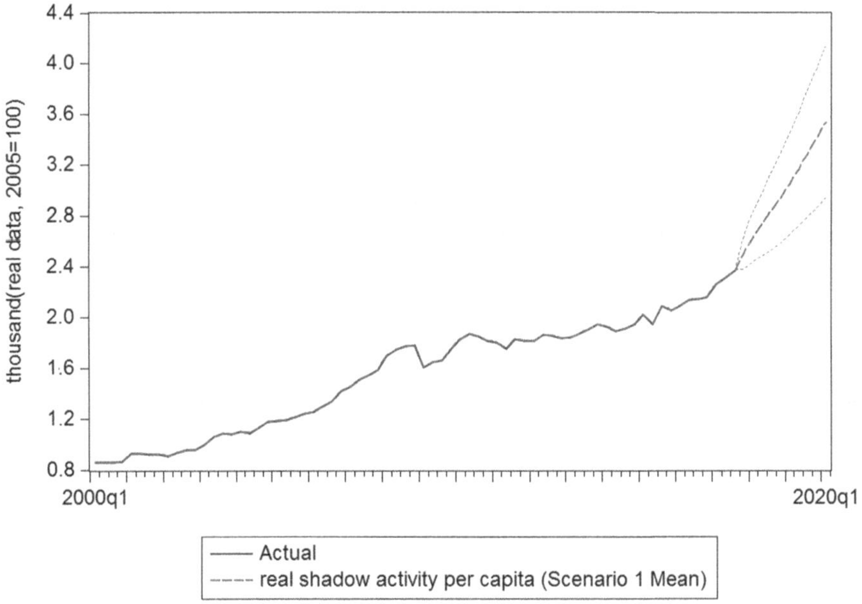

Fig. 3 The empirical results of the Scenario 1

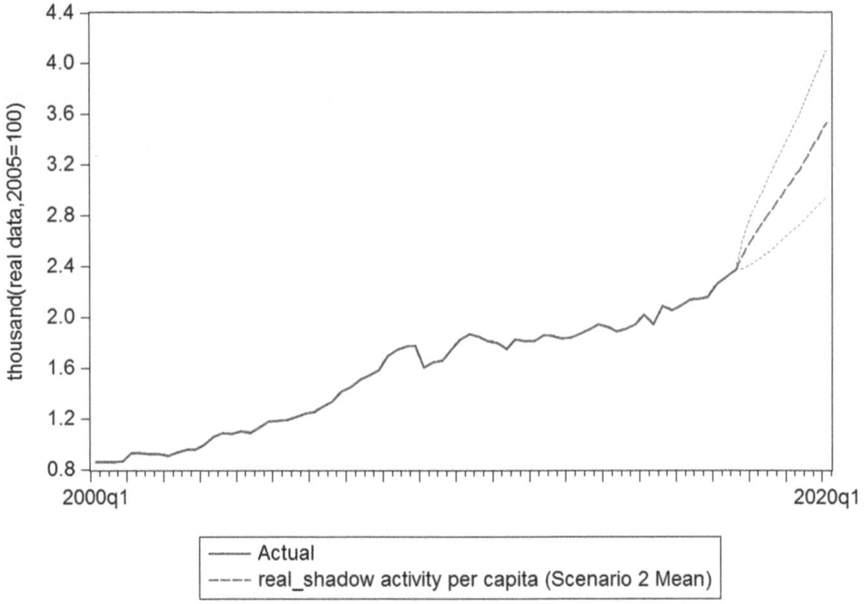

Fig. 4 The empirical results of Scenario 2

economic growth of 4% and an unmodified level of the employed persons having a second job, will lead to a new increase in informal economic activity, causing a loss of jobs primarily for low-skilled employees who will search for work in the unofficial sector (Fig. 5).

Therefore, future increases in the minimum wage need to be regarded with caution, especially if these increases seem not to take into account the labor market developments. Thus, these increases should not be encouraged before assessing the potential effect that such a measure might have on the economy for all actors involved.

4 Conclusions

In light of the latest successive increases in the minimum wage, the aim of this chapter has been to analyze the way in which a new potential increase in the minimum wage would affect the shadow economy activity in Romania using three forecasting scenarios and having as starting point two of our previous researches: the study of Davidescu and Schneider (2019) regarding the impact of minimum wage of the Romanian shadow economy and the research of Popescu, Davidescu, and Huidumac (2018) regarding the main determinants of Romanian shadow activity and its estimate related to official GDP.

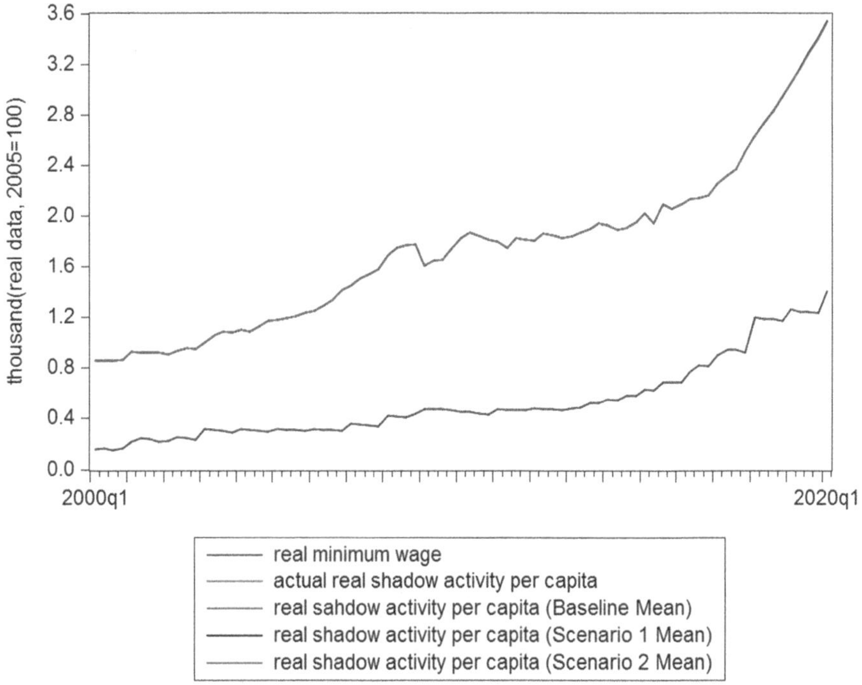

Fig. 5 Comparisons between the three forecasting scenarios

The empirical results revealed the existence of a direct relationship between both economies in the short run and in the long run and also highlighted the significant impact of the minimum wage on the magnitude of shadow economic activity but only in the long term. Therefore, the results confirmed the findings of Davidescu and Schneider (2019) according to which the minimum wage acts as a long-term supporting factor of the shadow economy, since companies will seek alternative methods of circumventing authorities and most likely at least a proportion of firms will decide to offer to their employees part of their salaries in cash, increasing in such a way the incidence of "envelope wage" pattern of informality. Another channel through which the increase of the minimum wage could lead to the increase of the incidence of informal activity is even the unemployment that pushes people into the informal sector.

Therefore, within the research, different increases of the minimum wage based on two scenarios (7% and 15%) have been simulated and their effects on the size of the Romanian shadow economy have been analyzed.

Both scenarios highlighted that a future increase in the minimum wage, under the hypothesis of a quarterly economic growth of 4%, will lead to a new increase in informal economic activity, causing a loss of jobs primarily for low-skilled employees who will search for work in the unofficial sector.

Furthermore, future increases in the minimum wage need to be regarded with caution, especially if these increases seem not to take into account the labor market developments. Thus, these increases should not be encouraged before assessing the potential effect that such a measure might have on the economy for all actors involved.

References

Bhorat, H., Kanbur, R., & Stanwix, B. (2014). Estimating the impact of minimum wages on employment, wages, and non-wage benefits: The case of agriculture in South Africa. *American Journal of Agricultural Economics, 96*(5), 1402–1419.

Carneiro, F., & Henley, A. (2001). *Modelling formal vs. informal employment and earnings: Micro-econometric evidence for Brazil.* Univeristy of Wales at Aberystwyth Management & Business Working Paper (2001–15).

Davidescu, A. A. (2014). Evaluating the relationship between official economy and shadow economy in Romania. A structural vector autoregressive approach. *Journal of Social and Economic Statistics, 3*(2), 57–65.

Davidescu, A. A. M., & Schneider, F. (2019). The minimum wage fuels romania's shadow economy? In *Subsistence entrepreneurship* (pp. 155–181). Springer.

Davidescu, A. A., & Schneider, F. (2017). *Nature of the relationship between minimum wage and the shadow economy size: An empirical analysis for the case of Romania* (No. 11247). IZA Discussion Papers.

Dell'Anno, R. (2003). *Estimating the shadow economy in Italy: A structural equation approach* (Working Paper 2003-7). Department of Economics, University of Aarhus.

Dell'Anno, R., & Solomon, O. H. (2008). Shadow economy and unemployment rate in USA: Is there a structural relationship? An empirical analysis. *Applied Economics, 40*(19), 2537–2555.

Dell'Anno, R., Gómez-Antonio, M., & Pardo, A. (2007). The shadow economy in three Mediterranean countries: France, Spain and Greece. A MIMIC approach. *Empirical Economics, 33*(1), 51–84.

Filion, K. (2009). Minimum wage issue guide. *Economic Policy Institute*, 21.

Gindling, T. H., & Terrell, K. (2005). The effect of minimum wages on actual wages in formal and informal sectors in Costa Rica. *World Development Elsevier, 33*, 1905–1921.

Gindling, T. H., & Terrell, K. (2007). The effects of multiple minimum wages throughout the labour market: The case of Costa Rica. *Labour Economics, 14*, 485–511.

Hazans, M. (2011). *Informal workers across Europe: Evidence from 30 European countries.* World Bank Policy Research Working Paper (5912).

Hijzen, A., Kappeler, A., Pak, M., & Schwellnus, C. (2018). Labour market resilience: The role of structural and macroeconomic policies. In *Structural reforms* (pp. 173–198). Springer.

Hohberg, M., & Lay, J. (2015). The impact of minimum wages on informal and formal labor market outcomes: Evidence from Indonesia. *IZA Journal of Labor & Development, 4*(1), 1.

Johansen, S. (1991). Estimation and hypothesis testing of cointegration vectors in Gaussian vector autoregressive models. *Econometrica, 59*, 1551–1580.

Krstić, G., & Schneider, F. (2015). *Formalizing the shadow economy in Serbia: Policy measures and growth effects* (p. 179). Springer Nature.

Lütkepohl, H. (2007). *New introduction to multiple time series analysis.* Springer-Verlag.

Magruder, J. R. (2013). Can minimum wages cause a big push? Evidence from Indonesia. *Journal of Development Economics, 100*(1), 48–62.

Maloney, W., & Mendez, J. (2004). Measuring the impact of minimum wages. Evidence from Latin America. In *Law and employment: Lessons from Latin America and the Caribbean* (pp. 109–130). University of Chicago Press.

Muravyev, A., & Oshchepkov, A. Y. (2013). *Minimum wages and labor market outcomes: evidence from the emerging economy of Russia*. Higher School of Economics Research Paper No. WP BRP, 29.

Neumark, D., Schweitzer, M., & Wascher, W. (2000). *The effects of minimum wages throughout the wage distribution* (No. w7519). National bureau of economic research.

OECD. (2012). *OECD Employment Outlook, 2012*. OECD Publishing. https://www.oecdilibrary.org/employment/oecd-employment-outlook-2012_empl_outlook-2012-en

Packard, T. G., Koettl, J., & Montenegro, C. (2012). *In from the shadow: Integrating Europe's informal labor*. World Bank Publications.

Popescu, G., Davidescu, A., & Huidumac, C. (2018). Researching the main causes of the Romanian shadow economy at the micro and macro levels: Implications for sustainable development. *Sustainability, 10*(10), 3518. https://www.mdpi.com/2071-1050/10/10/3518/htm

Pesaran, H. H., & Shin, Y. (1998). Generalized impulse response analysis in linear multivariate models. *Economics Letters, 58*(1), 17–29.

Schneider, F., Buehn, A., & Montenegro, C. E. (2010). New estimates for the shadow economies all over the world. *International Economic Journal, 24*(4), 443–461.

***Eurostat, Minimum wages, https://ec.europa.eu/eurostat/web/products-eurostat-news/-/ddn-20210205-1?redirect=%2Feurostat%2F

***Tempo database, National Institute of Statistics

Adriana AnaMaria Davidescu is a full professor in the Department of Statistics and Econometrics of the Bucharest Academy of Economic Studies and senior researcher at the National Institute for Scientific Research in Labor and Social Protection, with over 14 years of experience in socio-economic research and labor market analysis. Adriana has a PhD from the Bucharest University of Economic Studies and has been a visiting scholar at the University of Salerno (Italy).

She has over 14 years of experience in the analysis of informal economy issues, coordinating or being a member of the research team of over 50 national and international projects. The main areas of interest include, among others: labor market analysis, sustainable development, regional development, analysis and evaluation of public policies and programs, human resources management, etc. Adriana Davidescu has coordinated as director numerous national research projects in the field of informality, holding in 2017 the position of senior expert of the European Commission in the project aimed at implementing the mission, objectives, and activities of the European Platform to strengthen cooperation in tackling Undeclared Work.

Uncovering the Main Characteristics of Shadow Economies in Romania and Moldova for Strengthening the Labour Market Resilience

Adriana AnaMaria Davidescu, Talis J. Putnins, and Arnis Sauka

Abstract In order to strengthen labour market resilience, it helps to focus on different kinds of labour market patterns. This enables new information to be obtained on resilient policies and practices that work. This chapter takes the view that labour market resilience is the result of entrepreneurial practices. Thus, an emphasis on understanding the main characteristics of the shadow economies is undertaken as a way of understanding resilience. The shadow economies of Moldova and Romania are examined in this chapter. The main objective of this research is to reveal the main nuances and characteristics of the shadow economies, analysing in a comparative way the size of the shadow economy for Moldova and Romania, its main determinants and components that dramatically influence the decision of operating in this part of the economy, having as main purpose strengthening the future labour market resilience. It is well known that the shadow economy acts as a safety valve for the official labour market, creating employment and income opportunities, causing increase in supply. This is a second-wave of shadow economy survey realised in both countries having two period of analysis 2015-2016 respectively 2017-2018.Our most recent results revealed that the size of the shadow economy in Romania registered almost the same proportion: 14.61% in 2018 respectively 14.96% in 2017, with a very small decrease of 0.35 pp, while for the case of Moldova, the shadow economy in Moldova was 27.5% of GDP in 2018 and 29.4% in 2017, with a significant decrease of 1.9pp. In Moldova wholesale is the sector with the highest proportion of shadow economic activity (34.7%) in 2018, while in Romania, the things seem to be balanced, with a small increase in the construction sector (18.3%). Micro, small and large companies tend to operate more

A. A. Davidescu (✉)
Bucharest Academy of Economic Studies, Bucharest, Romania
e-mail: adriana.alexandru@csie.ase.ro

T. J. Putnins
University of Technology Sydney, Ultimo, Australia

A. Sauka
Stockholm School of Economics, Stockholm, Latvia

J. Leitão, V. Ratten (eds.), *Strategic Innovation*, Contributions to Management Science, https://doi.org/10.1007/978-3-030-87112-3_11

in the shadow activity in Moldova, while in Romania this type of activity is more widespread in large companies..

1 Introduction

The main objective of this research is to reveal the main nuances and characteristics of the shadow economies, analysing in a comparative way the size of the shadow economy for Moldova and Romania, its main determinants, and components that dramatically influence the decision of operating in this part of the economy, having as main purpose strengthening the future labour market resilience. It is well known that the shadow economy acts as a safety valve for the official labour market, creating employment and income opportunities, causing an increase in supply (Davidescu & Schneider, 2017). In this context, it becomes fundamental to know the main determinants, components, estimates and attitudes regarding this phenomenon.

Therefore, the chapter explores the main characteristics of the shadow economy in Moldova and Romania for the period of 2017–2018 and the main determinants using the methodology developed by Putniņš and Sauka (2015), which allows us to compare the size of the shadow economy in Moldova and Romania with shadow economies in the Baltic countries (Estonia, Latvia, and Lithuania) and Poland. This is a second-wave of shadow economy survey realised in both countries having two period of analysis 2015–2016, respectively, 2017–2018 aiming to offer more insights about this type of phenomenon being relevant for the main stakeholders in order to support the policy decisions. As in the previous report, the shadow economy refers to "all legal production of goods and services produced by registered firms that is deliberately concealed from public authorities" (Putnins et al., 2019, p. 89).

The report offers valuable insights on the most recent estimates of the shadow economy in Romania and Moldova for the period 2017–2018, highlighting the main determinants that influenced the decision of entrepreneurs to go in the unofficial sector, being based on national representative surveys that are mainly based on three components: misreported business income, undeclared employees and unreported "envelope" wages that will be used to compute the size of the shadow economies in these countries.

The report is organised as follows. The next section presents briefly the methodology used for building the index of the shadow economy, while the third section presents the estimates and shedding light on the main pattern of shadow activity. Section 4 explores the main drivers of shadow activity and offers valuable information about the entrepreneurs' attitudes towards shadow activities, and the last section is dedicated to the main conclusions.

2 Methods Used in Constructing the Index

2.1 *The Survey of Entrepreneurs*

In order to build the synthetic index of shadow economy, the raw information is provided by the entrepreneurs from Moldova and Romania. Thus, two national representative surveys among managers were conducted during the period January–February 2019 for Moldova, respectively, October–November 2019 for Romania collecting information about the shadow activity 2 years ago (2017–2018). Based on stratified random sampling through the CATI method have been collected a total sample of 505 interviews in the case of Moldova, respectively, 303 interviews for Romania, interviewing only companies with more than five employees.

As in the previous research of Putnins et al. (2019), the questionnaire kept the same four sections: (i) external influences and satisfaction; (ii) shadow activity; (iii) company and owner characteristics; and (iv) entrepreneurs' attitudes. A detailed description of all questions in the questionnaire together with their scales of measurement is provided by Putnins et al. (2019).

It is worth mentioning that the indirect approach has been used for questions about informal business, asking the managers about "firms in their industry" rather than "their firm."

In the assessment of the shadow activity, three main components are relevant to be estimated: the degree of underreporting of business income (net profits), underreporting of the number of employees and underreporting of salaries paid to employees.

2.2 *Calculation of the Index*

This synthetic measure of informality quantifies the magnitude of the shadow economy as % of official GDP using an income approach, which computes GDP as the sum of gross remuneration of employees (gross personal income) and gross operating income of firms (gross corporate income). Therefore, the computation process requires three main steps:

- To estimate the degree of underreporting of employee remuneration and underreporting of firms' operating income
- To estimate each firm's shadow production as a weighted average of its underreported employee remuneration and underreported operating income, with the weights reflecting the proportions of employee remuneration and firms' operating income in the composition of GDP
- To calculate a production-weighted average of shadow production across firms

The underreporting of firm *i*'s operating income, $UR_i^{OperatingIncome}$, is estimated directly from the survey through question Q7, while underreporting of employee remuneration is based on "envelope wages" (Q9) and unreported employees (Q8). Therefore, the firm *i*'s total unreported proportion of employee remuneration is[1]:

$$UR_i^{EmployeeRemuneration} = 1 - \left(1 - UR_i^{Salaries}\right)\left(1 - UR_i^{Employees}\right) \tag{1}$$

Then, the unreported proportion of the firm's production (income) is computed as a weighted average of underreported personal and underreported corporate income:

$$ShadowProportion_i = \alpha_c UR_i^{EmployeeRemuneration} + (1 - \alpha_c) UR_i^{OperationIncome} \tag{2}$$

where α_c is the ratio of employees' remuneration (*Eurostat* item D.1) to the sum of employees' remuneration and gross operating income of firms (*Eurostat* items B.2g and B.3g). Due to the lack of data for Moldova, we have used the figures for Hungary on employees' remuneration and gross operating income (51.2% in 2017 and 50.9% in 2018). In Romania, the ratio of employees' remuneration to the sum of employees' remuneration and gross operating income was 40.8% in 2017 and 42.5% in 2018.

In the last step, a weighted average of underreported production, $ShadowProportion_i$, across firms in country *c* is computed to arrive at the Shadow Economy Index for that country (Putniņš & Sauka, 2015):

$$INDEX_c^{ShadowEconomy} = \sum_{i=1}^{N_c} w_i ShadowProportion_i \tag{3}$$

The weights, w_i, are the relative contribution of each firm to the country's GDP, and due to the lack of information, we used a simple arithmetic mean of the $ShadowProportion_i$ for both countries.

Table 1 presents the distribution of sample companies, both Moldavian and Romanian, highlighting some specific distributions between both countries. Thus, if Romania has an overwhelming weight of micro-enterprises (65%) and only 5.6% of them are medium size or 3.6% of them being large companies, the situation is a little bit different among Moldavian firms. Therefore, if 41% of Moldavian companies from the research were micro-enterprises and about 19% are medium-size companies and only 7% are large companies.

[1] In deriving the formula, we make the simplifying assumption that wages of unreported employees are on average equal to those of reported employees.

Table 1 Distribution of the sample companies by the number of employees

Employees		Number	%
Moldavian companies	1–10 employees	206	40.8
	10–50 employees	171	33.9
	50–250 employees	94	18.7
	More than 250 employees	34	6.6
	Total	505	100.0
Romanian companies	1–10 employees	197	65
	10–50 employees	78	26
	50–250 employees	17	5.6
	More than 250 employees	11	3.4
	Total	505	100.0

Source: authors' own calculations

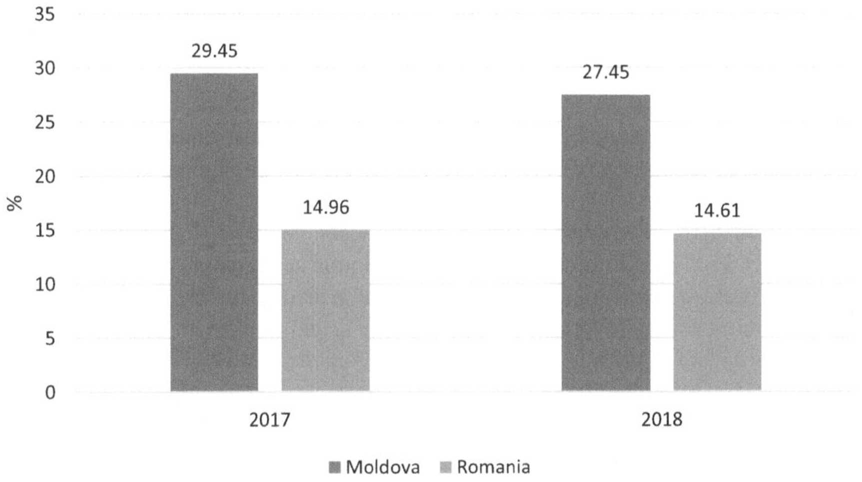

Fig. 1 Shadow economy index in Moldova and Romania (% of GDP), 2017–2018

3 Shadow Economy Index for Moldova and Romania for the Period 2017–2018

Figure 1 presents the aggregate size of the shadow economies in Moldova and Romania in 2017–2018. The table shows that the shadow economy in Moldova was 27.5% of GDP in 2018 and 29.4% in 2017, with a significant decrease of 1.9 pp. The shadow economy in Romania registered almost the same proportion: 14.61% in 2018, respectively, 14.96% in 2017, with a very small decrease of 0.35 pp.

Table 2 presents the punctual estimated together with the confidence intervals at 95% (in parentheses) for the size of the shadow economies, highlighting also in the first row the change in the relative size of the shadow economy from 2017 to 2018.

Table 2 Size of the shadow economies for the period of 2015–2018

	Moldova	Romania
Change (2018–2017)	−1.99% (−3.40%, −0.87%)	−0.344% (−0.773%, 0.084%)
2018	27.45% (23.92%, 30.98%)	14.61% (13.12%, 16.10%)
2017	29.45% (25.70%, 33.19%)	14.96% (13.31%, 16.6%)
2016	29.7% (26.9%, 32.5%)	29.8% (27.0%, 32.6%)
2015	33.3% (30.4%, 36.3%)	35.6% (32.2%, 39.0%)

Source: Putnins et al. (2019)

Figure 2 presents the components of the shadow economy index in both countries in 2018, highlighting that if in Moldova the unreported business income exhibited the highest proportion (52.8%) followed at large distance by the envelope wages (25.8%) and lastly the unreported or unregistered employees (21.4%), in Romania, the contributions are a little bit different, unreported business income, accounted for almost 45% of the total shadow economy, whereas the proportion of envelope wages was much closed to this value, 40.5% while underreported employees registered only 14.8%.

In comparison with 2015–2016, the differences are significant, in 2016 in Romania the main component of the shadow economy was also unreported business income but in proportion of 56.8%, whereas the proportion of envelope wages and underreported employees was comparably lower: 20.7% and 22.5%, respectively. In Moldova, in 2015, unreported business income accounted for 39.7% while envelope wages only 31.8%, followed by unreported or unregistered employees (28.6%).

Figure 3 illustrate the underreporting of business income (profits), underreporting of the number of employees (percentage of the actual number of employees) and underreporting of salaries (percentage of actual salaries) in Moldova and Romania for both years 2017 and 2018.

Figure 3 shows that underreporting of income has the highest proportion in Moldova – 26.7% in 2017 and characterised by a small decrease in 2018 (25.2%). The empirical findings also suggested that envelope wages decreased slightly in 2018 as compared to 2017, i.e., from 20.1% to 18.2%, whereas underreporting of employees is estimated at around 15.2% in 2018. Companies in Moldova most often underreport 11%–30% of actual salaries (Figure 4) and more than 25% of them underreport between 11%–30% of their business profits.

In Romania, the most commonly encountered form of undeclared work is the envelope wage with a proportion of 17% in 2017 and characterised by a small decline reaching the value of 14.2% in 2018. Underreporting of employees seems to be a little bit under-evaluated with a small proportion of only 4.9% in 2018. More than half of the Romanian companies underreport their income, while the almost 30% of companies underreport between 76% and 100% of their salaries (Figs. 5 and 6).

Figure 7 indicates that the magnitude of bribery in in 2018, the empirical results revealing similar figures in both countries regarding the percentage of revenue spent on "'getting things done" quantified to be around 14.5%–16.4%. Regarding the

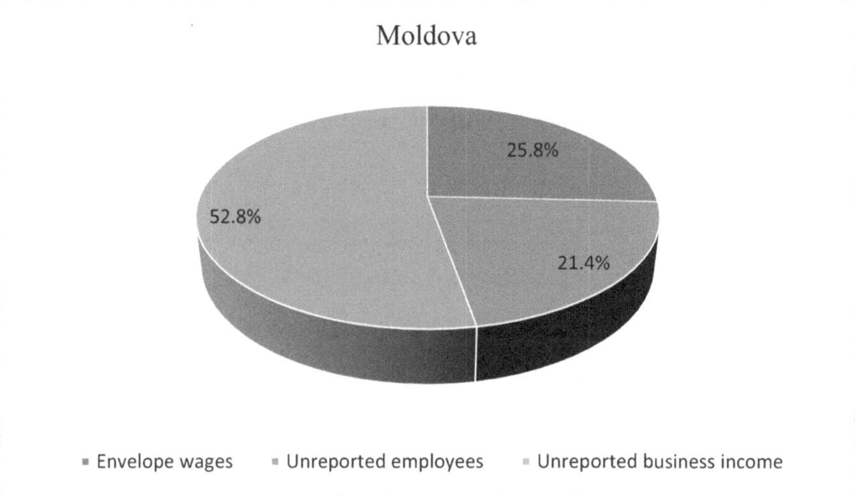

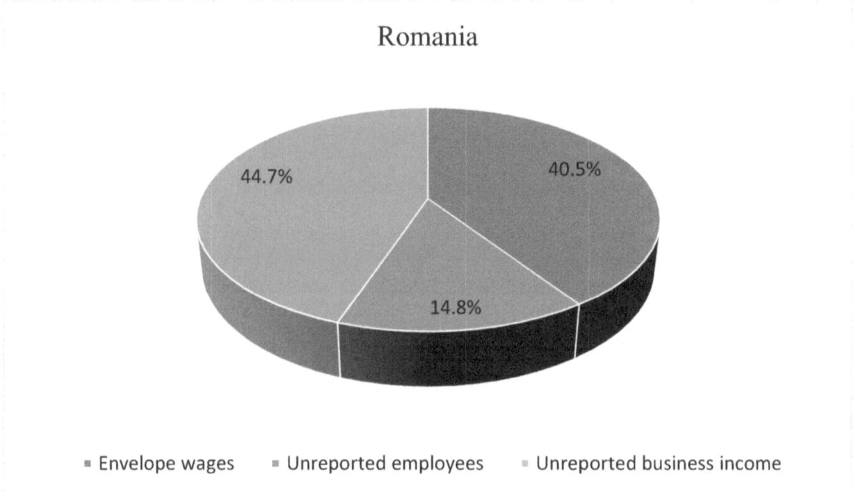

Fig. 2 Components of the shadow economies in Moldova and Romania, 2018

percentage of the contract value that firms typically offer as a bribe to secure a contract with the government, there are significant differences between Moldova and Romania. If in Romania, this percentage is relatively high (22.5% on average), in Moldova this percentage is very small only 8.15% of the companies admitting of using this type of behaviour.

The distribution of bribery: to "get things done" and securing contract with the government in both countries reveals that almost 20% and 18% of the Moldavian companies pay in bribes more than 75% of the revenue or contract value. In the case of Romania, almost 58% of the firms pay in bribes between 50% and 75% of the

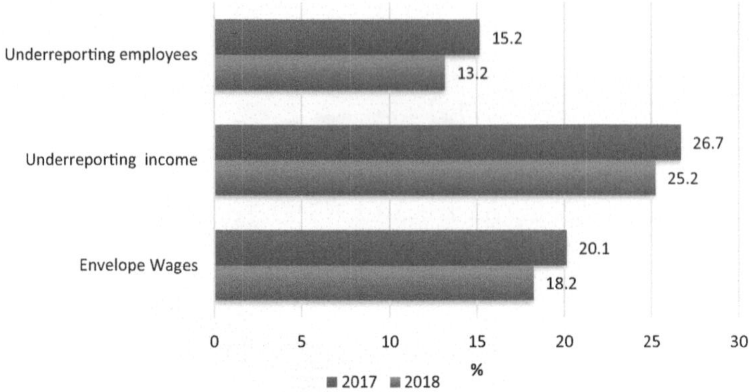

Fig. 3 Underreporting of business income (percentage of actual profits), the number of employees (percentage of the actual number of employees) and underreporting of salaries (percentage of actual salaries) in Moldova, 2017–2018

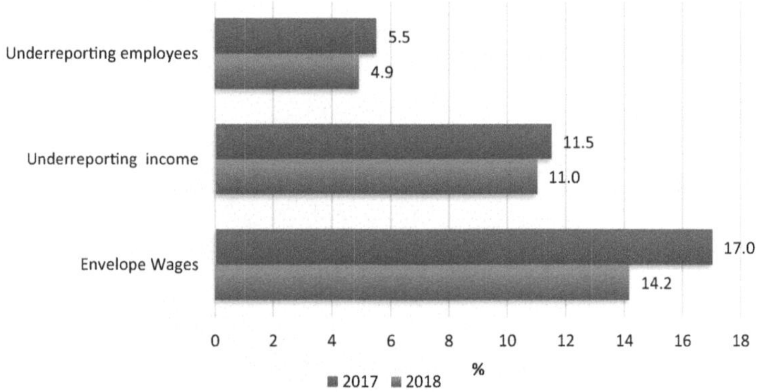

Fig. 4 Underreporting of business income (percentage of actual profits), the number of employees (percentage of the actual number of employees) and underreporting of salaries (percentage of actual salaries) in Romania, 2017–2018

revenue to secure the contract whereas 48% of the firms pay to get things done more than 75% of the revenue.

Finally, regarding the proportion of unregistered enterprises in Moldova and Romania, it accounts for 26% of all enterprises in Moldova and almost 8% in Romania (2018) (Table 3). The table shows point estimates and 95% confidence intervals of unregistered enterprises as a percentage of all enterprises in Moldova and Romania.

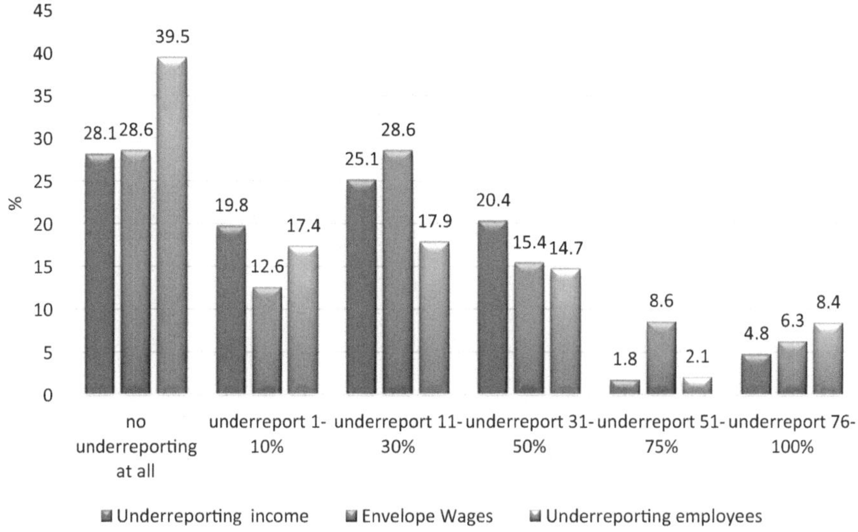

Fig. 5 Underreporting of income (percentage of actual profits), underreporting of the number of employees and underreporting of salaries in 2018 in Moldova. The vertical axis measures the percentage of each country's respondents underreporting within the range given on the horizontal axis

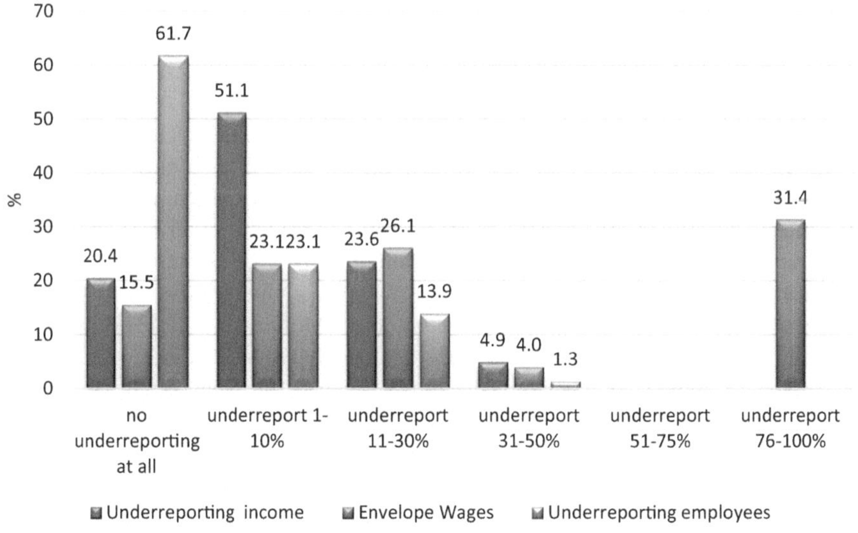

Fig. 6 Underreporting of income (percentage of actual profits), underreporting of the number of employees and underreporting of salaries in 2018 in Romania. The vertical axis measures the percentage of each country's respondents underreporting within the range given on the horizontal axis

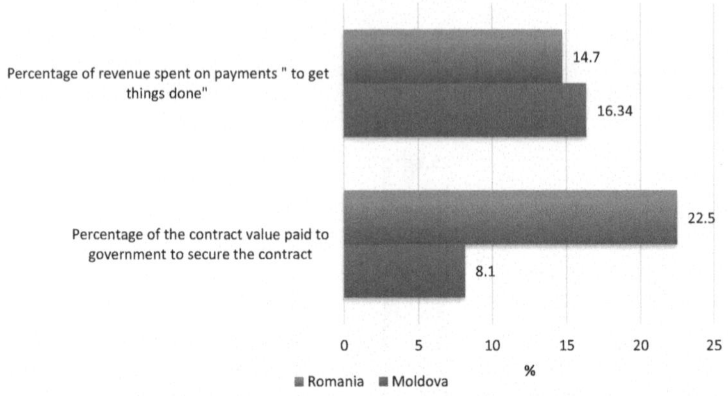

Fig. 7 Bribery (percentage of revenue spent on payments "to get things done") and percentage of the contract value paid to government to secure the contract in 2018 in Moldova and Romania

Table 3 Proportion of unregistered enterprises in Moldova and Romania, 2015–2018

	Moldova	Romania
2018	25.7% (21.8%, 29.7%)	7.73% (6.45%, 9.01%)
2017	28.9% (24.7%, 33%)	8.48% (7.04%, 9.91%)
2016	15.5% (13.3%, 17.7%)	14.4% (12.3%, 16.4%)
2015	15.7% (13.5%, 17.9%)	15.3% (13.0%, 17.7%)

4 Determinants of Shadow Activity

4.1 Company Characteristics

The highest proportion of shadow activity in Moldova in 2018 was registered in the South region and Chisinau (28.1%), while at the opposite side there was the Centre region with an average proportion of 22.6%. In the case of Romania, there are significant regional discrepancies regarding the incidence of such a phenomenon, with regions characterised by small proportion of shadow activity (Bucharest-Ilfov, 10.3%) and also regions with a high level of shadow activity (South-East, 19.9% and respectively South-Muntenia, 17.1%). Therefore, in Moldova wholesale is the sector with the highest proportion of shadow economic activity (34.7%) in 2018, followed by services (29.5%). In Romania, the things seem to be balanced, with a small increase in the construction sector (18.3%). Although there is a large proportion of shadow economic activity in micro and small companies in Moldova (around 31%), this type of activity is present also in large companies with less than 200 employees in proportion of 32.3%. In Romania, the highest proportion of shadow activity occurs also in large companies with almost 200 employees (18.8%) followed by medium-size firms (15.6%).

4.2 *How Attitudes and Perceptions Affect Shadow Activity*

It is worth analysing if the decision of participating in the shadow activities is influenced by the risk of detection, the value of penalties, by the level of fiscal morality or by the institutional framework.

4.2.1 Probability of Being Caught and Potential Consequences

The results on perceived probabilities of being caught and expected consequences revealed that the perceived risk of being caught when underreporting income, salaries and employees is relatively higher in Romania compared with Moldova. A high probability associated with the underreporting profits (76–100%) is more spread among Romanian individuals (76.24%) compared with Moldavians (49.5%). Also, in the case of briberies, significant discrepancies are encountered between both countries; 62% of respondents from Romania consider that the probability of being caught bribing is very high (greater than 76%), while only 34.5% of the Moldavians respondents think the same. The perceived probability of being caught while underreporting salaries seems to be higher in Romania. Only 20% of Moldavians declared that the probability of being caught underreporting salaries is between 31% and 50% compared with almost 36% in the case of Romanian respondents.

Interesting results were obtained from the analysis of responses regarding the expected penalties for deliberate misreporting. The proportions are quite similar for all categories. Therefore, almost 16% of the respondents from both countries consider that the expected sanction is only a small fine for deliberately underreporting, while around 45% of them agree that a serious fine, affecting competitiveness is most likely the expected sanction. The risk insolvency created by a serious fine has been mentioned by almost 26% of Romanian respondents and 31% of Moldavians.

4.2.2 Tax Morale

Based on Luttmer and Singhal (2014), Torgler (2003), Torgler et al. (2010) and Torgler and Schneider (2009), entrepreneurs' tax morality has been quantified through two questions regarding tax avoidance tolerated behaviour and their tolerance towards bribery.

4.2.3 Satisfaction with the Government and the Tax Authority

The satisfaction with the government and the tax authority has been explored within the questionnaire through four questions regarding satisfaction with the State Revenue Service, the government's tax policy, business legislation and the government's support for entrepreneurs. Some differences of perception among entrepreneurs from both countries can be revealed. If Moldavian entrepreneurs tend to be more satisfied with the activity of the State Revenue Service and tax policy, the Romanians are more likely to be satisfied with the quality of business legislation and the governmental support, but the differences among Romanian entrepreneurs' opinions are not very high.

The differences have been highlighted better by the distributions of responses for 2018. Therefore, Moldavians are less satisfied with the governmental support, while the Romanians are very dissatisfied with the activity of State Revenue Service.

4.2.4 Social Identity

The entrepreneurs' perception regarding the belonging to the state and how they identify themselves within the country is very important in their decision of going in the shadow economy.

The results show that entrepreneurs from Moldova on average possess very high community belonging and perceive their contribution to the economy also to be high. It is not the case for the Romanian entrepreneurs, who are not so attached to the community and who do not have the perception of contributing so much to the economy and society in general.

4.2.5 Institutional Environment

In order to assess the strength of formal and informal institutions in both Moldova and Romania, 11 elements have been taken into consideration. Our findings suggest that in Moldova, the biggest obstacles were perceived to be political instability, corruption and anti-competitive practices of other competitors. At the opposite side, we found business licencing and permits, trade and custom regulation, tax administration and functioning of the judiciary/courts.

In the case of Romania, the things are a little bit different. Romanian entrepreneurs perceived tax rates, trade and custom regulation and tax administration as biggest obstacles affecting the operations of a company, while at the opposite side, there were mentioned anti-competitive practices of other competitors.

5 Conclusions

Using the methodology developed by Putniņš and Sauka (2015), the report presents the most recent estimates of the shadow economy index for Romania and Moldova combining unreported business income, hidden employees, and "envelope" wages. This report is a second-wave of shadow economy survey realised in both countries for two periods of time, the years 2015–2016, respectively, 2017–2018.

Our most recent results revealed that the size of the shadow economy in Romania registered almost the same proportion: 14.61% in 2018, respectively, 14.96% in 2017, with a very small decrease of 0.35 pp., while for the case of Moldova, the shadow economy in Moldova was 27.5% of GDP in 2018 and 29.4% in 2017, with a significant decrease of 1.9 pp.

In the case of Moldova, underreporting business income represents in 2018 almost 25.2% while the envelope wages represent almost 18.2%, while in Romania things look a little bit different: envelope wages represent almost 14.2% of official GDP, while the underreporting income registered 11% of GDP. If in Moldova, approximately 13.2% of employees are unreported or working unofficially, in Romania this figure represents less than half (4.9% in Romania in 2018).

The empirical results highlighted similar pattern of bribing in both countries: the magnitude of bribery (percentage of revenue spent on "getting things done") is found between 14.7% and 16.3%%, whereas percentage of the contract value that firms typically offer as a bribe to secure a contract with the government in Romania is 8% while in Moldova is almost 23%.

The highest proportions of shadow activity in Moldova were registered in the South region and Chisinau, while in the case of Romania, South-East and South-Muntenia were the regions exhibiting the highest levels of undeclared activity.

In Moldova wholesale is the sector with the highest proportion of shadow economic activity (34.7%) in 2018, while in Romania, things seem to be balanced, with a small increase in the construction sector (18.3%).

If Moldavian entrepreneurs are relatively satisfied with the State Revenue Service and tax policy, Romanian entrepreneurs were more satisfied with the quality of business legislation and government support.

Romanian companies with a smaller number of employees being for a long time of the market and operating mostly in sectors such construction and services tend to be more involved in the shadow economy activity while in the case of Moldova, younger firms were more likely to be involved in this type of shadow economic activity.

Appendix 1. Questionnaire Form Used in Moldova and Romania

Entrepreneurs' Satisfaction with the Business Climate/Informal Entrepreneurship in Moldova and Romania

My name is ... from .... We are conducting a survey aimed at understanding entrepreneurs' satisfaction with the entrepreneurship climate in ***Romania and Moldova***. The main interest of the study is to find out how various policy initiatives implemented within the country and entrepreneurs' satisfaction with the business climate influence entrepreneurial behaviour, including tax avoidance.

I would like to emphasize that we are only interested in your expert opinion and in no way are we indicating, for instance, that your company is involved in any type of tax avoidance activities.

The interview will last approximately 15 minutes. We guarantee 100% confidentiality as neither your name nor your company's name will appear in the data analysis. Data will be analysed using a computer program without any reference to the data source. If you are interested, we can also send you the summary of the survey results once the survey is complete.

If the respondent hesitates or says 'no':

This survey is very important for fostering knowledge about entrepreneurship in ***(Romania / Moldova)***. By participating in this survey, you are helping to improve such knowledge. All your answers will be 100% confidential and no one will be able to trace them back to you or your company. Moreover, we are interested in your expert opinion and what you say will be attributed to the industry or your competitors, not your firm.

Questionnaire Form

External influences

Q1. Please evaluate your satisfaction with the performance of the State Revenue Service with regard to tax administration in *(insert country)* during 2018.

1	2	3	4	5
Very unsatisfied	Unsatisfied	Neither satisfied nor unsatisfied	Satisfied	Very satisfied

Q2. Please evaluate your satisfaction with the government's tax policy in *(insert country)* during 2018.

1	2	3	4	5
Very unsatisfied	Unsatisfied	Neither satisfied nor unsatisfied	Satisfied	Very satisfied

Q3. Please evaluate your satisfaction with the quality of business legislation in *(insert country)* during 2018.

1	2	3	4	5
Very unsatisfied	Unsatisfied	Neither satisfied nor unsatisfied	Satisfied	Very satisfied

Q4. Please evaluate your satisfaction with the government's support to entrepreneurs in *(insert country)* during 2018.

1	2	3	4	5
Very unsatisfied	Unsatisfied	Neither satisfied nor unsatisfied	Satisfied	Very satisfied

Q5. Tax avoidance is tolerated behaviour in *(insert country)*.

1	2	3	4	5
Completely disagree (entrepreneurs do not tolerate involvement in tax avoidance)	Disagree	Neither agree nor disagree	Agree	Completely agree (entrepreneurs highly tolerate involvement in tax avoidance)

Q6. Bribing is tolerated behaviour in *(insert country)*.

1	2	3	4	5
Completely disagree	Disagree	Neither agree nor disagree	Agree	Completely agree

Government policy and amount of informal business

Q7. Please estimate the degree of underreporting business income (profits) by firms in your industry in 2018_______ % (Q7.1) and in 2017 _______ %. (Q7.2)

Q8. Please estimate the degree of underreporting number of employees (% of actual number of employees) by firms in your industry in 2018_______ % (Q8.1) and in 2017 _______ % (Q8.2).

Q9. Please estimate the degree of underreporting salaries paid to employees by companies in your industry (for instance, if in reality an employee receives EUR 400, but the reported salary is EUR 100, then underreporting is 75%; if EUR 400 and EUR 200, then underreporting is 50%). Firms underreported actual salaries by approximately ____ % in 2018 (Q9.1) and ____ % in 2017 (Q9.2).

Q10. On average, approximately what percent of revenue (turnover) did firms in your industry pay in unofficial payments to 'get things done' in in 2018_______ % (Q10.1) and in 2017 _______ % (Q10.2).

Q11. When other firms in your industry do business with the government, approximately how much of the contract value would firms typically offer in unofficial payments to 'secure' the contract? (year 2018)_____%

Q12. In some industries, in addition to registered companies such as yours, unregistered enterprises also operate but do not report any of their activity to authorities. In your opinion, what percentage of your industry's total production of goods/services is carried out by unregistered enterprises in 2018?_____ % (Q12.1) in 2017? _____% (Q12.2).

Q13. What is the size of the average unregistered enterprise in your industry compared to your company (e.g., if the average unregistered enterprise is half as big then record 50%, if twice as big then 200%)?

In 2018_____% (Q13.1)

In 2017_____% (Q13.2)

Q14. For a typical company in your industry, what would you say is the approximate probability (0–100%) of being caught if the company were to:

Q14.1. underreport its business income? ______%

Q14.2. underreport its number of employees? _____%

Q14.3. underreport the amount it pays to employees in salaries? _____%
Q14.4. make unofficial payments to 'get things done'? _____%

Q15. If a company in your industry were caught for deliberate misreporting, what would typically be the consequence to that company?

Nothing serious	A small fine	A serious fine that would affect the competitiveness of the company	A serious fine that would put the company at risk of insolvency	The company would be forced to cease operations
1	2	3	4	5

Company / Performance/ Value Creation

Q16. What is the approximate percentage change in your operating profit, turnover and total employment in 2018 compared to 2017?

	1 Operating profit (Q16.1)	2. Turnover (Q16.2)	3 Total employment (Q16.3)
Change (increase or decrease in %) as compared to 2017. For example: +20%, −15%, 0 (no change)			

Q17. Approximately, what was the operating profit of your company in 2018?

EUR __________

Q18. Approximately, what was the turnover of your company in 2018?

EUR __________

Q19. Approximately, how many employees are currently employed in your company (full time equivalent, including you)?

_________ employees

Q20. Approximately what was the average reported salary in your company in 2018_______ EUR (Q20.1)/ month and in 2017 _______ EUR/ month (Q20.2)?

Q21. In which year did your company start operation?

Year________.

Q22. What is the main activity (i.e. sector) that your company is engaged in?

□ Manufacturing
□ Wholesale
□ Retail
□ Services (please specify______________________________)
□ Construction
□ Other (please specify______________________________)

Q23. In which region does your company conduct most of its business?
(Insert regions of your country- preferably bigger areas, not counties)

Attitudes / tax morale / barriers to business

Q24. For each of the following statements, please indicate on a scale of 1–5 whether you agree (1 means you completely disagree, 5 means you completely agree):

	Strongly disagree	Disagree	Neither/ nor	Agree	Strongly agree
Q24.1. Businesses such as yours contribute a lot to growth of the *(insert country)* economy and society in general	1	2	3	4	5
Q24.2. Companies in your industry would think it is always justified to cheat on tax if they have the chance	1	2	3	4	5
Q24.3. Being a member of the Latvian/ Lithuanian/Estonian community is important to me	1	2	3	4	5

Q25. As I list some factors that can affect the current operations of a business, please tell me if you think that each factor is No Obstacle, a Minor Obstacle, a Moderate Obstacle, a Major Obstacle, or a Very Severe Obstacle to the current operations of this establishment.

	No obstacle	Minor obstacle	Moderate obstacle	Major obstacle	Very severe obstacle
Q25.1. Tax administration	0	1	2	3	4
Q25.2. Tax rates	0	1	2	3	4
Q25.3. Trade and custom regulation	0	1	2	3	4
Q25.4. Business licencing and permits	0	1	2	3	4
Q25.5. Functioning of the judiciary/courts	0	1	2	3	4
Q25.6. Uncertainty about regulatory policies	0	1	2	3	4
Q25.7. Corruption	0	1	2	3	4
Q25.8. Anti-competitive practices of other competitors	0	1	2	3	4
Q25.9. Political instability	0	1	2	3	4

References

Davidescu, A. A., & Schneider, F. (2017). *Nature of the relationship between minimum wage and the shadow economy size: An empirical analysis for the case of Romania* (No. 11247). IZA Discussion Papers.

Luttmer, E. F., & Singhal, M. (2014). Tax morale. *Journal of Economic Perspectives, 28*(4), 149–168.
Putniņš, T., & Sauka, A. (2015). Measuring the shadow economy using company managers. *Journal of Comparative Economics, 43*, 471–490.
Putnins, T. J., Sauka, A., & Davidescu, A. A. M. (2019). Shadow economy index for Moldova and Romania. In V. Ratten, P. Jones, V. Braga, & C. S. Marques (Eds.), *Subsistence entrepreneurship the interplay of collaborative innovation, sustainability and social goals* (pp. 89–130). Springer. ISBN (Print) 9783030115425.
Torgler, B. (2003). Tax morale, rule-governed behaviour and trust. *Constitutional Political Economy, 14*, 119–140.
Torgler, B., Schaffner, M., & Macintyre, A. (2010). Tax compliance, tax morale, and governance quality. In J. Alm, J. Martinez-Vazquez, & B. Torgler (Eds.), *Developing alternative frameworks for explaining tax compliance* (pp. 141–173). Routledge.
Torgler, B., & Schneider, F. (2009). The impact of tax morale and institutional quality on the shadow economy. *Journal of Economic Psychology, 30*, 228–245.
Eurostat National Accounts Database.
STATA 14 software.
SPSS 22 software.

Adriana AnaMaria Davidescu is a full professor in the Department of Statistics and Econometrics of the Bucharest Academy of Economic Studies and senior researcher at the National Institute for Scientific Research in Labor and Social Protection, with over 14 years of experience in socio-economic research and labour market analysis. Adriana has a Ph.D. from the Bucharest University of Economic Studies and has been a Visiting Scholar at the University of Salerno (Italy).

She has over 14 years of experience in the analysis of informal economy issues, coordinating or being a member of the research team of over 50 national and international projects. The main areas of interest include, among others: labour market analysis, sustainable development, regional development, analysis and evaluation of public policies and programs, human resources management, etc.

Adriana Davidescu has coordinated as director numerous national research projects in the field of informality, holding in 2017 the position of senior expert of the European Commission in the project aimed at implementing the mission, objectives and activities of the European Platform to strengthen cooperation in tackling Undeclared Work. E-mail: adriana.alexandru@csie.ase.ro

Talis J. Putnins is a Professor at UTS Business School (Sydney, Australia) and Stockholm School of Economics in Riga (Latvia) as well as Research Associate at the Baltic International Centre for Economic Policy Studies (Latvia). His research interests include financial economics, market microstructure, market manipulation, tax evasion, and partial detection modelling. Tālis has a Ph. D. from the University of Sydney and has been a Visiting Scholar at Columbia University and New York University. E-pasts: talis.putnins@sseriga.edu, www: https://www.sseriga.edu/putnins-talis-j

Arnis Sauka is Professor, Director of the Centre for Sustainable Business at the Stockholm School of Economics in Riga. His main research interests include shadow economy, competitiveness and internationalization of companies. Arnis has a Ph.D. from the University of Siegen (Germany) and has been a Visiting Scholar at Jönköping International Business School (Sweden) and University College London (U.K.). E-mail: arnis.sauka@sseriga.edu, www. https://www.sseriga.edu/sauka-arnis

The manufacturer's authorised representative in the EU is Springer Nature Customer Service Centre GmbH, Europaplatz 3, 69115 Heidelberg, Germany. If you have any concerns regarding our products, please contact ProductSafety@springernature.com

Printed and bound by CPI Group (UK) Ltd, Croydon, CR0 4YY
30/09/2026
02225706-0001